Thorough surveillance

MANCHESTER
1824

Manchester University Press

Thorough surveillance

The genesis of Israeli policies of population management, surveillance and political control towards the Palestinian minority

Ahmad H. Sa'di

Manchester University Press
Manchester and New York
distributed in the United States exclusively by Palgrave Macmillan

Published by Manchester University Press
Oxford Road, Manchester M13 9NR, UK
and Room 400, 175 Fifth Avenue, New York, NY 10010, USA
www.manchesteruniversitypress.co.uk

Distributed in the United States exclusively by
Palgrave Macmillan, 175 Fifth Avenue, New York,
NY 10010, USA

Distributed in Canada exclusively by
UBC Press, University of British Columbia, 2029 West Mall,
Vancouver, BC, Canada V6T 1Z2

British Library Cataloguing-in-Publication Data
A catalogue record for this book is available from the British Library

Library of Congress Cataloging-in-Publication Data applied for

ISBN 978 0 7190 9058 5 hardback

First published 2014

Typeset
by SPi Publisher Services, Pondicherry, India
Printed in Great Britain
by CPI Antony Rowe Ltd, Chippenham, Wiltshire

Contents

Figures and tables

Figure

Tables

Acknowledgements

For a long time, I have been interested in the methods used by Israel to control its Palestinian citizens. In fact, the first article I published more than twenty years ago was on the politics of Palestinians' categorizations by the Israeli state and Israeli social scientists. Since then, I have published quite extensively on this subject. Yet, beside the long and Sisyphean archival research, the work on this book was conducted in three periods. A substantial reading and reflection on the methods of surveillance and political control in comparative perspective was made in January–March 2007 during my stay as visiting senior lecturer in the Institute of Islamic Area at Waseda University, Tokyo, Japan. I am therefore indebted to my Japanese friends for their encouragement, support, unique Japanese hospitality and interest in my research. In particular, I am thankful to my friends Professor Akira Usuki and Professor and Mrs. Nagasawa. Moreover, I am thankful to the late Professor Tsugitaka Sato, the then director of the centre, for inviting me and enabling me to spend a memorable period in reading and reflection without burdening me with duties or assignments. I also wish to mention the fellow researchers and the staff of the centre for their enormous help and collegiality and Professor Hidemitsu Kuroki for his collegiality and friendship.

I had the chance to examine some of my ideas in the workshop 'States of Exception, Surveillance and Population Management', which took place on 6–7 December 2008 in Larnaca, Cyprus. I wish to thank the organizers – Professor Elia Zureik, Professor David Lyon and Professor Yasmein Abu-Laban – for enabling me to present some of my ideas before an audience of specialists. This occasion might be ideal to express my thanks to Professor Zureik for his long-standing support, encouragement and friendship. Following this workshop, I composed a report that was commissioned with a grant from the Surveillance Studies Centre at Queen's University in Canada, and some of its findings and arguments are presented in chapters 3, 4 and 5.

The bulk of the book – chapters 1 to 6 – was written during two months, August–September 2011, which I spent as visiting senior research fellow at the Middle East Institute of the National University of Singapore. I wish to thank the institute's director, Professor Michael C. Hudson, for inviting me to spend two months in this unique institute during which I devoted all my time and energy for writing. I would also like to thank the then research fellows of the institute for attending the presentations I gave on various chapters of the book and for engaging critically with my ideas. Moreover, I wish to thank the institute's administrative and technical staff. During my stay in Singapore, I also benefited from the friendship and the support of Professor Syed Farid Hussein Alatas.

This book, like any other, is the product of years of accumulative research and intellectual influences. Several people affected my thinking in many and diverse ways. As always, I wish to mention with affection and appreciation Dr. Paul Kelemen, a mentor, friend and a great humanist. His deep and unfailing belief in justice and human dignity has been to me a shining example of commitment to these ideals. Professor Lila Abu-Lughod has also been a sincere and generous friend. Her support and advice are immensely valued. Among many other things, Professor Abu-Lughod read and commented on various chapters, which she did as always with great insight and wisdom.

I am also thankful to Mr Anthony R. Mason, senior editor in Manchester University Press, and his production team for the efforts they made to bring this book to publication in its current form. Mr Mason has been an ideal editor; his understanding, support, attentiveness and open-mindedness throughout the publication process are highly appreciated. Moreover, a note of thanks is due to two anonymous reviewers for reading the manuscript; particularly I owe a special note of thanks to Lianne Slavin, managing production editor, for reading the manuscript several times and for making very insightful suggestions. My thanks also go to Ms Uma Shankar, project manager, SPi Global, for overseeing the copy-editing and the preparation of the manuscript for publication. Yet, needless to say, I assume full responsibility for the arguments and data presented in the book.

Along the way, I benefited from the friendship of many people. The list of such friends is fortunately long. From this list, I would like to mention Ahmad and Rudena Muslih, Elizabeth Muawad, Nimer Samniah, Izzat Darwazeh, Rachel Pollard-Darwazeh and Andre Mazawi. Moreover, my colleagues in the Department of Politics and Government at Ben-Gurion University should be credited for maintaining a sense of normalcy despite adverse conditions.

My parents Hussein Hassan Sa'di and Fatima Samniah-Sa'di, although having endured the horror of the 1948 War and having lived through depressing sociopolitical realities, maintained their faith in human virtues. This book partly dwells on the stifling conditions they have gone through and faced with steadfastness and bravery.

Last but by no means least, my thanks go to Sylvia Saba-Sa'di for being loving, supportive and understanding throughout my long engagement in this project. She read and commented on several drafts of the book and accompanied it from beginning to end. Yara and Sari who have always seen their father interested, beside them, in books, papers and pens are now university students. Their love, their cheer and even their critique of their father's ideas make life, despite many discontenting, even vile, elements, delightful.

Introduction

Widely regarded as an expert in techniques of surveillance and political control, Israel has been successful in controlling a native population for a long time. Despite tremendous challenges, it has maintained a tight grip over a large Palestinian population in the territories it occupied in the 1967 War. Moreover, it has effectively contained the Palestinian minority inside its 1948 borders. Although members of the latter group were granted Israeli citizenship, through various policies, they have been blocked from challenging the state's Jewish identity. While colonial control of native populations represents a significant aspect of the history of the nineteenth and twentieth centuries, Israel's continued administration of a large Palestinian population into the twenty-first century, long after the demise of colonialism, represents a serious challenge for scholars and theorists of colonial forms of political control (Azoulay and Ophir, 2008; Gordon, 2008; Ophir *et al.*, 2009).

Several of the political objectives associated with population management and political control – such as how to alter the country's ethnic composition – are as old as the idea of establishing a Jewish state in Palestine itself. These became particularly pressing during the British Mandate over Palestine. The Zionist movement had to come up with a solution to what it called the 'Arab problem' – the fact that the country was overwhelmingly populated by native Arabs. Transfer of Palestinians as a strategy to transform the composition of the country's population loomed large in discussions among Zionist leaders since the early 1920s. The predicament of the 'Arab problem' was solved by war. The 1947/1948 War led to the transformation of Palestine from an overwhelmingly Arab country to a divided one, in which a Jewish state was established on the major part of the land – 78 per cent of Mandatory Palestine. Of the 900,000 Palestinians who had lived in the part of Palestine that became Israel, only 156,000 eventually remained. Moreover, some 500 Arab villages and cities were depopulated, and a social fabric that evolved through centuries was shattered (Pappe, 2006; Sa'di and Abu-Lughod, 2007). Although of great import, these events will not be examined in this book. Rather, they will comprise its backdrop.

This book deals with the period that extends between the summer of 1948 and circa 1970. Its aim is to describe and analyse the genesis and unfolding of

Israeli policies to control the Palestinians who became citizens of the state after 1948. The study of the foundational moment of the Israeli discourse of control – that is, the conceptual framework, mindset, methods and institutions – serves to elucidate the way in which this system worked during this particular historical period but also might shed light on the key elements of contemporary Israeli thinking on surveillance and political control.

Despite the importance of this pivotal moment for understanding future developments, most Israeli social scientists have argued that no state policy had evolved during that period. This argument not only denies the existence of systematic thinking and consistency in the state's actions, which the evidence from my archival research contradicts, but also removes from the field of inquiry any consideration of the forms of power that characterize modern states, namely their use of what Michel Foucault has called 'bio-politics': that is, the management of the size, natural growth, ethnic composition, age structure, spatial distribution, health, literacy and educational levels and economic conditions of their populations (see, e.g., Curtis, 2002; Foucault, 2009).

The consensus that the new Israeli state had no systematic policy towards its native Arab population and was not intent on managing it is articulated, for example, by Eli Rekhess (1991) in his article on Israel's attitudes towards the Palestinian minority in the first year after the state's foundation. He argues:

> The cabinet did not discuss policy towards the minorities as such, had no recognized process of decision making on the subject, and laid down no detailed guidelines for its agencies to follow. In addition to the need to respond to daily problems which might arise, the agencies were concerned with maintaining a general sense of loyalty to the principles of equal citizenship and integration while at the same time providing security for all. (109–10)

Similarly, Benziman and Mansour (1992), writing about the status of the Arab minority in Israel and the official policy towards it, concluded that

> State's leaders have not discussed systematically the fundamental questions regarding Jewish–Arab relations inside the Green-line, they have neither set for themselves long or medium term objectives nor did they devise plans for the achievement of these goals. (211)

Even the sole article written by an Israeli academic on the new state's policy of controlling the Palestinian minority does not depart from this conception. Sammy Smooha states:

> The establishment itself has, nevertheless, neither the interest nor the time to deal with Arab matters. Since it has no positive expectations of them, such as becoming equal and active partners in Israeli society, it does not define this situation as a state concern that requires planning, allocation of resources and ongoing daily care. (1982:75)

And since 1990, Smooha has become less interested in Israel's policy of control and has instead come to view Israeli domination on racial/national grounds as part of a democratic regime he labels 'ethnic democracy' (Smooha, 1990, 1997, 2002).

To counter such assertions, Ilan Pappe (1995) has examined the will to control the population. Yet he sets the historical moment of such policies later than I will in this book. He writes:

> Far from having a grand design or an ideological master plan, the policy-makers in the early years kept arguing and challenging each other about the desired policy and executed it flimsily once it had been concurred upon. It is in the next decade of Israel's history – the 1960s – that one can discern patterns of clear policy such as co-option, internal colonialism or modernization. (635)

The widely held view that Israel lacked policy guidelines or plans not only runs counter to the common understanding that the principal function of the modern state is to govern, and to govern indigenous population in situations of settler colonialism, but contradicts a constitutive image of Zionism as embodying European modernity and rationality. These features that are thought to set it apart from its Arab environment and constitute the basis of its deep affinity with the West, if recognized in the execution of rational racialized policies towards the native population, risk casting shadows on the state's morality. Were the practices of surveillance and control in which it engaged in the early period seen to be planned, it might suggest that Israel was far from being democratic and modernizing. As a way out of this predicament of rationality/irrationality, some researchers and commentators have claimed that the unfortunate political outcomes for Palestinians resulted from lapses and inconsistencies that occurred because of the seriousness and complexity of the issues with which the young state had to grapple.

For example, some have argued that the policies towards the Palestinians were relegated to the bureaucrats and commanders in the Military Government who ruled the Palestinians between 1948 and 1966. This contention resonates with the notion of 'deep state' or 'state within the state' (e.g. Freely, 2007), where an unelected group determines the state's agenda and dominates the policy-making in certain areas. Thus, when the Military Government through which Israel ruled the Palestinians was revoked, Israeli politician, activist and journalist Uri Avnery stated:

> A complete government ... was created in the Arab sector, a secret government, unsanctioned by law ... whose members and methods are not known ... to anyone. Its agents are scattered among the ministries and government. ... It makes fateful decisions affecting [Arab] lives in unknown places without documents and communicates them in secret conversations or over the telephone. This is the way decisions are made about who goes to the teachers' seminar, or who will

> obtain a tractor, or who will be appointed to a government post ... or who will be elected to the Knesset, or who will be elected to the local council – if there is one. (Cited in Jiryis, 1976:70)

This description was reaffirmed by Amnon Linn (1968), who was all along a member of this 'ghostly government' as an Arabist, first in the Histadrut's Arab Department and later as a member and between 1965 and 1969 as the chairperson of Mapai's[1] and Ha-Ma'arach's[2] Arab departments. He argued:

> Since the establishment of the state, the Jewish public tended to be passive regarding this issue [the Palestinian minority], and left the dealing with it exclusively at the hands of a group of 'experts' who have been labeled 'Arabists' (experts in the problems of the Arabs). The public trusted us and gave us freedom of action, from which no other group in any field of our life has enjoyed. (Linn, 1968:68)

> In the course of time, we achieved a special status in the state as experts and thus no one dared to challenge our opinions or deeds. We are found in all the ministries, in the Histadrut and in the [political] parties. Every office or association has its 'Arabists', and, only they are allowed to act among Arabs in the name of their dispatchers. (*Ibid.*:69)

Does this mean that the actions of these Arabists were arbitrary, anchored neither in a strategy nor in a defined set of policy principles? Many Israeli scholars explained the official policies largely by referring to personal dispositions or attitudes of certain Arabists or politicians (e.g. Smooha, 1982; Kafkafi, 1998; Bauml, 2007; Reiter, 2009). But can such principles be detected by analysing the state's ideological foundations or by classifying the regime's practices and finding patterns? The archives from the 1940s to 1970 are very revealing. Moshe Sharett, who served between 1948 and 1956 as a Foreign Minister and for a short period as Prime Minister, and was one of the principal architects of the official policy towards the Palestinians, dismissed the claim that policy issues were left to the whims of individuals. Discussing Arab affairs in a meeting of the government on 12 July 1950, he commented: 'Although officially sanctioned principles regarding this issue have never been laid down, however, sometimes things take shape without formal principles' (quoted in Avivi, 2007:27). Sharett's remark, which is corroborated by ample archival documents that this book examines, suggests that there were common understandings regarding the official policy towards the Palestinians. This shared understanding was translated into modes of action and representation – something social scientists might call a discourse.

Indeed, various scholars have discerned patterns in Israeli policy towards the Palestinians. Chief among these are Elia Zureik (1979) and Ian Lustick (1980). Zureik has characterized its underlying logic as a form of internal colonialism. That is, the state's policies were geared towards the creation and reproduction of domination and a hierarchical division of labour along national lines. Lustick (1980), on the other hand, has analysed the regime's practices as a system of control comprised of three mutually reinforcing components: segmentation, co-optation and dependency. Yet, he stops short of describing this system as deliberate state strategy. Instead, he sees this model as a theorization of actual practices:

> The system metaphor ... helps avoid the suggestion of comprehensive conspiracy by permitting analysis of how specific policies, because of the structural and institutional contexts within which they are adopted, tend to have *unanticipated* consequences which also reinforce one or another component of control. Thus the 'system of control' described and analyzed in this study is offered as an analytical construct for interpreting a complex social, economic and political reality. (Lustick, 1980:78–9)

Lustick was the first researcher to analyse, systematically, questions relating to Israeli state power, political control and surveillance. However, his behavioural and positivist approach combined with the absence of the archival data available to a later generation of scholars hampered his ability to see that his 'system of control' was not just a metaphor or an abstraction from practice.

Recent research has not only confirmed that the Israeli state employed strategies of surveillance and population management in relation to the Palestinian minority but has highlighted that such strategies were methodically devised as early as 1920, when the Jewish population composed a mere 10 per cent of the country's inhabitants. These strategies aimed to destabilize and disorganize the indigenous Arab community (Cohen, 2004:18). Moreover, techniques of data collection and surveillance – of the population and its property, and particularly land – were widely employed before 1948 by specialized Zionist bodies (Danin, 1987; Pappe, 2006; Fischbach, 2011). Indeed, when Israel was established, it relied extensively on a rich knowledge of control and surveillance practices as well as personnel trained in these techniques.

Two recent books by Cohen (2006) and Bauml (2007) rely on considerable archival material on the state's policies of controlling the Palestinians. Yet neither tries to generalize about Israeli policies or to theorize the nature of its power. Cohen's book *Good Arabs* is subtitled *The Israeli Security Agencies and the Israeli Arabs, 1948–1967*, indicating that its main focus is on the way in which the security services interacted with and governed the Palestinian minority. From his presentation, the reader would not be able to determine whether these security agencies were implementing state policy or whether they were acting within the law, outside it or in the grey area between legality and illegality. Moreover, Cohen's method of presenting a plethora of cases related to each of the subjects he discusses (e.g. education, collaboration), with little analysis or background information, risks misleading readers. For example, Cohen shows that the state was able to exercise tight surveillance due to the many Palestinian collaborators and informers it recruited. But he does not investigate what brought ordinary Palestinians including teachers, parents, young pupils and even passengers on public transportation to spy and pass on information to the authorities about their colleagues, neighbours and friends. Nor does he ask what the sociopolitical context was that made such a behaviour pervasive.

Bauml, on the other hand, limits his study to the second decade of statehood. The picture it renders is thus partial. He offers extraordinary details of the subjects he discusses in this history study but at the expense of any larger theorization and any comprehensive perspective on the decade. The book's arguments shift erratically as Bauml interprets the data as revealing sometimes a process of modernization and sometimes political control. As I will argue, these processes are not necessarily antithetical as modernization can increase the scope and the efficiency of schemes and apparatuses of control.

Despite these limitations, these two books have added a wealth of data to the previous research on the Israeli system of control by Zureik and Lustick and another important book by Sabri Jiryis (1976). Jiryis was principally interested in the way in which the laws could be (ab)used as a tool of domination (Jiryis, 1976, 1981). Jiryis' attempt to demystify the law and place it within, rather than above or outside, the matrix of power relation in the state has had significant impact on the understanding of Israel's governance (*ibid.*). Although the book was first published in 1966, it is still an indispensable source for understanding the discussed period (Jiryis, 1976). Jiryis' critique of Israel's domination by law came from the formal legal discipline itself, not from a Marxist perspective that might view the law as simply superstructural and reflective of the material conditions.

Alongside these advances in the study of Israel's governance of the Palestinian minority, the techniques and theories of governance and surveillance in other contexts and more broadly have received much attention during the last four decades. Questions of population management and surveillance have become focal interests for researchers, policymakers and commercial and financial agencies in an increasingly digitalized and globalized world (Lyon, 2007). Insights regarding the modern (rather than the postmodern) modes of surveillance have informed my analysis of the historical archive. Indeed, concepts, notions and metaphors employed by Bentham (1995) and Foucault (1991, 2009) as well as Deleuze (1992) must comprise a cornerstone for any endeavour like mine.

An additional theoretical paradigm that is closely related to, though not part of, the kind of work done in surveillance studies that provides the framework of this study is the examination of exceptionalism that Schmitt initiated (Schmitt, 2005) – a discussion which has recently been revived and elaborated upon by Giorgio Agamben in *State of Exception* (2005). Schmitt and Agamben analyse the State of Exception, such as the reliance on emergency regulations as a condition wherein the distinction among the different powers (executive, legislative and judicial) is blurred; the executive branch dominates and becomes the regulator of the other two. Moreover, the rule of the normative law is curtailed in favour of decisionism (arbitrary exercise of authority by state officials or military officers). This discussion provides the potential to widening the theoretical perspective implied by Jiryis' thesis of domination by law and can be applied to Israel as in the historical period under question, it relied explicitly on emergency regulations.

Thus, far from dealing with the Israeli policies, strategies and tactics of population management and control towards the Palestinian minority as a metaphorical model or as a theorization from observed practices, this book systematically describes the emergence, evolution and implementation of these policies. Relying on some hitherto unpublished archival material, I shall point to dates and forums in which the debates on the control of the Palestinians took place. Moreover, I shall name the participants, analyse their different approaches, summarize their conclusions, reveal their plans of control and outline the policy principles they devised. Additionally, I shall analyse how these plans were implemented and affected various spheres of Palestinians' lives. Furthermore, I shall examine the relationships between these schemes and practices and the democratic principles to which Israel proclaims adherence.

While this analysis has great import for our understanding of the methods through which the Palestinian minority in Israel was governed and contained, it may also advance our knowledge of the dynamics and techniques of internal colonization and states' production of racialized social-political orders elsewhere. I rely on various concepts that ought to be defined. These concepts are population management, surveillance, political control and the Palestinian minority. Following Michel Foucault, I use *population management* to refer to the deployment of mechanisms to affect the size, structure, ethnic/racial composition, spatial distribution, well-being, mobility, wealth, occupational distribution, patterns of family structure and family planning policies. My use of *surveillance*, in line with David Lyon's (2007) definition, refers to systematic attention to and gathering of personal and categorial data through a variety of means, including face-to-face surveillance – that is, spying – and bureaucratic information collection. While some of the data about the Palestinian minority was gathered by official or semi-official organizations for their own purposes, such as car licensing, some was used for political control, including through social sorting and disciplining. By *political control*, I refer to the structuring of a field of action through the deployment of state power in order to regulate, modify or alter the conduct of a certain group of citizens in such a way as to further the state's political goals or plans, without necessarily trying to shape the thoughts or the dispositions of this group. Political control is not inevitably premised on consent or free will.

It should be noted that the use of the term panopticon in the book does not mean that the official policy was premised on the principles of the panopticon, as charted by Jeremy Bentham. In fact, in chapter 3, I argue that Israeli policy had followed these principles only partially. Nevertheless, I employ it to highlight the desire for achieving total surveillance and control by those who ran the official and semi-official control and surveillance agencies, a wish which could be discerned throughout the book but is particularly conspicuous in the first three chapters. As to the last concept, *the Palestinian minority/citizens*, it refers to the native Arabs of Palestine who after 1948 resided in the area on which Israel was established, though not all of them became Israeli citizens in the discussed period. Some (particularly present absentees), although residing in Israel all along, were given Israeli citizenship in later stages.

In the first chapter, I discuss the foundation of an Israeli discourse about the Palestinian minority, which Israeli leaders called *birour* or clarification, and the circumstances of its emergence and crystallization. Various conditions and contingencies affected this discourse, including the Israeli application to the UN for membership, questions of borders and refugees, the Israeli elections for the first Knesset held in January 1949 and the status of the Jewish minorities worldwide. This discourse developed because the bulk of the Palestinians who remained within the territories controlled by the Jewish state were in Galilee, a region which had been designated for the Arab state according to the UN partition plan. The fate of this minority therefore was not only an Israeli internal affair but also an issue of concern to the international community. More significant for this study is that this discourse, which had taken shape during the first four years of statehood, laid down the framework, the limits and the parameters within which the Palestinian minority would be discussed and dealt with.

This discourse, I will argue, was not confined to the realm of ideas and debates. Rather, it was intimately associated with the deployment of state power to monitor and manage the Palestinian population. Thus, in chapter 2, I deal with the translation of this discourse into policy guidelines, principles and comprehensive plans. The existence of these policy guidelines and plans refutes the dominant consensus in the scholarly literature, as outlined earlier, regarding the absence of a state policy vis-à-vis the Palestinians.

In chapter 3, I describe and analyse the legal and institutional frameworks through which the Palestinians were governed. These were the tools for implementing the policy guidelines and plans. The control processes put into motion by these frameworks are analysed in relation to two well-theorized forms of modern political control: the panopticon and the state of exception. That the two models were operative is revealed by the metaphors and arguments which appeared in the writings of witnesses, commentators and scholars who have dealt with the period.

Chapters 4, 5 and 6 examine specific aspects of the state's policy of control and surveillance of the Palestinians. In chapter 4, I discuss the policy of constructing the Palestinians both as non-Jews and as an assortment of insular minorities. In this chapter and in the following one, I analyse the role of state power in categorizing the Palestinians. While the principles according to which these categories were constructed were not artificial or imaginary, the emphasis on certain divisive principles and their manipulation, and the hierarchical ordering of the various categories (including by their awarding differential benefits and rights), bolstered certain identities and created chasms among the various groups. In this chapter, I describe how such categories were reinforced as a result of explicit deliberations and carefully planned policies.

In chapter 5, I analyse the ways state control and surveillance were implemented at the level of the locality. At this micro-level, the state used the intimate social unit of the *hamula* (clan) to practise its control of the population. While this social unit has been essentialized by researchers and has become a hallmark of Palestinian social structure, I shall describe official plans and policies to revive and strengthen the influence of the hamula and the 'dignitaries'. The hamula, whose traditional role was to provide moral and social support to its members, was turned into a unit through which state control was practised. Its perpetuation had become essential for the economy of control and surveillance. The control of Palestinians through their hamula affiliation and the manipulation of social relations at the local level through hamula politics, including the promotion of competition and rivalries among hamulas, led to the walling off of Palestinians from each other on the basis of social and blood affiliation.

While the policies of segmentation worked at the social level, dividing Palestinians by ethnicity, religion and blood, the Israeli state sought to shape Palestinian consciousness through educational policies. Thus, in chapter 6, entitled 'The power of mind over mind',[3] I analyse the way state educational policy not just fostered the segmentation described earlier but promoted among students and educators what Syed Hussein Alatas (1974) has called a 'captive mind'. Alatas argues that in colonial situations, what has been produced is the 'uncritical and imitative mind dominated by an external source, whose thinking is deflected from an independent perspective' (quoted in Alatas, 2006:47). My emphasis will not be on the manifestation of such a mode of consciousness but rather on the mechanisms and methods of its construction. Given the historical backdrop of the establishment of Israel and the status of the Palestinian minority, those in charge of the Palestinians questioned the efficacy of such a policy. While the educational system might provide a setting for the cultivation of 'captive minds', they feared that literacy would open up the horizons of educated Palestinians and enable them to read critical or 'subversive' writings. Indeed, the role of education in the state control and surveillance system had been discussed at length among those in charge of Arab affairs.

This chapter offers a systematic analysis of the ambivalence and the tentative solutions offered.

Chapter 7 takes up the question of political rights and their meaning under the rule of Military Government. Indeed, the granting of political rights to the Palestinians and their participation in the first elections bolstered the image of Israel as a robust democracy. But can those who live under a state of exception determine the nature of the political system? If democracy and a state of exception are antithetical, how can the political right be empowering to those living under military rule? Or maybe giving political representation to the subordinate population might have other ends than influencing the political system. Colonial regimes, for example, primarily the British, had fostered compradorian – or intermediary – native elites in the colonies. Yet, for a long time, many of these elites played other roles than struggling for liberation. Does the role of Arab members of the Knesset (MKs), particularly those who were elected on Mapai's (the ruling party) affiliated slates, correspond to this interpretation of the role of native elites under colonialism? Such queries about representation, authority and legitimacy faced those in charge of Arab affairs. In this chapter, I discuss how Arab MKs were chosen and what authority and representativeness they had in light of the building and maintenance of a control system. A look at Palestinian opposition to the system through official political channels and alternative venues of contestation reveals the political dynamics and the modes of resistance that this minority has offered.

The book concludes with personal reflections on the thousands of minutes, protocols, reports, plans and personal messages, which I have read and some of which I summarized in this work. I focus particularly on the issues which those in charge of the surveillance agencies were oblivious to or preferred not to tackle. I probe their self-reflections on what they were doing and the implication their actions might have. I conclude by considering the impact that this book – which reveals the deliberate policies put in place to control the Palestinian minority and analyses the various techniques and methods of control used by the Israeli state – might have on future research about state–minority relations in Israel as well as the theoretical field that addresses other unwelcome minorities and native populations in deeply divided societies.

The particular contribution of this book lies in its reconstruction of a wide-ranging scheme of surveillance that existed over a relatively long time and the glimpses it offers into the world of those who took part in this endeavour. While concepts such as control, surveillance and oppression of subaltern communities are widely used in social science literature, there are very few substantive studies of how these concepts take shape and materialize in everyday reality. This book aims to show their embodiment in state–minority relations in Israel in the first two decades. The analysis is intended to go beyond abstractions, theorization and jargon and to deal with the way in which population management, control and surveillance were embodied in the 'ordinary' thrust of life.

Notes

1 Mifleget Poalei Eretz Yisrael in Hebrew, meaning the Workers' Party of the Land of Israel.

2 Meaning 'alignment' in Hebrew. It was an alliance of two left-Zionist parties, Mapai and Achdut Haavoda, and in the 1970s, they were joint by Mapam. It existed between 1965 and 1991.

3 This metaphor is taken from Bentham (1995).

1

The formation of a discourse

The need for a discourse

In the autumn of 1948, while the eventful war was drawing to an end, David Ben-Gurion, who led the organized Jewish community – the *Yishuv* – to what has been described until recently in the media and history books as a miraculous victory, began his moves for the next stage. At the personal level, he had to reaffirm his leadership through a popular vote. In the international arena, he had to manoeuvre for international recognition of Israel without making concessions on the two key issues of international concern – the borders and the Palestinian refugees. Israeli policy towards the refugees was clear: their return had to be blocked under all circumstances. And various activities to this end had already been undertaken, including the destruction of empty or partially empty Arab villages (Morris, 2004:342–95; Pappe, 2006:188). Moreover, not only was Israel not ready to yield the territories it occupied outside its boundaries defined by the 1947 UN resolution, it had also laid claims to regions which had not been occupied.

One thing however did not fit in the new reality – the existence of Palestinian citizens. What is the appropriate discourse for dealing with them? This question became unavoidable as a call for general elections to be held in late January 1949 was issued. Should these Palestinians be allowed to establish their political parties and take part in the forthcoming elections as ordinary citizens? Or should the racial boundaries that had been promoted by Zionism during the British Mandate be reinstated (Sa'di, 2004a)? Yet, maybe a Machiavellian alternative could be found in which these opposite solutions would ostensibly be reconciled. To this end, Ben-Gurion summoned the 'Arabists' – those who had gained intimate knowledge of the Arabs through their work in various institutions and participated in the implementation of the Zionist policy – for consultations.

Yaakov Shimoni of the Middle East department in the Ministry for Foreign Affairs argued that principally they should not be given political rights. However, three days earlier, he composed a memorandum in which he outlined three alternatives regarding the non-participation of Palestinians: (A) to find a security excuse for denying them political rights; (B) to argue that, in the absence of appropriate conditions, elections in the Arab localities cannot be held, yet the government would appoint Arab representatives in the Knesset, in proportion to the Arab population; and (C) to establish a sectarian system wherein each national group – Israeli Jews and Palestinians – elects its representatives. To these options, he added a fourth – that the state persuade Arab 'dignitaries' to call upon the Arab population to refrain from taking part in the elections. Similarly, Yehoshua (Josh) Palmon maintained that the state should not give the Palestinians political rights as they do not wish to become Israeli citizens. Meanwhile, Abba Hushi recommended the establishment of three Arab lists along 'ethnic', that is, religious, lines – Muslims, Christians and Druze. Yet, as the majority of the Druze had not by then received identity cards, and therefore were ineligible to vote, he suggested the establishment of one list, which would be composed of two Muslims, two Christians and one Druze (Pappe, 1995:644; Avivi, 2007:331). However, given Israel's precarious position, Ben-Gurion decided against the advice of the experts on Arab affairs, maintaining that 'we cannot start national discrimination, while the whole world is discussing the problem with Israel and the rest of Palestine' (quoted in Pappe, 1995:644). Then, Israel's application to UN membership was discussed and the Galilee, which was allotted to the Arab state according to the UN resolution, was not officially considered part of Israel. Rather, it was referred to – including by Israeli officials – as the 'administered territories'. Explicit in this debate was the absence of a conception of citizenship rights and universalistic principles. The awarding of political rights to Palestinians was not conceived as a means for them to have an impact on the political sphere. Rather, it was seen as a means through which the state would influence them.

Yet, Ben-Gurion's decision to give the Palestinians political rights was viewed by some Israeli leaders as erroneous and unrealistic, for political rights usually followed rather than preceded the normalization of the citizen's everyday life. For example, in a discussion held in Mapai's political bureau on 10 November 1948, Yehiel Duvdevany commented:

> If the government wants to do justice with the Arabs, it ought to stop murdering them after the end of the fighting. This week Arab women and children were killed in the Galilee because there is no firm supervision on the commanders who ought to prevent our soldiers from acting in a lawless manner.
>
> I understand that there is an international milieu, which compels us to give the Arabs living in the country the right to vote ... [however] the law exists first of all for us. (The Political Committee, 10 November 1948:6)

Duvdevany highlighted two points of immense significance: the meaning of political rights in a state of exception where the rule of law is curtailed and the racial bias of the state.

Beyond this, the fundamental question was why these Palestinians remained. Why was their fate dissimilar to that of the refugees? This question has been part of an intense debate among historians on the 1948 events and the Palestinian refugee problem. Chief among these is Benny Morris (2004), who argued that the Palestinians' exodus was born of war rather than by design. The compelling war conditions made the expulsion of Palestinian civilians and in some cases their massacre unavoidable. Criticizing Morris' thesis, Masalha (1991, 1992, 2009) contended that the expulsion of the Palestinians was not carried out in a void; rather, the transfer idea had been deeply rooted in the minds of Zionist leaders and was embedded in Zionist political thought all along. Lately, Pappe (2006) has made the case that the expulsion of the Palestinians was an act of ethnic cleansing, which was guided and supervised by Ben-Gurion and a small group of his aids. Nonetheless, the fact that Palestinians remained in Israel, particularly in the Galilee, which was occupied at the end of the war, needed an explanation. Morris cited this fact as a vindication of his thesis and a refutation of his critics. Hillel Cohen (2008) went one step further by crediting Palestinian collaborators with the survival of Palestinian villages in the Galilee:

> In Western Galilee, veteran Druze collaborators worked with Muslims and Christians from the region. For the most part, the people involved had been in contact with the Zionists for several years.
>
> Surrender negotiations are a classic situation in which opposite concepts of what is treason and what is patriotism come to the fore ...
>
> The Zu'biyya villages east of Afula – Nin, Na'ura, Sulam, Tamra ... are prominent examples of those who surrendered of their own volition consenting to live under Israeli rule. The ruling family in these villages, the Zu'bis, maintained close relations with the Jewish settlements in the region over the course of many years ...
>
> There were similar cases in the Western Galilee, some involving Muslims and others Druze. (245–6)

Cohen's reasoning is flimsy. It is easy to bring many counterexamples where, despite the cooperation of Palestinian villages with neighbouring Jewish settlements or the collaboration of Palestinian chiefs with the Haganah, these villages were not spared destruction and in some cases massacres. Deir Yassin, Dawayima, Lifta, Huj, Ghabisiya and Kafr Bir'im stand as good examples. Moreover, the ideological tenets of Cohen are transparent and equally feeble.[1] The straightforward conclusion one might draw on the basis of his narrative is that had Palestinians collaborated with the Yishuv and accepted to live peacefully in the Jewish state, they would not have been driven out.

Although of direct bearing, this debate does not give a direct answer to the question posed: Why did Palestinians stay in specific regions and not others? Chiefly, why were they allowed to stay in the Galilee? In a meeting of the secretariat of Mapai with the party's Knesset members (MKs) on 18 June 1950, Moshe

Dayan, one of the key commanders of the 1948 War and Chief of Staff and Minister of Defence later, stated that Palestinians stayed in the Galilee because of the nature of the Israeli military operation there. According to Dayan, this operation took the shape of a pincer (double) movement, which resulted in many Palestinian villages finding themselves within Israeli controlled territory. However, had it taken a different form, the fate of Galilee Palestinians would not have been different from those of other regions who were driven out (The Secretariat's Meeting with [Mapai's] MKs, 18 June 1950:1/4).[2]

Moshe Sharett, the Foreign Minister, emphasized that a different course, which would have brought different results, was not possible:

> This process occurred in stages, and the circumstances surrounding the Arab exodus or uprooting in the first stages are not the same as in the final ones. Two facts – on the one hand the Galilee was the last area to be conquered and on the other it has the main concentration of Arabs who remained. The co-existence of these two facts is not accidental; rather it is a cause and effect. ... We shouldn't deceive ourselves by assuming that we could have managed this affair differently. *When we confronted strong villages with deep roots that refused to move, we did neither spare military power nor moral strength or diplomatic valor.* (Emphasis added by AHS. *Ibid.*:1/2)

As for the Triangle where a large Palestinian population continued to live, it was transferred from Jordanian to Israeli rule under the 1949 Armistice Agreement, with the stipulation that its population would not be expelled or harmed. In other words, as Dayan put it: '... the borders there were demarcated in a technical way. Had the borders been set differently they would have become part of an enemy state' (*ibid.*:1/2). In addition, few Palestinian Bedouins remained in the Negev desert, and some remained accidentally in a few villages and townships such as Al-Majdal (which would be depopulated within a year). Other villages which remained are inhabited by Druze and two villages by Circassians (*ibid.*). These authoritative explanations clarify the circumstance which made the Palestinians' presence in Israel possible. But they hardly support the theses of either Morris or Cohen.

Israel's willingness to tolerate a large Palestinian minority was tested in one case. An Egyptian initiative which was discussed at the end of the war proposed the transfer of the Gaza strip with its population to Israel, a move rejected by Israel – '... we preferred to give up the Gaza strip and not to increase the size of the Arab population by such [large] numbers[3]', explained Sharett (*ibid.*:1/2).

Awaiting the next stage

Beyond the contingencies of the first elections, the question regarding the existence of a Palestinian minority in Israel needed thorough evaluation. Indeed, various meetings took place throughout the next three years – 1949 to 1952 – with the participation of leading politicians and Arabists. Moshe Sharett was the guiding figure in this examination (they referred to it as *birour*, clarification). In the meeting of the secretariat of Mapai with the party's MKs held on 18 June 1950 (The Secretariat's Meeting with MKs, 18 June 1950), he predicted that a Palestinian minority, concentrated in the regions mentioned earlier, will continue to exist for some time despite the Israeli state's policies which would be geared to internally relocating Palestinians. However, he conceived its existence as temporary, thus stating that

> the state of Israel, by a stroke of fate, will include for a certain period of time, a sizeable Arab minority. I do not know the length of this period nor do I know what changes are expected in the turbulent future. ... However until the next upheaval ... we will continue to have among ourselves a sizeable Arab minority. (2–3/2)

Given this, the impending questions, according to Sharett were: What should the nature of the governance arrangements be during this transitory period? What should their scope and severity or leniency be? Yet, he maintained that deciding on these arrangements was not a simple task, as they might impinge on various spheres which are important or sensitive to Israel. Sharett identified four such spheres: the morality of the state (by that he meant the socialization of the young Israeli generation), the security of the state, the international standing and reputation of the state and the plausible implications of its policies on the well-being of the Jewish communities worldwide. Sharett thought that any Israeli policy would impinge on one or more of these spheres, thus generating paradoxes and dilemmas. For example, there is contradiction between Israel's international commitment of granting these Palestinians equal rights and the security risk entailed in this approach, as they might become a fifth column in times of emergency.

The security risk was even greater, as they are part of the Arab majority of the country – the refugees – who still live in dismal conditions across the borders. If Israel treats the Palestinian minority decently, it will increase the attraction of the country to the refugees. However, if it intervenes in their lives arbitrarily and harshly, the lure of the country to the refugees might decrease, and in this way the state's security would be bolstered. Yet, accepting the security consideration as the overriding one might adversely affect the morality of the state (i.e. the values transmitted to the younger generations), its international standing and the status of the Jewish communities in other countries (*ibid.*:3/2–1/3). Out of this dialectical thinking, he concluded that 'This question [of the Arabs in Israel] is very complicated and our approach to it should be multifaceted and sophisticated' (*ibid.*:1/3).

Thus, he suggested five policy principles for the transitory period. First, to continue the transfer of Palestinians when the circumstances permit, thus arguing:

> if currently there is an opportunity to decrease the number of the Arab minority which numbers 170,000 by one thousand – it should be done, however, it

> depends on how [should it be done]. Sometimes there are few such opportunities. However this shouldn't be done on a wide scale and by deprivation. First in this way, the objective will not be achieved and, if it will, it will work for a limited number only. (*Ibid.*:3/4)

Second, to establish a clear-cut distinction between Palestinian refugees and those who remained, pointing out that severe measures should be taken against the refugees who would attempt to return. Third, to supply the Arab minority with its 'minimal cultural needs' (*ibid.*:4/4). Fourth, to establish dependency of the Palestinian minority on the state through the provision of state services:

> I don't profess for hasty [measures for] equality, rather a constructive concern of the state. I argue for a [state's] concern which will make the Arabs dependent upon the state.
>
> I argue that for such a concern which will make the Arabs dependent on the state for the improvement of their living conditions. They ought to know 'the hand which gives them life' and what does this require them to do in term of their internal adjustment. (*Ibid.*:5/4–1/5)

Fifth, to support the rise of an Arab leadership which would be subservient to Mapai but be capable of influencing Arab public opinion (*ibid.*:2/5). Such a leadership, he estimated, would not emerge from the ranks of the League of Arab Workers – a front organization established by the Histadrut during the Mandate era to influence the Palestinian workers' movement and revived after 1948.

Moshe Dayan, who took part in this debate, unlike Sharett, thought that the temporality, uncertainty and vulnerability of Palestinians' existence in Israel should be accentuated as the eventual goal was their expulsion. Thus, he argued:

> I think that the Party's [Mapai's] policy should be that the fate of the 170 thousand Arabs has not been decided yet. I hope that in the coming few years an opportunity will rise to transfer these Arabs from the country and, as long as such an opportunity is still probable, we should not take any action that might hamper it. These 170 thousand are part of the rest of the Arab population [of the country]. (*Ibid.*:2/2)

Meanwhile, no positive steps to normalize their conditions should be taken. On the contrary, the tenuousness of their existence should be increased:

> [W]e should not accept them in the army, we should not give them identity cards or permanent citizenship, we should not give them back property or pay compensations. We should declare that we are allowing them stay in the same conditions, and that we are not going to progress towards a constructive solution, this despite the danger that they might be harmed by local [Jewish] forces. (*Ibid.*:3/2)

Dayan saw that the question of the Palestinian minority was part of the wider political reality which had not been entirely settled. He argued that the status of the Palestinian minority should be linked to two other issues: the demarcation of the final borders and the settling of the refugees. In case an Arab state (or Arab states) was found to settle the 700,000 refugees, it (they) should also settle these Palestinians as they are part of the country's Arab population. In other words, the change in the status of the Palestinian minority would take the shape of their transfer and resettlement in the Arab world along with the fulfilment of Israel's demand with regard to the refugees and the borders (*ibid.*:3–4/2).

The differences between the approaches of Sharett and Dayan should not be exaggerated, however. They differed on tactics and style rather than on substance. Both viewed the Palestinians' existence in Israel as impermanent. The difference was on the nature of the temporary period within which Palestinians would live in Israel. While Dayan seemed to have paid little attention to it, Sharett wanted to shape Palestinian lives even within its limits, a stand that could be gleaned from a series of questions he posed to Dayan:

> Should we allow Arab kids to go to school or shouldn't we? And if we do allow them, should or shouldn't we make sure that the school becomes a means of influencing them? And there is the question: should or shouldn't we give them work? And if we do give them work, should we ensure that their workers' organization becomes a means of influence, or should we disregard this option? (*Ibid.*:3/2)

The third intervention in this debate was by Yehoshua (Josh) Palmon who then held the position of Advisor to the Prime Minister on Arab Affairs. His presentation was composed of two parts. The first included a description of the official bodies through which the state governed the Palestinians and their functioning. These bodies were the Office of the Prime Minister's Advisor on Arab Affairs, the Military Government, the Arab departments in the various ministries and quasi councils (which were most likely the security committees). The second represented a sociological analysis of the Palestinian minority and the plausibility of migration of the different groups during the transitory period. He divided the Palestinians into three class categories. The first comprised of 15 per cent of the population and was made up of big merchants, large landowners and high-ranking civil servants. The second comprised of 20 per cent of the population and was made up of professionals and small landowners who held 25–35 dunams. They were self-employed or employed one or two paid workers, besides their family members. The third comprised of 65 per cent of the population and included landless peasants and workers.

Palmon predicted that the first group would find it hard to continue living in the new reality: 'During the British Mandate they lived in a paradise and this paradise is not going to return. ... There are cases of migration; anyway many of them are willing to leave' (*ibid.*:5/1). This had partly to do with actions taken by the state. For example, it had undermined the businesses of the merchants who marketed the agricultural produce of the Triangle. As for the second group, he expected that its members would experience problems of psychological adjustment due to their loss of comfort and freedom. They were also inclined to leave. As for the third group, its members would not leave even if they were persecuted due to their low standards of living. Moreover, they were not easily governed because they were capable of corrupting the Jewish staff which governs them (*ibid.*:1–3/2).

Similarly to Sharett, Palmon thought that those who would leave during the transitory period should be used to further the goals of the state and the party:

> I think it is logical to establish a movement ... which should include groups that do not join the League [of Arab Workers]. I am talking about the 15 per cent who might leave in the future, yet I think that a movement should be established from the most progressive and intelligent groups among the Arabs. I am not deterred by the fact that after 3–5 years they have to leave the country, yet in the meanwhile we can establish a worthwhile workers' movement. (*Ibid.*:1/3)

He claimed that such a group has already been established (*ibid.*).

Four years after the state's establishment and almost two years after this meeting, Israeli leaders realized that the transitory period in which a Palestinian minority would live in Israel could be much longer than they hoped for. Therefore, a need emerged to rethink and modify their discourse and the state's goals. Moreover, they could no longer defer various laws such as the nationality (citizenship) law under which Palestinians would gain rights that could complicate future schemes of transfer. Yet, the law and the protection it grants should not be fetishized. Carl Schmitt (2005) noticed this long ago and Israeli leaders were well aware of that. Indeed, Israel continued expelling Palestinians until 1959 – eleven years after the state's establishment and seven years after the passing of the citizenship law (see chapter 2). Still, mass deportation of citizens would be hard to defend in the international arena.

A thorough discussion that extended over two long meetings took place in Mapai's Political Committee in 1952. The aim was to reassess the official discourse regarding the temporality of Palestinians' existence in Israel and to amend the state's policies. In the first meeting which took place on 24 January 1952, Ben-Gurion was the first speaker. His presentation, largely contradictory and inchoate, included his perception of the Palestinian minority. He argued that various characteristics of the Palestinians are inherently problematic. These have to do with their perception and their religions. They do not see themselves as a minority, but rather as part of the region's majority, and they view Israeli Jews as oppressors who dispossessed them, and for this, they are not going to forgive. Even if some would forgive and forget, their forgiveness should not be accorded much weight as long as the majority's perception remained unchanged. But change, according to Ben-Gurion, was not forthcoming. Their majority is comprised of Muslims who, due to their militant religious socialization, will not be ready to accept the Israeli state. Meanwhile, their minority is composed of Christians, among whom the Catholics – the dominant group – are inimical to the idea of independent Jewish nationhood because the Jews rejected Christ's annunciation and crucified him. As for Orthodox Christians – the minority within the minority – given their religious affiliation, they are likely to be influenced by Russia.

These characteristics are not the only factors that determine Israeli policy towards the Palestinians. There were external factors as well: the multiple connections – primarily through the Jewish communities – to the international community, without which Israel would find it hard to survive. Therefore, Israel is demanded to maintain high international standing and moral potency. However, in the international arena, there were also enemies who would capitalize on Israel's mistakes or maltreatment of Palestinians. These are the Vatican, the Muslim countries and the anti-Semites (The Political Committee, 24 January 1952:1–2).

Moreover, the benign discourse of Arab MKs seemed to trouble Ben-Gurion as it invalidated his beliefs. Their statements seemed a mismatch with his perception of the Palestinians:

> The hate of the Arabs in Israel for the state of Israel and for the Jewish people has now a respectful guise ... now the hate is dressed in the costume of communism or (supposedly) of Mapam. When I hear (Knesset member, MK) Bustani (of Mapam) or MK Tawfiq Tubi (of the Communist Party) speak, I hear the Mufti speaks through their throats. But they speak in the name of progress and in the name of pioneering revolutionary Zionism. (*Ibid.*:2)

In the light of this, Ben-Gurion offered four policy principles. First, security should be given priority over all other considerations. Practically, this meant the continued imposition of the Military Government on the Palestinian-populated areas and the denial of the refugees' right of return. Second, equality between Jews and Palestinians in Israel should be instituted both de facto and de jure. Third, Palestinians, particularly the Muslims, would be converted to Judaism, if this would become plausible. Ben-Gurion was referring to his theory, according to which Palestinian peasants are originally Jews who stayed in the country and converted to Islam during Islamic rule. He proposed to explore the plausibility of their return to Judaism. However, if this proved to be impossible, they should be brought as close as possible to Israeli Jews through acculturation. Fourth, the establishment of a Jewish–Arab organization, which would attract Palestinians and minimize the influence that the communist party had on them (*ibid.*:3–4).

Unlike Ben-Gurion, who spoke in broad terms and expressed his ideological convictions, Moshe Sharett explored concrete issues. He raised the question of

Palestinians' loyalty to the state. Given the historical backdrop, he wondered whether Palestinians – or at least considerable sections among them – could become loyal. Although he was pessimistic with regard to the majority, he believed that some sections might become loyal. Along with that, he reiterated his support for the 'soft transfer' and for giving security a priority over all other considerations. He also contended that the Palestinians' discontent stemmed from their psychological condition of being a minority. Moreover, while he opposed an application of Ben-Gurion's theory of Muslims' mass conversion to Judaism, he supported a policy of gradual integration (*ibid.*:5–7).

Then, Sharett discussed the issue of governance. He underscored the need for coordination between the various bodies which dealt with Palestinians and called for the establishment of Arab departments in the various governmental offices (in fact, a separate bureaucracy for the Palestinians; see chapter 2). However, official bodies are not capable of sorting out all social and political issues; therefore, he foresaw a need for societal organizations. He pointed to the need for establishing a framework which would give the Palestinians the '*illusion that they have their own project and their own movement*' (*ibid.*:2/2). Moreover, besides the need for mystification, Sharett referred to the absence of popular Palestinian leadership which would collaborate with Mapai. In this regard, he was raising again the issue of Palestinian leadership which he and Palmon highlighted two years earlier. It seems that Mapai's leaders were particularly concerned about the absence of a credible Palestinian collaborative elite (see chapter 7). The problem, as Sharett put it, was that 'most of the leadership of the past is not in the country, and in case there are some, they are disqualified [by the state] on loyalty grounds and a new strata of leadership has not emerged yet, but there are all kinds of groups and there is a tradition of infighting among them' (*ibid.*:2/2). Sharett also pointed out that the party's [Mapai's] approach should be binding to all those who deal with Arab affairs (*ibid.*:3–4/2).

The absence of a single, clear party approach was underscored by Reuven Barkatt, a long-standing Histadrut official and Arabist. He argued that the official policy had hitherto been erratically moving between the two lines – referring to the approaches which were proposed in 1950 – one of uprooting the Palestinians (i.e. Dayan's line) and another which came to be known as constructive (i.e. that of Sharett). The result was failure (*ibid.*:8/2). This reached a point where, during the elections, personnel of the Military Government, who were party members, acted contrary to the party's directions (*ibid.*:11/2). Barkatt argued that the constructive approach, which Sharett and Ben-Gurion proposed and which he supported, enhanced the security of the state (*ibid.*:8/2). Then, Barkatt approached the question of loyalty which had surfaced as a main issue during the debate. He claimed that there were already Palestinians who were either loyal or potentially so. They came from the ranks of the fellahin and the workers. Meanwhile, the urban population had remained inimical.

Did Barkatt's appraisal result from the fact that nationalism is more pronounced in the cities than in the countryside in Palestine, as elsewhere? Or maybe it reflected his ideological bias, as a self-styled socialist? Whatever the reason, he was gratified with the shift of the Palestinian sociopolitical centre after the establishment of Israel from the cities to the villages. As for the instruments of governance, despite his position and sphere of influence in the Histadrut, he did not have much of an illusion about the League of Arab Workers. He described it as a 'function' of the Histadrut and as no more than an 'instrument' for implementing the constructive policy (*ibid.*:8–9/2). In case a club was established, as Ben-Gurion suggested, he foresaw that it should fulfil defined tasks, other than those of which the League was in charge of. Furthermore, Barkatt described a failed endeavour to put together an educated collaborative elite and the institution of a Palestinian leader that he and Abba Hushi had undertaken:

> Abba Hushi and I had an experience of trying to find intelligentsia on the election's eve. ... I am sorry to say that even five virtuous men we didn't find. ... There was someone in the name of Nemri (most likely he was referring to Nimer Hawari, see chapter 7) who was supposed to fill in the role of leader, he betrayed us, then he returned, in the meanwhile, however, it became clear that he is worthless in the Arab community. (*Ibid.*:10/2)

Another approach was put forward by Issar Harel, who between 1952 and 1963 simultaneously headed both agencies of Israeli intelligence: the General Security Services – commonly known as Shin Bet – and the Mossad. Unlike previous speakers, who explained the position of the Palestinians in psychological terms, he referred to the recent history which made Palestinians' identification with the state almost impossible:

> I think that the Arab community is, nonetheless, a fifth column. And the reasons are known. We cannot fix what we have done to them. ... I am sure it is wrong to assume [that they are devoid of nationalist sentiments]. The Arabs will never forgive us for what we've done, even if we treat them in a good way; develop them socially or in another field. (*Ibid.*:12/2)

His straightforward conclusion was to keep them underdeveloped and marginal, as their development would help in creating a sophisticated fifth column. But he sensed that throughout the debate, his true sentiments and those of his colleagues were not boldly stated: 'we should be brave and say it openly – we want to see the Arabs out of the state of Israel. This is the [our] wish' (*ibid.*). However, as this cannot be achieved through a direct action due to the international milieu, he asked why, instead of spending money in organizing the Palestinians and establishing a club for them, it could not be used to elicit them to migrate.

However, if the existence of a Palestinian minority in Israel is principally accepted, Harel contended, why should the government undertake actions which aggravate them and eventually push them to the communist party, which provides an 'outlet to [their] feelings of discrimination and injustice' (*ibid.*:1/3)? He pinpointed various forms of exploitation to which Palestinians were subjected by Jewish contractors, firms and marketing companies (mainly those which marketed their agricultural produce). Harel's main contention was that the Palestinian community was mostly composed of proletariat, who should be given basic social services such as employment and medical care. These services should be provided by the League of Arab Workers, which is conceived by Palestinians as an instrument of the government (*ibid.*:1/3). Moreover, he aired pessimism regarding the impact that a club or a movement, which Mapai would establish, could have on solving the Arabs' problems (*ibid.*:2/3).

MK Zalman Aran raised two points: the first, on the Arab leadership, a focal point in the emerging Israeli discourse; and the second, regarding the representations and the stereotyping of Palestinians in Israeli society and media, an issue which would be disregarded for several decades. On the question of Palestinian leadership, he distinguished between two groups of Arab MKs: the MKs of Mapam and the communist party on the one hand and the MKs of Mapai's affiliated lists on the other. He rhetorically asked: Why are the members of the first group intelligent and give a good impression, while there is no single righteous or intelligent one in the second? He went on to describe the Arab MKs affiliated to Mapai as 'orphans', isolated and discarded. It seems that Aran was offering an alternative, though not a counter discourse. His premise was that there is a fundamental flaw in the way the Arab affairs are managed, thus adding: 'A Jew like me cannot talk with them [Mapai's affiliated Arab MKs] since I cannot – I'd have talked to them with the help of an interpreter – however I don't talk because I know that I cannot be truthful with them' (*ibid.*:2/3). He saw his personal case as an epitome of the wider reality: 'The problem is that I don't see any intelligent, righteous and decent Arab who in the current state of affairs would become a leader of a movement which identifies with our party or with the state' (*ibid.*:2/3).

Aran's reflective and critical remarks were supplemented by the intervention of Professor Ben-Zion (Dinaburg) Dinur – Minister of Education from 1952 to 1955. Dinur tried to shift the discussion back to the issues which Ben-Gurion, Sharett and Barkatt excluded, namely, an acknowledgement of the political origins of the current state of affairs and specifically the Palestinian calamity of 1948. With regard to loyalty, he stated: 'We shouldn't have illusions about their loyalty; let's put ourselves in their place. We forget that the Arabs are a historic nation, a people with a past and memories, and as we teach them more they will see their own history' (*ibid.*:3/3). His last comment would raise long discussions in the future regarding the impact of education on the political attitudes of Palestinians. Would it increase their national sentiments or draw them closely to the state and the Jewish Israeli society?

In contrast to Dinur, Palmon was less bothered by the loyalty of the Palestinians. Rather, as always, he was interested in questions of governance, which he raised back in 1950. These included the need to establish an Arab movement in line with Ben-Gurion's suggestion and the pervasiveness of corruption in the systems which governed the Palestinians (see chapter 3). Yet, he tackled one issue which would become an everlasting topic of theorizations in Israel, namely, how could democracy and equality exist in a state where the laws are biased? He answered Ben-Gurion's demand of full equality by asking how equality can prevail when Palestinians who live in the country are treated as absentees and their property is confiscated, and where Palestinian land is transferred to the ownership of faraway Jewish settlements (such as the transfer of Al-Lujoon lands which were owned by Umm al-Fahm's residents to the Zikhron Yaakov settlement).

New citizens?

By August 1952, Israeli leaders were still in the middle of their debates – the second meeting – and an operative consensus, regarding the conceptualization of issues at hand had not been reached. Mapai's Chairman, Meir Argov, urged the participants to round up the discussions in the light of impending events, including the final stages of the discussions on the Land Acquisition (Validation of Acts and Compensations) Law, under whose clauses the state ought to compensate Palestinians for confiscated lands.

Sharett began by admitting that his expectations regarding the transitory period were dashed. Moreover, some Palestinians acquired Israeli citizenship by virtue of the nationality law which was passed on 1 April 1952, and their demands began to focus on the normalization of their status. They demanded freedom of movement, joining the trade union in order to improve their work conditions, etc. Sharett argued that they could also use their rights as political people usually do by supporting any party they wished. Despite that, he believed that Mapai still had enough leverage, mainly through its dominance in the government, to control the Palestinians and at the same time to get their votes. To achieve this, he saw 'a need for trickery calculations in every step. ... Even if guidelines are set, there is a need to think when to apply [certain] policy and to give directions to the in charge persons, and to use the Party's influence in the government' (The Political Committee, 3 August 1952:4–6).

Similarly to Sharett, Barkatt admitted that his expectations were not met, particularly with regard to the size of the Palestinian minority and its survivability:

> I am afraid that today the Arabs number 200 thousand. This means that all the measures we undertook to decrease their number in the country were unsuccessful. The majority of the Arabs do not think of leaving the country. And the Arabs surrounding us [i.e. the refugees] are still attracted to it. ... Today we don't have much choice. ... The Arabs attained rights and various political and economic achievements. We cannot turn the clock back. We cannot go back to square one and plan our policy towards the Arabs. We cannot withdraw what we have already granted. (*Ibid.*:8)

However, to amend the current course of action, Barkatt proposed two measures: first, to encourage the ascendance of new sociopolitical forces to lead the Palestinians, instead of the mukhtars, and second, to create mechanisms for returning the money, or at least some of what Arab workers earned, to the Jewish economy. This question of siphoning the money had become – according to Barkatt – urgent in the light of a governmental decision to equalize the prices of Arab and Jewish agricultural produce and to equalize, at one stage, the salaries of Jewish and Arab workers.

In addition to these suggestions, he raised two issues. First, how should the problem of Palestinian commuter workers be approached? Should they be encouraged to live in Jewish or mixed cities, or should they be retained in their villages? Second, should Palestinians be allowed to join the Histadrut in the future, particularly in the light of the rapid decline in new membership, as Jewish immigration had dwindled? And if they were to be accepted, how would their voting likely affect Mapai's dominance (*ibid.*:8–11)?

Yitzhak Ben-Zvi, a politician and Arabist and later the second President, highlighted certain aspects of the Israeli discourse, particularly with regard to demography. His premises would become the cornerstone in future debates on this issue. After expressing the disappointment he shared with his colleagues for having an Arab minority in the country and for Israel's inability to conduct a wide-ranging transfer or an exchange of population with the Arab countries, he underscored the need for a demographic policy which would keep the rate of the minority population stable at 10–11 per cent. Moreover, he explicitly underlined the need for rearranging the spatial distribution of the Palestinians through 'removal and resettlement which should be conducted according to a plan' (*ibid.*:12–13). Along with that, he maintained that the Palestinians should adapt to Israeli reality through 'cultural assimilation' (*ibid.*). On the other hand, stiff measures such as expulsion should be taken against those who show disloyalty. Ben-Zvi's principal argument was that the

Palestinians should not be allowed to compose a single unified group. In addition to their dispersion, various groups of Palestinians should be treated according to the danger they *potentially* pose to the state. While the Muslims, as part of the majority in adjacent countries, might establish a secessionist movement, the Druze are a minority in these countries too, and they are not likely to threaten the state's integrity. As for the Arab leaders in Mapai's affiliated lists, he argued that 'they are viewed as an unnecessary burden' (*ibid.*:14). However, he called for various face-saving measures, which would show that 'they are being consulted' (*ibid.*).

Some of Ben-Zvi's ideas were elaborated upon by Yosif Efrati (the Deputy Minister of Agriculture). In his intervention, he highlighted two issues. First, the lack of interest or desire by Israeli Jewish institutions – such as agricultural schools or Tnova marketing company of agricultural products – to deal with Arabs, an attitude which might hamper Ben-Zvi's vision of 'cultural assimilation'. Second, the fragmentation of the Palestinian minority ought to be pursued, among other means, by '*inserting Jewish settlements between the Arab villages*' (*ibid.*:19–20, emphasis added). Efrati mentioned in particular Nazareth, the sole remaining large Arab city, arguing that 'We should make Arabs leave it and settle Jews in it' (*ibid.*:19). In a similar vein, Namir wondered what could be the Zionist interest in leaving Nazareth as an Arab city (*ibid.*:21).

Besides the issues of demography, loyalty, leadership, education and identity, ideas relating to methods of governance were also raised. For example, HaCohen wondered why, instead of passing oppressive laws to confiscate Palestinians' lands, heavy taxes were not imposed on them and in this way compelling them to sell their lands (*ibid.*:15). On another issue, Namir thought that the way for 'cultural assimilation' passes through the schools: 'There is an opportunity to educate the young generation to Israeli patriotism' (*ibid.*:21).

The debate on the Palestinians' existence did not only take place in Mapai's Political Committee but in various other forms as well, principally in the meetings of Mapai's secretariat with the party's MKs. The default option which emerged in this debate was summed up by the novelist and MK Yizhar Smilansky:

> What I've heard of our attitude towards the Arabs can be summed up in four lines. A) It is too bad that Arabs remained in the country. B) It would have been better had they not remained and we are sorry that they are so numerous as to comprise one sixth of the population. C) It would have been better had we been able to decrease the number of the Arabs currently residing in the country. D) The Arabs are not allowed to complain because what they already have is more than enough. It is the same as saying that it would have been better had we been separated from them; however we are obliged by law to tolerate them. (The Secretariat's Meeting with MKs, 9 July 1950:8–9)

An Israeli discourse of the Arabs

These debates reflected certain worries, problems and dilemmas that Israeli politicians faced during the first four years of Israeli statehood. And they can be analysed as such – namely, how did the founders of Israel respond to the challenge of the existence of a Palestinian minority and what kinds of solutions did they offer? Yet, such a reading would be partial at best. These debates did not only refer to their time, but they shaped the mindset and the starting point for the way in which issues relating to the Palestinians in Israel had been approached and treated. Moreover, they had also been associated with institutions – such as the Military Government, the Shin Bet, the Office of the Prime Minister's Advisor, the Histadrut, Arab departments in various ministries – and with a legal framework – principally, though not exclusively, the emergency regulation.

Moreover, this debate did not take place at the margins of the Israeli political, security, bureaucratic and executive circles: rather, some of the most senior politicians, security figures and Arabists took part in it, including Moshe Sharett, David Ben-Gurion, Yitzhak Ben-Zvi, Moshe Dayan, Yigal Alon, Shimon Peres, Ben-Zion Dinur, Abba Eban, Issar Harel, Josh Palmon, Ziama Divon, Shmouel Tolidano, Mishal Shikhter, Uri Lubrani, Abba Hushi, Reuven Barkatt and Amnon Linn. These and others had dominated the Israeli scene for a long time, and some influenced the daily life of Palestinians directly for many years. In summary, the debate was about power and its exercise. The adoption of any approach to a certain issue, such as Arab education, would influence the attitudes and behaviours of Palestinians, as it entailed the setting up of the Arab department at the Ministry of Education, supervising the content of textbooks, training and selecting teachers, etc. Moreover, by becoming a point of reference for future discussions and policies, these debates set the limit to what should be discussed and what should not, what is considered appropriate for the Arabs and what is not. In this regard, these debates were enabling for the state's action – they made sense of the exercise of state power, the setting up of institutions and the fashioning of certain acceptable modes of action. But at the same time, they were limiting, as they precluded other approaches, viewpoints and attitudes, which would probably have created a different set of state–minority relations.

In short, my argument is that these debates were constitutive of an Israeli discourse of the Palestinians. In this, I follow the approaches of Michel Foucault (1981, 1991) and Edward Said (1978, 1983) in the analysis of discourses, where power generates certain modes of thought which attained a status of truism, or official truth; even some such discourses become what Antonio Gramsci (1986) had called common sense (see the discussion of Robinson, 2005a). If my argument is correct, the opinions and attitudes which had been aired in the course of these debates would be echoed, repeated and recirculated in the future in different forms – such as laws, policies and public statements – by those who dealt with Arab affairs. Although they might not use the same wording, they would stay within the limits which these debates had set. In this regard, Said (1983) stated: 'Over and above every opportunity for saying something, there stand a regularizing collectivity ... called a discourse' (186).

Conclusion

In the *birour* or clarification discussed in this chapter, the Palestinians were treated as the 'other' and were the object of an evolving power/knowledge discourse. At first, the official discourse was one of exclusion. The Palestinians were considered ad hoc residents whose expulsion was imminent. Therefore, the discussions among those in charge of Arab affairs focused on their management during the transitory period. Yet, the prolongation of a reality that was considered fleeting – it took four years – along with the imperatives of institutionalizing and formalizing the state's institutions, procedures and the legal system, rendered a revision of the discourse unavoidable. Thus, while exclusion remained the favourite option, the dominant discourse focused on the plausible impact of various processes and changes on the control of the Palestinians. These include the impact of education on their consciousness, their identity, their spatial distribution, the plausible role and impact of compradorian elite and the factors that might elicit voluntary migration. Moreover, the *birour* touched on questions regarding the relationships between democracy, equality and the role of law. Yet, the discourse of citizenship has never been taken seriously. Sharett was the one who advanced the notion that political rights can be emptied of their content through the creation of separate bureaucracies, through the dependency of the Palestinians on official bodies as well as through manipulations and trickery manoeuvres. In short, the Israeli discourse moved gradually from emphasis on exclusion to control. Laying the foundation for the Israeli governance of the Palestinians, this discourse, I argue, was simultaneously enabling and disenabling: while it gave a structure, rationale and legitimacy to Israeli policy towards the Palestinian minority, it precluded alternative perceptions and modes of coexistence. Such alternatives had become unimaginable or simply beyond the pale.

However, to be enabling, the emergent Israeli discourse had to be translated to mental images, official policy guidelines, principles, plans and practices. These revolved around principles of exclusion, supervision, control and surveillance. This translation of the discourse to operative plans and guidelines is the subject of the next chapter.

Notes

1 On various occasions, Cohen expressed sympathy for Palestinian collaborators; see Cohen (2010:231–3) and Dudai and Cohen (2007).

2 Page numbering refers to the number of the page written by the person who wrote the minutes. Although they worked consecutively, each of them began from page 1. Thus, for example, page 1/4 refers to page 1 which was written by the fourth person who noted the minutes.

3 According to Sharett, the population in Gaza was then estimated to be between 250,000 and 300,000.

2

Policies

The realm of policies

In the first chapter, I argued that an Israeli discourse was formed through the thorough discussions, *birour*, which were held during the first four years after Israel's establishment, in which senior politicians and Arabists took part. This debate has continued, yet its boundaries have rarely been breached or amended. In this chapter, I shall discuss the way in which this discourse was translated into clear and firm policy principles.

Although Foucault (2000, 2009) has argued that population has become the main concern of all modern states, for Israel, the size, natural growth, structure, migration and spatial distribution of Palestinians and Israeli Jews have had a fundamental import to its functioning, even to its very survival. As a Jewish state, Israel is premised on racial/national domination (Sa'di, 2004a); therefore, it has devised different, even opposing, principles of governmentality for Palestinians and Jews. Intentionality, elaborate planning and learning, therefore, are at the heart of how Israel handled populations. As the Palestinians were, from the start, considered an unwanted minority, Israel would follow strategies employed in European societies in treating 'abnormal' populations, namely, through exclusion, quarantine or surveillance (Foucault, 1991). These strategies, according to Foucault (2000:332), work simultaneously at the collective and individual levels. In the case of Israel, they could take the form of removal through expulsion, ghettoization or the imposition of surveillance and control techniques. These latter techniques were intended to mould the indigenous population's identity, culture, consciousness and modes of economic activity, most noticeably through regular (and occasionally mundane) practices aimed at keeping them subordinate. Actual policies would not follow these archetypes; rather, they would mostly be hybrid, as the rest of this chapter will illustrate.

The first decade

Already during the 1948 War, Israeli leaders endeavoured to achieve the ethnic cleansing of the majority of Palestinians. Through the statistical–bureaucratic means of registration, the emerging demographic reality was to be objectivized, and the population was divided into categories characterized by hierarchies of entitlements and rights to citizenship. Thus, in November 1948, the first census – doubling as a registration process – was carried out.

Although presented as a 'snapshot' of the population at a given point in time, it was in fact constitutive of the social reality. Its major aim was to present a coherent legal position to deny the refugees the right of return at the end of the war, as Leibler and Breslau (2005) explained:

> If now, in late 1948, all those remaining in the country, Jews and Arabs alike, were universally granted citizenship, it would be possible to observe international norms [of territory based citizenship] while turning the distinction between Arabs who had stayed and who had left into a permanent, legal divide. (892)

In an administrative move that was indicative of future state strategies, the census/registration also aimed to create the political basis for a hierarchical system of citizenship in Israel, according to which pre-1948 Jewish settlers were placed at the top while Palestinian 'present absentees' were relegated to the bottom (*ibid.*:896–7).

The main binary of Jews versus Arabs (i.e. dominants versus subordinates) was underscored by the 'present absentees' category, which included Arabs only. It comprised Palestinians who resided, on 27 November 1947, in the territory upon which Israel was established but who were not registered as citizens in the census/registration. This group included Palestinians who, in response to the fighting, fled to safer areas inside the territories controlled by Israel or to areas which were captured later. It also included Palestinians who simply were not present when the registration took place as well as Palestinian refugees who managed to return. This categorization allowed the state to expropriate their property, particularly their land, and prevented their return to their villages. In 1949, they numbered 81,000 (*ibid.*:896).

Yet, despite the dramatic demographic transformation of Palestine as a result of the 1948 War, the remaining 156,000 Palestinians who eluded the ethnic cleansing campaign (Pappe, 2006) were viewed by Israeli leaders with apprehension and abhorrence. In line with the atmosphere which prevailed throughout the *birour*, early debates on how to handle this minority lamented the incompleteness of the transfer campaign. Yitzhak Ben-Zvi, who was to become Israel's second President, observed that 'there are too many Arabs who remained in the country' (Segev, 1998:46). Other Mapai leaders made similar observations. Eliyahu Carmeli, a Member of Knesset (MK) pointed out: 'I'm not willing to accept a single Arab and not only an Arab but any gentile. I want the state of Israel to be entirely Jewish.' Yehiel Duvdevany, MK, maintained: 'If there was any way of solving the problem by way of a transfer of the remaining 170,000 Arabs we should do so.' And Onn, another Mapai leader, commented: 'The landscape is more beautiful – I enjoy it, especially when traveling between Haifa and Tel-Aviv, and there is no single Arab to be seen' (*ibid.*:47). This approach would later be translated into plans to decrease the minority population through various means, including transfer.

Indeed, the first state's set of goals, which was formulated in 1949, focused on three issues that would comprise the basis of future state strategy: decreasing the size of the minority population, rearranging its spatial distribution and subjecting it to a tight regime of control and surveillance. The state's objectives were articulated as follows:

1. To prevent the return of Palestinian refugees and expel those who succeeded in returning.
2. To relocate (and occasionally to transfer) the population of partly empty villages and neighborhoods and Palestinian villages adjacent to the new borders, and transfer Palestinian-owned lands to Jewish settlements.
3. To establish political control over the Palestinians and segregate them from the Jewish majority. (Segev, 1998:52)

Ben-Gurion, the first Prime Minister, adopted these goals and his directions would ensure their implementation. The following describes how these goals were translated into practice.

While the issue of the refugees is multifaceted and was fought on various fronts, one way of blocking the Arabs' return to Israel was to settle Jewish immigrants on their lands and, in many cases, in their houses. This was part of a policy later labelled 'Judaization'. Indeed, according to Peretz (1958:143): '[O]f 370 new Jewish settlements established between 1948 and 1953, 350 were on absentees' property. In 1954 more than one third of the new immigrants (250,000) settled in urban areas abandoned by Arabs.'

The second goal led to the development of two processes: the continuation of transfers and the spatial rearrangement of Palestinians. As to the first, research on the expulsion of the Palestinians usually refers to the massive ethnic cleansing of Palestinians during 1947–48. However, this process continued intermittently and on a smaller scale until 1959, eleven years after Israel's establishment. The most well-known cases are the expulsion of the inhabitants and refugees from Faluga and Iraq al-Manshiya (3,100 people in 1949), the transfer of Al-Majdal's citizens who acquired ID cards and voted in the first elections – numbering some 2,600 – mostly to Gaza during February–October 1950 (Morris, 2004:528–9) and the expulsion of 12,000–15,000 refugees who remained in the 'Triangle' area following its handover from Jordanian to Israeli rule in accordance with the 1949 Rhodes Armistice Agreement (*ibid.*:529–33). The last documented expulsion was the deportation of hundreds of Bedouins from the al-'Azazma tribe to Jordan and Egypt in 1959 (Jiryis, 1976:82; Cohen, 2006:223). According to Morris (2004:536), Israel's policy of cleansing the borders of Palestinians resulted in the expulsion of 30,000–40,000 Palestinians.

These overt and coercive transfers were accompanied by silent initiatives as well. The Higher Council for Arab Affairs (a coordinating body of state control–surveillance agencies, established in July 1952) estimated that the aggressive stick-and-carrot policy intended to elicit massive Palestinian migration had led, by 1965, to the exodus of some 3,000 Palestinians (Cohen, 2006:120). Various unsuccessful clandestine attempts at transfer were revealed some years later by scholars and journalists; others might still be hidden, either because they have not been discovered yet or they were not formalized and put on paper. The best-known transfer plan, which carried the codename 'Operation Yohanan', aimed at transferring Galilee Christians and settling them in Brazil and Argentina. The plan began to take shape in the autumn of 1950 but culminated in failure in early 1953. It was engineered by Yosef Weitz, the director of the Jewish National Fund's Land Settlement Department, and he received the active collaboration of the Foreign Minister Moshe Sharett – a long-standing advocate of 'soft transfer' – and the blessing of Prime Minister Ben-Gurion. Various tactics regarding the management of the transfer were devised. A letter from Sharett to Weitz on 4 November 1952 disclosed some of these:

> In reply to your letter dated 6 October [1952] and after I have consulted the Prime Minister and other colleagues in the Foreign Ministry, who accepted my opinion, I here inform you that we approve of the implementation of the plan, which it has been agreed to call 'Operation Yohanan' (the emigration of Christian Arabs from the Upper Galilee to Argentina and Brazil). It seems to us that it is absolutely desirable to keep this matter secret for the time being. In any case, we should promote matters in a way which would enable us, at a time of need, to present this movement [publicly] as emigration of individuals conducted on the initiative and responsibility of those concerned – similar to the emigration of the Maronites from Lebanon – and not as a government operation. We assume in advance that the departees would leave and arrive at their destination as subjects of Israel and until their naturalization in the new country the Israeli embassy would extend to them all the required assistance. Thus the permission to begin implementation has been given and I ask you to inform me about any progress. (Quoted in Masalha, 1996:30)

These tactics, as shall be illustrated in chapter 4, carried the fingerprints of Israeli presentation. They aimed to absolve the Israeli state of liability for the actions of its agents.

Another unfulfilled plan was hammered out by Ariel Sharon in 1964. Then an Israel Defence Forces (IDF) Colonel, he planned to expel some 300,000 Palestinians residing in Galilee in the course of a war that would be waged with Syria. The plan reached the operational level as he inquired about the number of vehicles needed to carry out the deportation (Melman and Raviv, 1988).

The second process of spatial rearrangements embodied the emptying of some villages in order to cleanse the border areas of Palestinians or transfer their land to Jewish settlements. The research on Palestinians' relocation inside Israel has remained patchy and inconclusive. The most famous cases are the displacement of the residents of the villages of Iqrit (7 November 1948), Kafr Bir'im (13 November 1948) and Ghabisiya (24 January 1950). Although the inhabitants of these three villages were promised early return, this has not materialized, despite official promises and several verdicts by the High Court of Justice (Morris, 2004:509–16; Sa'di, 2005; Pappe, 2006:185–7). Other cases include inhabitants of Saforyya, Fardia and Kafr 'Anan (Pappe, 1995:644). Meanwhile, in mixed cities or in Arab cities which became mixed after the war – Haifa, Jaffa, Lydda, Acre and Al-Majdal (until the expulsion of its residents) – Palestinians were quarantined in poor neighbourhoods (Morris, 2004; Pappe, 2006:207–8).

Having transformed the country demographically and constructed a ring of Palestinian-free areas along the new borders, the state had isolated Palestinians in Israel from the refugees and the rest of the Arab world. The third goal, then, was to govern them through an effective control and surveillance system. They were to be governed not by the ordinary state bureaucracy, but rather by a Military Government and through the British Mandatory Emergency Regulation, primarily enacted to fight Jewish terrorism. Besides the spatial isolation of Palestinians, their institutional segregation aimed to enhance the effectiveness of the technologies of surveillance through which they were to be governed. A letter from Foreign Minister Sharett to his fellow ministers, dated 24 February 1950, underscored the need to maintain this segregation:

> There is a growing number of cases of Arab citizens of Israel applying directly to members of the government and the central offices not via the authorized officials, i.e., the military governor or the local officers in charge of Arab affairs.
>
> When there is a direct application by Arabs who are residents of Israel, your offices should firstly verify the details of the case in question with the appropriate local military authorities and not respond to the applicants until the matter has been clarified, and then do it in full cooperation with the authorized local government. Also, it would be preferable if the answer would not be given to the applicants directly, but that the final decision should be transmitted via the local military governor or the regional officer for Arab Affairs. (Quoted in Segev, 1998:65)

Three years after the formulation of these objectives, Mapai's Political Committee reformulated them in a way that would reflect the new reality. By 1952, it became clear that a mass expulsion of Palestinians along the 1948 lines was impossible. This, however, did not mean that the idea or the planning for transfer was abandoned; as a case in point, 'Operation Yohanan', mentioned earlier, was under way when these objectives were formulated. Another failed attempt, with tragic results, was plan *Hafarferet* (Mole) (or military plan number S-59), which was seemingly implemented by mistake in Kafr Qasim on 29 October 1956 on the eve of the war that Israel, in collaboration with France and Britain, launched against Egypt. This operation resulted in the death of forty-nine Palestinians. While the official version was that soldiers and commanders misinterpreted the instructions, the language, the operational planning and the objectives that the perpetrators revealed in the court unambiguously echoed the plan that Moshe Dayan, who in 1956 was Chief of Staff, outlined in 1950. The plan, as described by the lawyer of one convict, was 'to construct fenced in areas to which Arabs will be forced in to prevent disorder during the war and then to let them escape eastward [to the West Bank]' (quoted in Rosenthal, 2000:16; for a detailed discussion, see also Pappe, 2011).

Thus, the new objectives which were outlined in 1952 reflected a shift of emphasis from transfer to control and surveillance. These objectives, and the reality on which they were based, were:

1. The expulsion of the Arabs is impossible.
2. The activities of the [Mapai] party and the government must be increased (among the Arab population).
3. The existing separate institutional frameworks ... should be strengthened in the interest of the state and the party. (Wiemer, 1983:37)

In addition to the change of emphasis, these objectives reflected the growing synchronization of various surveillance and control apparatuses (SCA), which included the Office of the Prime Minister's Advisor on Arab Affairs, the Military Government, Mapai's Arab Department, the Histadrut's Arab Department, the police and the General Security Services (Shin Bet). This synchronization also reflected the Mapai leadership's view of the overlap between the state and Mapai goals.

The second decade: the first comprehensive plan[1]

Almost ten years after the establishment of the state, a committee composed of central figures in SCA was established to study and analyse the state's strategy and goals towards the Palestinian minority and to present a comprehensive plan for dealing with it. It was headed by Reuven Barkatt (a leading figure of Mapai in the Histadrut and the head of the Histadrut's Arab Department) and included Issar Harel (head of the Shin Bet and since 1952 the head of the Mossad as well), Ziama (Shmuel) Divon (the Prime Minister's Advisor on Arab Affairs), Eliahu Aghasi of the Histadrut's Arab Department, Amnon Yanai (the commander of the minority's battalion in the IDF), Mishal Shikhter (the head of the Military Government), Yaakov Eini (a leading figure in Mapai and in charge of the relationships with Arab MKs and Arab municipal affairs) and Uri Lubrani (of the Office of the Prime Minister's Advisor on Arab Affairs, later an Advisor) (The Arab Affairs' Committee, 30 January 1958:11).

The Committee submitted its plan to Mapai's Arab Department for discussion and approval on 30 January 1958. The minutes of the meeting give a clear picture of the state's strategy and methods of implementation.

The plan was premised on three assumptions. First, transfer in normal circumstances is not possible, but it is not to be overruled under certain conditions, such as war ('[during] catastrophe [i.e. war] all kind of scenarios can emerge', the document states) (The Arab Affairs' Committee, 30 January 1958:2–3). Second, integration of the Palestinians as equal citizens is not possible, and only their partial incorporation is plausible. Third, security considerations should always prevail, although the authors of the document acknowledged that such concerns were unjustifiably invoked in the past.

These assumptions drew the limits of the strategies available to Israel. In the absence of a real expulsion option, two alternatives remained: ghettoization, and control and surveillance. What followed in the plan, therefore, details the array of methods and tactics which would serve these two strategies. These methods will be divided, for analytical purposes, into five non-exclusive categories:

(A) Political control

This embodies, among other things, creating insurmountable legal or practical hurdles in order to prevent the establishment of an organized political body/bodies to voice the opinions and concerns of the minority. The document under discussion cites three such methods:

1. The mobilization of local groups of collaborators (called in the document 'public cells'), which would help obstruct any drive by Palestinians for separation from the state. Moreover, through these groups, Jewish–Arab disputes would be presented by the state as intra-Arab rivalries, as these groups would be mobilized to act against trends deemed unfavourable by the state. They would also be assigned to spy and pass on community information. These groups, however, were to be kept localized: '... we are not talking about nationwide frameworks, however we are interested ... that in every area a cell is established on which our economic activity rely, and in this way we can convert this cell to the operator of anti-clandestine activities in the Arab community' (*ibid.*:4–5).
2. To prevent the establishment of Arab organizations in any form.
3. To disallow the establishment of an independent Arab political party. Even the possibility of establishing a party under Mapai's auspices was precluded. Thus, the document states: The establishment of a [political] party [affiliated to Mapai] at this stage will not solve the problems, will not be helpful; it will only complicate [matters] because such a party will be devoid of content, it will be the target of attacks. ... However the idea of establishing a social club by the Party [Mapai] or linked to it can be considered, ... not an ideological framework, but a cultural social one. (*Ibid.*)

(B) Segmentation of Palestinians

This tactic refers to two processes: spatial ghettoization by severing the territorial continuity of Arab communities and the balkanization of the Palestinian minority. Thus, the document points to the following tactics:

1. Disrupting territorial continuity of the Arab community by implanting 'serious Jewish wedges'.
2. Encouraging the fragmentation of the Arab minority rather than its treatment as a single totality. The state should endeavour by all possible means to nurture in every 'ethnic' (i.e. religious) group particularistic interests: 'Through favoritism, the state should bolster particularistic interests of the various groups. And, wedges should be created by all possible means between the [various] ethnic groups so as to ensure that they would not comprise a single entity' (*ibid.*:4).

(C) Economic dependency

Economic dependency refers to the creation of conditions whereby individuals or collectives are compelled to compromise their political or moral beliefs to ensure their economic survival or material interests. The plan in this regard made this swap explicit:

1. At the personal level, Palestinian individuals are to be directly connected to the state through personal interests. The document states further that '[these] favors, however, should be awarded in such a way as to commit them [the receivers] to the relationship with the state' (*ibid.*).
2. The Palestinians as a collective were to be incorporated into the periphery of the Israeli economy through various means, including economic activities of state and Histadrutic enterprises in the Arab sector, which ought to be highly profitable to these companies but will turn Arabs who will engage in them into an oppositional force to any Arab separatist movement; an increase in the number of Palestinians incorporated in the Israeli economy; and an increase in the workers' and farmers' fund's activity (*ibid.*:6–7), which was controlled and managed by the state and comprised the financial source for the side benefits it grants collaborators.

(D) Provision of services and local-level administrative changes

Given the continuous and routine operation of the bureaucracy, and its neutral image, it comprises an effective tool for control and surveillance. Extending the operation of the official bureaucracy in the Arab community took two forms: the provision of basic services (dubbed 'modernization') and the establishment of elected local authorities. Thus, the plan recommended:

1. Providing water, electricity and health services.

While providing these services is essential for the development of the minority, its dark side has rarely been acknowledged, let alone highlighted, although it was a crucial consideration for the plan's authors. Barkatt, who presented the plan, spoke in almost Foucaultian terms of surveillance, explaining:

> The electrification of the Arab village has an immense value not only in economic-cultural terms; it has also a significant security value. When you pass by Wadi-'Ara street [that crosses the Triangle area, which is inhabited by Palestinians] at night you see a hostile darkness ... if we glow this darkness, we take them out of the darkness and place them under our supervision. The same is true with regard to streets and transportation. (*Ibid.*:9)

Moreover, supplying these services – water, electricity and health – by official or semi-official bodies simultaneously increased the dependency of Palestinians upon the state. In fact, on various occasions, these services were introduced by the Military Government, regardless of the residents' consent (*ibid.*:35).

2. Pressing ahead to establish local authorities. The motivation for establishing local elected Arab authorities was to create jobs for the growing strata of educated young Arabs and thus avert their adoption of undesirable ideologies or political behaviours.

(E) Enforcement of the hegemonic order

Israel, as a Jewish state, cannot propagate a hegemonic ideology that would present the interests of the ruling Zionist group as the shared interest of all the citizens due to the hierarchical order of citizenship between Jews and Palestinians – a hierarchy which directly stems from the Zionist ideology. Therefore, a need has emerged to create a minimal hegemony – an ideological structure for the Palestinians that focuses on what Gramsci called 'common sense' (Robinson, 2005): in this case, personal advancement within the existing power structure (Sa'di, 2005a). Due to the injustice embedded in the very notion of minimal hegemony, by which inequality and domination are the norm, there is a need for what Fanon (1961) called 'mystification'. Indeed, the plan highlighted the need for propaganda (*Hasbara*) organs and methods, calling for

1. Intensifying the operations of the various *Hasbara* branches.
2. Setting up a worthwhile daily newspaper in Arabic.
3. Encouraging the establishment of clubs for workers and farmers, to be run by the Histadrut's Arab Department – an arm of the control system.
4. Establishing a youth club by the Histadrut's Arab Department.
5. Establishing a department for *Hasbara* and for the raising of educational services' standards.

6. Encouraging vocational training for Arab youth. This policy aimed at giving Mapai an edge over its left-Zionist rivals – Mapam and Achdut Ha'avoda – in the struggle to win over Arab votes. Thus, Barkatt explained that the aim was '...to bring as much Arab youth as possible to our agricultural settlements. Mapam is doing so intensively. Even Achdut Ha'avoda, which "excels in the love of Arabs, almost as much as we do", began to do so' (The Arab Affairs' Committee, 30 January 1958:8–9).
7. Planning how to handle youth and the intelligentsia. The emerging Palestinian educated strata challenged the state's ability to control and manipulate the Palestinians. Employing the 'intelligentsia' aimed to avert their criticisms of state policies or even to mobilize it in institutionalizing the official discourse. Thus, the document states:

> nowadays there is a secondary and higher education, and an intelligentsia is emerging, which can collaborate with the state; however it is becoming a proletariat intelligentsia, very dangerous to the state, and if the problem remains unsolved, it will be a leading [force] of rebellion and a movement of separation. ... There is a need to solve this problem and not to be contented with formulas only; we request that the government, the Histadrut and other public offices arrange within a short time to employ 100 Arabs from the intelligentsia. (*Ibid.*:8)

This plan was introduced when a *state of exception* had already existed for a decade (see chapter 3). The military governors had maintained near-absolute power over Palestinians, who were obliged to have permits – from the Military Administration – for any activity outside the boundaries of their villages, including working in their fields. Moreover, they were subjected to curfews and various arbitrary measures. Given their isolation and the state of uncertainty in which they lived, fear and confusion prevailed. Thus, while the Military Government managed the everyday lives of Palestinians and executed the state's dictates and programmes, the plan aimed to introduce structural changes among them: to alter their collective identity, to change their modes of life and to rearrange their spatial distribution. The end result was to incorporate them as small, marginal and subordinate collectives devoid of a collective identity, vision, will or resisting ability, in Foucaultian terms, to render them docile bodies.

Another plausible explanation might be found in the conception of Ben-Gurion and his colleagues of the Palestinians. Pinhas Lavon – a senior Mapai leader and senior Israeli politician – understood that they envisaged two non-exclusive ways of dealing with the Palestinians. The first implies the ghettoization of Palestinians and the confiscation of their land for the building of Jewish settlements or expulsion (Kafkafi, 1998:356). The second meant the ghettoization of Palestinians which would not only render their control easier but would also make their expulsion, once an opportunity surfaced, easier to conduct. '...[Mapai's leaders] do not believe in the possibility of co-existence between Jews and Arabs, and therefore believe that in the final analysis transfer will be the solution. They profess the need for segregation in order to make evacuation easier when time comes' (*ibid.*:352).

Yet, the discrepancy between the discursive and the pragmatic levels should not be overlooked or underestimated, particularly since Israel has always endeavoured to present the image of a democratic, enlightened and moral state. Therefore, issues relating to presentation, mystification, discourse and perceptions were embedded in the plan and were also part and parcel of its wider context. A discussion of these issues, even as they relate to the period under discussion, could be wide-ranging and is beyond the scope of this chapter. However, I shall briefly explore two issues: the functions of the Military Government and the role assigned to the emerging educated Palestinian strata.

The Military Government

The imposition of the Military Government on the Palestinian populated areas was justified by pressing security considerations. The severe living conditions of Palestinians under this regime were deemed unavoidable. Yet, as shall be explained later, this *state of exception* was consciously tailored to meet various objectives other than security, particularly after 1952. In the course of the discussion of the 1958 plan, Mapai member and Chairman of the Foreign and Defence Committee in the Knesset, Meir Argov (who was taken on a tour of Arab localities before the discussion), was both uncomfortable with, and understanding of, this *state of exception*, explaining:

> The reality seemed to me more horrible than I imagined it before. ... The Military Government in its current form cannot continue to exist. It has two dimensions: the Zionist dimension and the security one. Palliatives to the security dimension could be found ... legal and operative [ones] ... [while] to the Zionist dimension I have no treatment, I am most doubtful. (*Ibid.*:16)

He then went on to pinpoint one Zionist dimension:

> All the Galilee is Arab and there is a Zionist goal of splitting it up and populating it by Jews. ... We cannot publicly justify the existence of the Military Government by this Zionist reason, since this would mean the taking of Arabs' land and settling Jews on it. ... 300,000 dunums which might be owned by Arabs [will be confiscated]. (The Arab Affairs' Committee, 30 January 1958:16)

Other Zionist 'dimensions' were divulged in the course of the discussions. Shikhter, for example, underscored the 'locking up' of the rapidly growing Palestinian proletariat in their localities in order to preserve jobs for Jewish workers. He also noted the gathering of information through espionage, stating that 'Arabs pass on information because they are dependent upon us;

had this dependency not existed, there would have not been cooperation between us and them' (*ibid.*:32).

Meanwhile, Issar Harel emphasized the Military Government's coercive function, which is the essence of the *state of exception*:

> We should let them understand [that] ... if there will be a rebellion or an uprising or lack of collaboration in order to harm the state, first of all the Arabs of Israel will be annihilated, and first of all their leaders will be wiped out before the state of Israel would be harmed. For years they have been living in fear, and they must understand that this fear is real. (*Ibid.*:26)

Argov's reference to the discrepancy between the declarative and the pragmatic 'dimensions' of the Military Government was not confined to this construct, but rather was inherent in the state's handling of the minority. Mordechai Namir (The Arab Affairs' Committee's Chairman) described this discrepancy as a scam (*Kontz*), stating that '[The state] does not oppose [the existence of] the Arabs as citizens of Israel and [simultaneously] being the Israeli state, which was established to solve the problem of the Jews – that is to do two opposite things at once ... [and] to try to divide, as much as possible, Arabs' unity [while] in Jewish eyes everyone who is not a Jew in the country is an Arab' (*ibid.*:17). Meanwhile, Michael Assaf, an orientalist and one of Mapai's leaders, suggested playing down this contradiction through obfuscation by 'maintaining the military government but changing the name, the military government, which has become a monster' (*ibid.*:24).

Palestinian intelligentsia

Although, throughout the debates on the plan, various discussants spoke in a dismissive tone of the emerging strata of educated Palestinians, they were nevertheless apprehensive of the latter's potential future role. This was particularly so because some speakers viewed the intellectuals in Leninist terms and believed they could potentially lead revolutionary social movements. For example, Namir stated:

> Already today we are in a condition in which the emerging intelligentsia might play a decisive role. In the world there is not much value to masses' rebellions. The slaves' uprisings in ancient Rome did not bring about any change, because they lacked a leadership, an intellectual leadership. It's not without a reason that the Soviet Union created a huge gap between the professor and the simple worker...; it understood well that 200 million persons, if they are devoid of intellectual leadership, they comprise a herd of slaves, particularly under a dictatorial regime.
>
> Buying the goodwill or at least the neutrality of the technical and pedagogical intelligentsia on the one hand and the political intelligentsia on the other – and these groups are dissimilar, although they can be similar – is of great importance. (The Arab Affairs' Committee, 30 January 1958:19)

To avert such a possibility, they proposed employing a hundred educated Palestinians in state and Histadrut offices. They further discussed ways of converting educated Palestinians into advocates of the official line in their communities and abroad. For example, Committee member David HaCohen thought they could comprise a propaganda tool for Israeli diplomacy:

> According to my understanding we could have employed 10 young men in the foreign ministry. They will not reach the levels of ambassadors or consuls; however they can do various jobs in the delegation to the UN as well as in embassies and this will be very beneficial. ... [H]ad we given guidance to a number of Arabs from the intelligentsia, we would have been able to send them in *Hasbara* activities. ... The echoes of the trial that was done with Kamal Mansour (a Druze) are remarkable. ... understandably had we been able to present him as a Muslim, it would have been more beneficial. (*Ibid.*:12–13)

Meanwhile, Namir argued for their employment in functions that would help divert the Palestinians' attention from their daily realities to more benign subjects. Therefore, he underscored the need '...to establish musical bands and entertainment groups, this gives expression to the feelings in the cultural field. ... This [recreation] is also an employment sector for students and secondary school graduates. ... The Roman slogan of "bread and entertainment" is not wrong' (*ibid.*:19).

Another way of obviating the undesirable influence of Palestinian intelligentsia was to change its class basis. They were not to be overwhelmingly drawn from the impoverished strata of merchants – the most economically affected segment among Palestinians in Israel as a result of the state's creation – as had customarily been the case. Rather, they were to be drawn from the *fellahin* (*ibid.*:13). In this way, the leading intelligentsia would not carry and articulate the grievances of a disfranchised group. Moreover, the educated Palestinians of *fellahin* origin would lack the historical leadership role traditionally assumed by the urban intelligentsia.

However, this approach towards educated Palestinians was reversed during the late 1960s and early 1970s. Instead of viewing them across the board as a potential threat, SCA's leaders began to explore ways of incorporating educated Palestinians on an individual basis into the system of patronage (Sa'di, 2003:81–6). Those incorporated were gradually to replace the old feudal collaborators, called *Nikhbadim* (dignitaries) by the regime. Consequently, the system of selection and screening, through which students passed at different points of their studies, was refined (see chapter 6). Those identified by the system as promising were assisted in their pursuit of postsecondary education and future employment. Moreover, a specialized culture of signs and double meaning, which reflect the minimal hegemonic ideology, emerged. Knowledge and internalization of this ideology, along with association with well-known collaborators, comprised the main factors in the selection processes (see Sa'di, 2005).

In short, as early as 1952, those in charge of the surveillance and control of the Palestinians began realizing that transfer was untenable as a strategy for dealing with the Palestinian minority. They never entirely abandoned transfer as an option, but what followed was mainly the elaboration of tactics pertaining to strategies of ghettoization and control and surveillance along with soft transfer tactics. The 1958 Plan represents a watershed in the conceptualization and development of these tactics.

The third decade and beyond

The 1958 Plan continued to comprise the basis for the state's strategy of dealing with the Palestinian minority during and beyond the next decade. While transfer remained the most alluring strategy, thus eliciting transfer plans under the cover of war, as Sharon's 1964 plan shows, the daily life of Palestinians was managed by tactics derived from the strategies of ghettoization and control and surveillance.

A comprehensive set of policies which were employed during the second decade was outlined on 20 June 1968 by Shmouel Tolidano, the long-standing Advisor to the Prime Minister on Arab Affairs (1965–77) (The Arab Affairs' Committee, 20 June 1968). Rebuking those who claimed that there was no clear policy towards the Palestinians, such as the Israeli academics who were quoted in the introduction, he maintained that '....our policy principles with regard to the Israeli Arabs ... contrary to what is thought, are very clear. And I'll count them one by one' (The Arab Affairs' Committee, 20 June 1968:4). Tolidano divided these policies into three aspects: the economic, the political security and the social. On the economic aspect, he basically described a five-year plan (1968–72) that the state was to launch. He believed it would narrow the socio-economic gaps between Jews and Palestinians (*ibid.*:1–2). Yet, the bulk, and the most revealing part, of his presentation referred to the second aspect, political security. It was hammered out in the 'Central Committee' – a security body which includes representatives of the IDF, the Shin Bet and the police, in addition to the Advisor's Office. According to it, the state acted to:

(A) Arab organizations

1. Prevent the establishment of independent Arab political parties or nation-wide Arab organizations. In this respect, [he appraised that the state] was successful. For example, we [always referring to the state] prevented the establishment of a political party by Elias Kussa. [we blocked] the Popular Front, Al-Ard movement and a separate students' union. We have succeeded in obstructing all these [attempts] during the twenty years of the state's existence. The question is whether we can inhibit this in the future.
2. Prevent nation-wide Islamic organizations on religious or national basis. We did not establish nation-wide Islamic religious organizations and disallowed (popular) Islamic rituals. In this respect we also were successful.

3. Prevent the establishment of Arab municipal organizations beyond the locality level. We said yes to local councils, and no to center for local governments and no to regional councils.
4. Prevent the establishment of large Arab economic enterprises – an independent bank, Arab labor unions, and chambers of commerce – [while] endeavoring to preserve the economic dependency on the Jewish sector (*ibid.*:4). In this respect we also were successful.
5. Prevent the establishment of independent social institutions and sport clubs. Instead, [we] encouraged the integration of Arabs in existing Israeli frameworks. They wanted to establish a sport club in the villages of the Triangle, we barred it. Now 20 years after the establishment of the State, there is no single Arab sport club.

(B) The second principle – reward and punishment – we acted according to the following guidelines:

1. Awarding preferential treatment in socio-economic development to certain villages and religious sects.
2. Giving side benefits to collaborators and withholding them from negative elements.
3. Cultivating leaders at various levels – Knesset members and heads of local authorities – by channeling side benefits through them (*ibid.*).

(C) In the third principle – demography – we acted according to the following policy guidelines:

1. The inculcation of the family planning notion among the Israeli Arabs.
2. The awarding of direct and indirect assistance to those who migrate.
3. The initiation of various measures for the liberation of women, particularly the raising of their educational standards and the elevating of the family-life more generally. *We reached a conclusion that an increase in the woman's education causes a decline in her fertility*. We faced a question: what is preferable – a large population with low national [consciousness] or small population, [but] more educated and more nationalistic? As education increases so does patriotism. We gave priority to the demographic issue. We said it is not important how nationalistic they might be, the main thing is demography.
4. In the field of internal migration we encouraged the settlement of Arabs and Bedouins in the mixed cities [located] at the center of the country (*ibid.*:5). We proposed [that] Jews [ought to move] from the city to the village and the Arabs from the village to the city. ... I say in some cases we were successful while in others we upheld this goal without accomplishing it.

5. It was decided to split up the demographic concentrations in the Galilee, the Triangle and the Negev by Jewish settlement or state's institutions, such as army and police [compounds] and civilian institutions. This guideline was partially achieved. The IDF established a school for infantry in Hazon, in accordance with the guideline of splitting the demographic concentrations by state institutions (6).

(D) With regard to the fourth principle – the ethnic group, the tribe and the Hamula – we determined that the disintegration of the tribe and the Hamula should be deceleration, however, without being committed to representatives who have no actual support. This means we shall try to preserve the Hamula and the tribe, yet if in reality this proves unattainable we should adopt other leaders; this is first. Second, singling out and giving preference to the Druze and Circassian communities and to a limited extent to the Greek-Catholic community. This prevailed until the six-day war [1967].

(E) With regard to lands we decided

1. To end up the claims of the present absentees. ... Soon we shall set a deadline for the submission of requests for compensation.
2. To conclude the land settlement in the North [the Galilee] and embark on such an arrangement in the Negev. ... After a thorough investigation we concluded that it is preferable to give the Bedouins holding of 100 thousand dunums, instead of allowing them to be in actual possession ... of 700 thousand dunums (*ibid.*:6).
3. To avoid land confiscation as long as it is possible. We saw that land seizure sparks off unrest. Therefore during the last three years we did our best not to expropriate land. ... I think this episode is about to end within 2–3 months as the army needs lands which we shall confiscate.

As to the third aspect of Jewish–Arab relations at the social level, he pointed to three policy principles:

(F) With regard to the Jewish–Arab tension, we reached the conclusion that frictions between Jews and Arabs should be prohibited.

(G) With regard to the disorderly building – This is a very painful issue, as thousands of dunums were occupied by illegal buildings. Following our investigation of this question we concluded that zoning plans for the villages ought to be prepared. ... In places where [such] plans exist, we shall begin the demolishing of houses [which were built outside the locality's boundaries].

(H) As to the Bedouins we decided to:

1. Move them northward in a collective and organized manner.
2. The sedentarization of the Bedouin and the change [of their source of living] from agriculture to wage labour. This process is currently under way.

3. Gradual elimination of their livestock. In this respect we have not been successful. We have not succeeded in decreasing the Bedouins' livestock, on the contrary it is increasing. (The Arab Affairs' Committee, 20 June 1968:7)

Tolidano presented these policy principles to MKs of Ma'arach (an alliance of Mapai and other small factions), ministers and Arabists one year after the Six-Day War where a new reality had emerged. State leaders, including the leading figures of SCA, were well aware that changes in these policy guidelines were needed. But what should the scope of these changes be? Tolidano pointed out that such a re-examination will take place within a few weeks with the participation of the Prime Minister and the Minister of Defence (*ibid.*:8). Three alternatives were to be considered. First, to pursue a liberal alternative; it will be modelled on the policy that has been applied towards the Palestinians in the occupied territories. In this regard, he commented that Palestinians in the occupied territories enjoyed more freedom of expression than the Palestinian citizens of Israel and they maintained control over the Islamic endowments (*ibid.*:9). Second, to keep the current policy unchanged in the light of its success. And third, to adopt a compromise between these two options. Moreover, he revealed that in preliminary discussions, the representatives of the various parties in the state SCA were divided as follows: representatives of the Office of the Prime Minister's Advisor and the IDF supported the first alternative with reasonable amendments, while the representatives of the Shin Bet demanded the continuation of the current policy for another decade or so. Meanwhile, the representatives of the police did not have a firm opinion although they inclined to option three, namely, the introduction of incremental change (The Arab Affairs' Committee, 20 June 1968:9).

The bulk of the policy guidelines which Tolidano presented are the same as those which were present in the 1958 Plan, though they were articulated with clarity and precision. For example, Tolidano listed the Arab organizations that the state prevented from being established, such as political parties, nationwide Islamic organizations, municipal associations beyond the local level, large economic enterprises (e.g. an independent bank, labour union and chamber of commerce) and independent social institutions and sports clubs. Yet, the tactic of containing the Palestinians demographically – through the education of Arab women and the introduction of family planning notions to the Palestinians – represented a leap in thinking and elaboration relative to the previous ones.

Two other policy guidelines which appeared in the Tolidano presentation and were not included in the 1958 Plan represented new emphases rather than novel principles. The first refers to the concentration of the Bedouins and the changing of the sources of their livelihood. This policy reflected the place that the Negev had acquired in the 1960s as a new frontier of colonization. Meanwhile, the second refers to the Hamula, which was considered a main component of the Palestinian social structure, through which the state exercised its control (see chapter 5). The doubts that Tolidano raised seem to reflect a belief regarding the crumbling of the old Palestinian social order.

The policy plan that Tolidano presented acquired a much longer lifespan than one would anticipate. It remained in place despite the changes in the conditions which ensured its implementation – principally, the termination of the Military Government and the end of Labour (previously Mapai) rule. Its principles were mentioned by the 'Central Committee' in 1969 as the policy guidelines towards the Palestinians and by Deputy Prime Minister Yigal Alon (who took part in the meeting in which Tolidano outlined it) (Avivi, 2007:280).

Moreover, Tolidano's principles were echoed in the memorandum, which the Northern District Commissioner Israel Koenig submitted in March 1976 to then Prime Minister Yitzhak Rabin. Besides shrill rhetoric, Koenig suggested three new tactics of control. The first was to contain Palestinians demographically by withholding social benefits paid to large Palestinian families and encouraging Palestinian students to study abroad while making it difficult for them to return and find employment. Second, students at universities, in the forefront of political consciousness, were to be channelled to the sciences, given the time needed for studies; they would not be able to engage in politics. Third, to restore the state's aura of power by implementing harsh law enforcement and tax collection measures and decreasing the dependency on Arab workers in vital economic enterprises.

According to Tolidano, his goals comprised the greater part of a memorandum he submitted to the government in 1973 which was adopted a year later as official policy. Moreover, it continued to constitute the basis of the official policy until 1991 (Sa'di, 2003b).

Conclusion

The 1948 War created excellent conditions to fulfil the transfer of Palestinians through coercive and bureaucratic means. However, the 1948 ethnic cleansing was incomplete: a small minority of Palestinians managed to stay within the boundaries of what became the state of Israel. At first, Israeli leaders hoped that these would also be transferred. However, as early as 1952, they realized that it would not be possible to transfer them under normal conditions. Therefore, a need emerged to adopt strategies which would simultaneously allow the development of Israel as a Jewish state despite the existence of a Palestinian minority and sustain an image of an enlightened democratic state. Consequently, an amalgamation of three strategies emerged: 'soft transfer', ghettoization, and control and surveillance. Within a decade, a comprehensive plan to realize these strategies was formulated.

The 1958 Plan was comprehensive in two respects. First, ghettoization and political control and surveillance were to be altered from specific state activities. Rather, they were integrated into the structural constraints imposed on Palestinians as individuals and as a collective, thus having the effect of individualization and totalization. Second, these strategies were in-built and diffused in the social, political, cultural and economic spheres. Moreover, given the *state of exception* under the Military Government, any programme of resistance became formidable. In short, the end result of this plan was to incorporate the Palestinian minority as subordinate collectivities devoid of an overarching identity, vision, will or ability to resist.

This combination of strategies prevailed despite the termination of the Military Government in 1966. According to Tolidano, it continued to exist till as late as 1991. In the meantime, as revealed in the Tolidano memorandum and Koenig report, refinements and innovations to the tactics were introduced.

Note

1 This plan is found in The Arab Affairs' Committee 'The Protocol of the Meeting of the Arab Affairs' Committee, 30 January 1958', *Labour Party Archive*. Files 7/32. All the references to this plan refer to this protocol.

3

Legal framework, institutions and approaches to power

The foundational moment

If discourses and policy plans were to be implemented, they ought to be couched within a legal framework and to be implemented by specialized institutions. While surveillance and political control usually take place in the grey area between legality and illegality, the Israeli discourse of control, discussed in the previous chapters, could not be reconciled with a reasonable interpretation of a liberal legal framework. Emergency laws therefore were the only accommodating alternative. Indeed, Israel's first piece of legislation passed soon after the declaration of Israel's independence was the *Law and Administration Ordinance* (1948); published on 19 May 1948, this affirmed the continuity of the legal system that had existed hitherto, including the Mandatory Emergency (Defence) Regulations of 1945, except those which restricted Jewish immigration. The declaration stated:

(A) If the Provisional Council of State deems it expedient so to do, it may declare that a state of emergency exists in the State, and upon such declaration being published in the *Official Gazette*, the Provisional Government may authorise the Prime Minister or any other Minister to make such emergency regulations as may seem to him expedient in the interests of the defence of the State, public security and the maintenance of supplies and essential services.

(B) An emergency regulation may alter any law, suspend its effect or modify it, and may also impose or increase taxes or other obligatory payments.

(C) An emergency regulation shall expire three months after it is made, unless it is extended, or revoked at an earlier date, by an Ordinance of the Provisional Council of State, or revoked by the regulation-making authority.

(D) Whenever the Provisional Council of State thinks fit, it shall declare that the state of emergency has ceased to exist, and upon such declaration being published in the *Official Gazette*, the emergency regulations shall expire on the date or dates prescribed in such declaration.[1]

Institutions and objectives

Although the state of emergency was declared during the war for three months, as Walter Benjamin has rightly suggested, such a regime often becomes the rule (Agamben, 2005:6). In fact, the state of emergency in Israel has never been revoked, and the emergency regulations, which curtail the rule of law, were enforced almost exclusively on the Palestinians between 1949 and 1966 by a Military Government that was imposed on the Palestinian-populated areas. The number of these regulations varies as, over the years, Israel has made some additions and omissions to the Mandatory ones. In the first two decades of the state, there were some 150 regulations (Segev, 1998:49). Yet, Mishal Shoham, who headed the Military Government, stated in 1958 that his apparatus relied mostly – though not exclusively – on six of these regulations: 108, 109, 110 and 111, '[which] are used against individuals and make possible their placement under police supervision', and 124 and 125, which relate to 'territories and crowd' (The Arab Affairs' Committee, 30 January 1958:5–6).

These regulations are quite restrictive. For example, according to regulation 110, an individual may be required to live in a specified place, to not leave the area of a town or village without permission, to present himself/herself at the police station at designated times and to remain within the confines of his/her home from one hour after sunset until sunrise (Kretzmer, 1990:142). Regulation 111 empowers the military commander to imprison a person for up to six months without trial or formal charges – a period that can be renewed after a formal review. Candidates for administrative detention may appeal to a military advisory committee; however, its recommendations are not binding. Moreover, evidence can be kept from the candidate and his lawyer for security reasons. Regulation 124 empowers the military to confine people to their homes or offices for an undetermined length of time. A military commander may, by order, require every person within any area specified to remain indoors between such hours as may be specified in the order, except those with a written permit by the military commander. Meanwhile, regulation 125 authorizes the military commander to issue a closure order on any area under his jurisdiction. Once a closure has been issued, no person within the area may leave, and no person outside it may enter without a permit; and indeed, Palestinians were not allowed to leave their areas of residence without a pass from the Military Government. Other regulations empower the military commander to banish a person or prevent him/her from acquiring certain articles – such as typewriters – to prevent him/her from communicating with certain people or to outlaw any association or organization.[2] Moreover, a combination of various regulations may also be enforced.

In line with these regulations, the Palestinian-populated areas were declared closed areas and a Military Government was established. Although it existed earlier, the Military Government was officially established on 3 September

1948. It was headed by a military general who was responsible for all aspects of Palestinians' lives. Hence, he was part of two hierarchies at once: the military and the civilian. On issues under military authority, he reported to the Chief of Staff; on civilian issues, he worked under the Minister of Defence. The area under military rule was divided into five regions at first but was divided into three from 1950 onwards: the northern district (the Galilee), the central district (the Triangle) and the southern district (the Negev) (Peretz, 1991:85). Each of the three regions was headed by a Military Commander. The Arab population which remained in the cities of Haifa, Jaffa, Lydda, Ramle and Al-Majdal (before their transfer during the early 1950s) was concentrated in poor neighbourhoods and was put under military rule (Segev, 1998:52–8) until 1 July 1949 (Ozacky-Lazar, 2002:111), when Jewish immigrants were settled in deserted Arab houses, thus converting some of these cities – which had all along been Arab cities – into mixed ones.

By the end of 1949, the Military Administration was composed of some 1,000 employees (Segev, 1998:48); however, its staff steadily declined. In 1958, they numbered 116 persons, 87 of which were assigned a variety of administrative and operational duties (such as liaison with the local population), while the remainder comprised three squads for escorting and patrolling (The Arab Affairs' Committee, 14 August 1958:9). This decreasing staff was responsible for a rapidly growing population. For example, in 1958, the staff of 116 persons ruled over 180,000 (*ibid.*:2) and had to fulfil the formidable duties which were entrusted to the Military Government. Indeed, on 14 May 1950, Prime Minster Ben-Gurion decreed that the various ministries would deal with Arab issues only through the Military Governor (Kafkafi, 1998:354). Ziama Divon, the second Advisor to the Prime Minister on Arab Affairs, detailed the following assignments which were entrusted to the Military Government, besides its main task of stopping the return of Palestinian refugees:

1. Imposition of emergency regulations: the closure of areas, military courts, administrative detention, imposition of curfews and confinement of movement.
2. Gathering of up-to-date information on the population under its jurisdiction.
3. Allotment of passes and work permits outside the areas of the [Military] Government.
4. Granting of licenses for carrying arms.
5. Establishment of local councils.
6. Appointment of *mukhtars.*
7. Giving advice in the appointment of teachers and civil servants.
8. Leasing of land.
9. Granting [of permits for the purchase] of tractors.

10. Granting of various franchises.
11. Encouragement for the establishment of development projects in the villages. (The Arab Department, n.d.:2–3)

Yet, perhaps the most salient feature of the Military Government was its projection of state power, which was occasionally no less significant than its deployment. In this regard, Uri Lubrani, the third Advisor to the Prime Minister on Arab Affairs, summed up the significance of the Military Government at the end of its first decade as follows:

1. It represented, to a frightened, segmented and distressed population, the new regime.
2. It presented to this population the military power which this regime has built.
3. It comprised the only address for all state branches which were active in the Arab sector. As such, every Arab citizen felt dependent in his everyday life on the military governor of his area.
4. Through mukhtars, sheikhs and heads of Hamulas, it had been able to rule over an entire population by a very small staff. (Bauml, 2007:224)

Lubrani's assessment might create the impression that this administration was reminiscent of Bentham's panopticon, where the projection of power induces compliance among a large and segmented population. Moreover, the small staff of the Military Government and the popular characterization of the areas under its rule as a prison might have amplified this image (Ozacky-Lazar, 2002:110; Eyal, 2006:162).

This metaphor of the panopticon merits further exploration. In fact, in various points, the Military Government was, I argue, strikingly different from the panopticon. First, it was different with regard to the goals. The objectives of the Military Government were not confined to surveillance and normalization as in the case of Bentham's panopticon prison; rather, they stemmed from a generalized conception of state security. In 1958, Mishal Shoham, the head of the Military Government, made a distinction between two conceptions of state security: overt/direct and covert/accumulative. The first includes the aims of preventing the return of the refugees, smuggling and espionage, preventing the establishment of Palestinian organizations deemed hostile to the state and the seizure of Palestinian lands for military training (when it was necessary and when it was not, he stated) (The Arab Affairs' Committee, 14 August 1958:6).

The second, the accumulative conception of security, encompassed five goals, which did not have immediate effect on security, but their accumulation, according to Shoham, bolstered it:

(A) To prevent the rehabilitation of deserted villages by their inhabitants who became internal refugees and who lived in nearby localities. For example, in the Galilee there were ninety-seven such villages whose 20,000 residents were scattered in fifty-four villages and the city of Nazareth.

(B) To stop the Palestinian workforce from reaching the labor market in the cities and Jewish settlements in order to keep the available jobs for Jewish migrants.

(C) To prevent Palestinians from moving in 'security-sensitive areas'. These areas were composed of the country's major part: from Benyamena (to the south of Haifa) to the south of the Negev.

(D) To limit the seizure of state-declared lands. These lands were frequently declared as closed areas, '[assigned] for military training or the disguise of training' [he emphasized that 'what was said here should not be mentioned outside this place']. Moreover, it was intended to facilitate land settlements with regard to the confiscation, registration and purchase of Palestinian lands.

(E) To protect newly established Jewish settlements that were physically and organizationally weak by preventing Palestinians from passing through their lands. (*ibid.*:7–8)

Another goal to which Shoham alluded but did not elaborate upon was the transfer of Palestinians should an opportunity for such a move emerge:

> They know that we shall not act like the Mandatory government in the 1937 events or similar to the way the French act in Algeria. Our way will be either us or them, therefore they are very cautious. (The Arab Affairs' Committee, 14 August 1958:4)

Indeed, in line with the dominant discourse and the 1958 Plan discussed in the previous two chapters, an internal memorandum of the Military Government specified that in the case of war, it should 'encourage and make it possible for certain parts of the population to move to neighbouring countries' (quoted in Eyal, 2006:154). Such an atmosphere trickled down to the level of the soldiers and policemen who were stationed in Arab localities. In the course of the court of the military personnel who took part in the Kafr Qasim massacre, which was carried out by the Israeli army on the eve of the Suez War in 1956, it was revealed that in line with the oral tradition – *Torah Shi-Ba'al Peh* – a leaflet distributed in the battalion stated: '[From here the Arabs ought to be] going to Jordan [i.e. the West Bank], maybe there would be a need to give a punch here and a slap there, to let them escape beyond the borders, [there] they can do whatever they like' (Rosenthal, 2000:18).

Shoham used a canonized conception of security, which means – in the words of Kretzmer (1990):

> [S]ecurity of the state is synonymous with security of the Jewish collective, and that is often seen as being dependent on promoting 'Jewish national goals'. Acts

> that strengthen the Jewish collective are perceived as acts that promote security. On the other hand, acts that tend to strengthen Arab national aspirations among Israeli Arabs are regarded threatening to the Jewish collective. (136)

Given these goals, it might be misleading to evaluate the Military Government according to its success in perfecting surveillance. Rather, it should be analysed in accordance with the political plans and schemes of the regime.

The second difference between the Military Government and the panopticon metaphor relates to the way in which power was practised. The Military Government was not based on routinized procedures or sets of rules and rituals as in the institutions described by Foucault; rather, in representing a state of exception, it was based on unrestricted arbitrary power. Indeed, the emergency regulations gave the military governors unlimited authority that was subject neither to administrative nor to judicial reviews. For example, the first head of the Military Government, Colonel Elimelech Avner, thought that these powers would make each governor an 'absolute monarch' in his small domain (Pappe, 1995:639). Later his main job would become protecting Palestinians from acts of revenge and looting by his own staff (Robinson, 2005b:89). The head of the Military Government, along with the Prime Minister and his Advisor on Arab Affairs, would not be bothered as much by the abusive behaviours towards Palestinians as by the collapse of discipline within the organization (*ibid.*:153:89). However, given the quality of the soldiers and the nature of their work, disorder and corruption were inevitable. The soldiers mostly came from the human surplus of the army: they were either unfit due to age or health or were injured in battles (Segev, 1998:51; Robinson, 2005b:89). The only body which could have imposed restrictions, the High Court of Justice, ruled that 'it cannot interfere in the military governor's absolute discretion when he is driven by security considerations, and that the military governors are not to be interrogated regarding their reasoning as this might endanger state's security' (Jiryis, 1976:20; Ozacky-Lazar, 2002:105).

The third difference between the Military Government and the panopticon model has to do with Bentham's main concern, namely, utilitarianism. The Military Government did not rule effectively over the Palestinians; rather, it was the outer layer of multiple control and surveillance apparatuses. However, it has drawn the attention of researchers because of both its visibility and the legal powers awarded to it by the emergency regulations. As Uri Lubrani put it, it was the symbol of the occupying army. In governing the Palestinians, the Military Government was aided by various bodies which were in charge of surveillance and security directly as well as with organizations employing subtle forms of power. These organizations include first and foremost the Shin Bet (General Security Services – *Sherut Bitachon Klali*). Established in the summer of 1950, the Shin Bet's main assignment has been the prevention of sabotage and espionage activities. Yet, it had engaged in wide-ranging surveillance of the various aspects of Palestinian lives: it monitored Palestinians in classes, offices, mosques, public spaces and social gatherings to learn about their political attitudes (regarding its current role of political surveillance, see, e.g., Yoaz and Khourie, 20 May 2007). Such activities were conducted besides the usual practices that such agencies commonly undertake including wiretappings, interception of mail and bugging communication systems. Additionally, the Shin Bet screened, and in many cases continues to screen, Palestinian candidates for positions in state and public sectors such as teachers, headmasters, inspectors, bureaucrats in state and Histadrut-related bodies and functionaries in Islamic religious institutions. Its recommendations, which are decisive, would be passed in the discussed period, to the Office of the Advisor on Arab Affairs. Additionally, the Shin Bet gave advice to policy-making bodies regarding the policy options towards the Palestinians available to them (Benziman and Mansour, 1992).

The second agency is the police. Besides its duty of maintaining law and order, it had additional assignments in the Palestinian-populated areas, including political surveillance and control. The police, particularly 'the department for special assignments' (*Matam*), was entrusted with surveillance over the Palestinians as well as coordinating police activities with the Shin Bet and the Military Government. The *Matam* operated sections at the district and the regional levels, known as *Latam*.

These three organizations – the Military Government, the Shin Bet and the police (*Matam*) – along with the Prime Minister's Advisor coordinated the running of Palestinians' everyday lives. This coordination was carried out at two levels: the Central Committee (*Hava'ada HaMerkazit*), through which the overall policies, conduct and activities of these bodies were coordinated; and the district committees (*Va'adot Mirchaviot*). The Central Committee was headed by the Advisor on Arab Affairs and included the head of the Military Government and representatives of the Shin Bet and the police. It dealt with general issues but also with specific cases. Its discussions revolved around, among other things, screening of candidates for teaching and dismissal of teachers on political grounds, deciding on the awarding of licences for taxis, trucks, the opening of businesses, etc. (The Arab Affairs' Committee, 14 August 1958:9; Cohen, 2006:244; Aviv, 2007:33–54). Meanwhile, the three district committees (corresponding to the areas under the Military Government) were composed of three representatives of the security agencies along with the head of the Regional Bureau of the Advisor's Office, and were headed by the Regional Military Government Commander. These committees were in charge of running the day-to-day activities of the Palestinians at the micro-level as well as composing recommendations to the Central Committee and to state offices.

While the functions of these organizations were to supervise, punish, inhibit, disallow, restrict, suppress and expropriate, and were directed towards preventing dissent and persuading collaboration, the Histadrut's goal was to incorporate Palestinians in state structures and in the economy as second-class citizens. Its role was formalized in August 1949. It was agreed with the Advisor on Arab Affairs that it would be in charge of, among other things, banking, marketing organizations, transportation, local cooperatives and the awarding of credit (Mol and Palmon, 21 and 25 August 1949). It was also stated that its role was to serve political ends: '*The development of the Arab economy has to contribute to the struggle against forces in the Arab community that oppose de facto or de jure the Israeli state, its security or development*' (*ibid*., emphasis added).

While it marketed Arab agricultural products in Jewish cities and settlements by setting up open markets, it was aided by the Military Government in establishing shops in Arab villages where Israeli products were sold in order to 'circulate' the money that Palestinians earn back to the Jewish economy (The Histadrut's Arab department, n.d.:1–2), as the following letter exemplifies:

15.2.56

To Atta Ltd. [textile company]
The northern district
Haifa

Permission [was given for the opening of an] Arab cooperative store in Deir Hanna, Nazareth district.
[It] was organized by our department and it comprises a tool for *the introduction of Israeli industrial products to Arab villages.*

Sincerely, Yaakov Cohen
(Cohen, 15 February 1956)

The Histadrut was also the main supplier of vital services. It provided health insurance and health services through its nationwide clinics 'Kupat Holim' and training for paramedical personnel. Moreover, as a workers' union, it provided protection for employees, after the acceptance of Palestinians to the labour federation since 1960 (A Review of the Histadrut's Arab Department n.d.:2–3). It also established sports clubs in Palestinian villages, particularly soccer teams – the most popular game among Palestinians – within the Hapoel sport network (5–6).

Alongside these activities, it aimed to influence Palestinian consciousness through wide-ranging educational and cultural activities. For example, it set up in some localities 'clubs [which] included a library, a reading hall, games and newspapers' (*ibid*.:4). These clubs also screened films, showed plays and hosted public lectures. As early as 1961, special attention was paid to Palestinian women because as one Histadrut report revealed: 'From our activity in this field, we learnt that Arab women are susceptible to our *Hasbara* and are ready to be incorporated in the Histadrut's and state's life' (*ibid.*:6). Therefore, various courses for women were opened – which were modelled on colonial education for native women – and focused on teaching house management, handicrafts and Hebrew (*ibid.*).

Moreover, in the realm of Hasbara, the Histadrut's Arab department assumed in 1960 the management of *Al-Yom*, the semi-official Arabic daily (*ibid.*:5). Additionally, it published a wide array of publications including Al-*Yom for Children*, which with the recommendation of the Ministry of Education was sold to schools, and the monthly *Al-Hadaf* (the Target), which was also launched in 1960 and offered political and social analysis, substituting *Haqiqat Al-Amr* (The Truth of the Matter), the long-standing Arabic propaganda publication of the Histadrut and the Jewish Agency. Other publications included the semi-monthly magazine for teachers *Sada Al-Tarbia* (The Echo of Education), which was distributed to almost all Arab teachers as members of the teachers' union. The Histadrut also published books in Arabic, mostly translations from Hebrew, as well as calendars which lay emphasis on Israeli dates and celebrations. Some of these publications were particularly meant to impress foreign audiences.

Moreover, the Histadrut tried to influence large Palestinian audiences (and not only the literate) through films which were screened in Palestinian villages either for the purposes of distractions or to transmit hidden messages.[3] Additionally, a theatre group of Iraqi Jews (Ohel group) was established and performed plays written by Arab playwrights, such as the classical romance 'Majnon Lila', the performance of which was launched in October 1956.[4] In fact, many of these activities were also meant as propaganda to the outside world.[5] Given these activities, one report stated that:

> The Histadrut is [viewed as] the main public body which materializes Israel's presence in the Arab villages year-long. In Arab villages there are almost no branches of governmental ministries or [Mapai] party's branches. The Histadrut is the only body that occupies buildings and centers of activities which show in practice, through signs, flags etc. the presence of Israel in the Arab villages, small as large, and this is important. I would say that the Histadrut became hegemonic in the social, cultural and political aspects. (The Arab Affairs' Committee, 6 June 1968:12)

The Histadrut was also a tool to enlist Arab support for Mapai. Amnon Linn – who served as director of Mapai's Arab department in the Northern district, between 1951 and 1965 and nationally between 1965 and 1969 – was unambiguous in describing its role:

> I remember ... [in the 1950s and early 1960s] Mapai's activity among the Arab population was carried out by the Histadrut's Arab department – this means by a subsidiary which we called Brit Po'ali Eritz Yzrael [The League of Arab Workers]. Although the Histadrut was a general [union], but the Arab department was more or less homogenous; and in a certain stage we expelled Mapam ... I am telling this because the Histadrut's Arab department executive was controlled by us; it was

> possible to use it as Mapai's instrument in the villages. Our delegates and the Histadrut institutions in the villages were our operative arm. Then we could do in the Histadrut all what we desired. (The Arab Affairs' Committee, 6 June 1968:3–4)

Despite this, the Histadrut activities did not bring about the anticipated success. Yaakov Cohen of the Histadrut's Arab Department had to admit on 24 June 1964:

> [The Histadrut's activities] don't affect wide audiences in the Arab localities. ... [It] ought to be considered, whether we are content with these dimensions (of participation) or require wider circles to collaborate and get immersed in cultural, social, sport or artistic activities of the Histadrut as a sign of identification with the state's values and orientation. (The Secretariat of the Arab Affairs' Committee, 24 June 1964:1)

It seems that these state values were the problem. Despite the persecutions of the founders of Palestinian clubs established in some villages in the Triangle area, they managed with meagre resources to compete with the Histadrut's clubs.

Panopticon practices

In various aspects, the Military Government, along with the other institutions described earlier, embodied and gave expression to conditions and practices of a panopticon. In three aspects, the Military Government could be compared to the panopticon: its fixing of the population to specific spaces, its use of polarities as bases for judgement and its close and continual surveillance and registration.

The majority of Palestinians lived in closed areas, where movement in or out required passes. The three regions under the Military Government were divided and subdivided into smaller units, which in many cases formed the boundaries of a single locality; for example, until 1954, the Galilee was divided into forty-six areas, and passes were required to move between them (Kafkafi, 1998:357). Even after the relaxation of restrictions, the areas under military rule were divided into sixteen units.

These spatial divisions were used as the criteria according to which the military commanders made decisions with regard to the allocations of permits, supplies, transportation and services. The social communications and relationships between the residents were consequently confined to their areas of residence, thus giving rise to localism (Eyal, 2006:156). Moreover, such divisions made it easier to control Palestinians through state-sponsored programmes. In this regard, Barkatt stated: '... clubs should be established and not only for youth and young people ... where they can play their games and drink coffee etc. In this way it becomes possible to concentrate, and [consequently] influence them' (The Confined Secretariat of the Arab Affairs Committee, 19 March 1964:9).

In line with this objective, mentioned in the 1958 Plan and the Tolidano set of policy principles discussed in chapter 2, various measures were taken to concentrate Palestinians in small areas. For example, on Ben-Gurion's request to settle Palestinian commute workers in Haifa, Abba Hushi set up a housing company with the bishop Hakim to build and market apartments, yet not much came out of it. Palestinian workers preferred to commute rather than be packed up in dense neighbourhoods. More generally, A. Becker (the Secretary of the Histadrut) stated: '... we should have an interest in the thinning-out of Arab villages. Otherwise, by our deeds, we would ensure the continual concentration of Arabs in one place [i.e. region]' (*ibid.*:6).

Yet the idea of having these subdivisions was intended to prevail after the end of the Military Government. The policies towards the Negev Bedouins and the plans for their forced settlement represent perhaps one of the clearest examples of this principle of fixing and concentrating Palestinians. Although they were confined to the *Seig* area after the 1948 War, two plans were hammered out to confine them to much smaller areas (less than 10 per cent of the areas in which they previously lived). There is no doubt that the plans for the Bedouins stemmed from the Zionist principle of 'liberating the land', yet they also reflect the principle of fixing the population in small fragmented zones.

The first plan, outlined by Moshe Dayan in 1960, was premised on the notion of settling the Bedouins in working-class neighbourhoods in the mixed cities of Ramle, Jaffa and the town of Beersheba. Meanwhile, the second, devised by Yigal Allon in 1962, aimed at concentrating them in a small number of townships. Both plans were premised on the spatial confinement of the Bedouins (see, e.g., Bauml, 2007:190–200). The minister Bechor Sheetrit thought that such plans ought to take into account the Bedouins' social structure. Thus, regarding Dayan's plan, he maintained that 'I was against this [plan]. If you don't uproot the whole tribe you achieve nothing. If [only] part of the tribe leaves, the tribe will grow again and nothing is achieved ... you achieve results if you move the [whole] tribe from one place to another' (The Confined Secretariat of the Arab Affairs Committee, 19 March 1964:4).

The second similarity between the Military Government and the panopticon is the employment of a binary classification. It is obvious from the previous two sections that a binary division of the population into Jews and non-Jews comprised a cornerstone in Israeli policy (this point is discussed in the next chapter).

In the following paragraphs, I explore the legal implications of this dichotomy. The imposition of the Military Government on Palestinian-populated areas meant, in the legal sphere, the establishment of two legal systems: one for Palestinians and another largely for Jews. Although the emergency regulations are stated in universalistic terms, their application was almost confined to Palestinians. For example, Military Governor Shoham stated in 1958 that the areas under the Military Government were drawn in such a way as to be imposed on Palestinian localities only; 'Understandably exempted from this [area are], the Jewish settlements, the Circassians [village] (Kafr Kama) and every person who served in the IDF and carry with him this certificate or he is in the reserve service or during a compulsory service' (The Arab Affairs' Committee, 14 August 1958:6). The discrimination in the application of the law was not only on spatial criteria but on ethnic grounds as well. Indeed, the state comptroller stated in his 1957/8 report:

> An order from the military governor declaring an area closed is, in theory, applicable to all citizens without exception, whether living in the area or outside it. Thus anyone who enters or leaves a closed area without a permit from the military governor is in fact committing a criminal offense. In practice, however, Jews are not expected to carry such permits and in general are not prosecuted for breaking the regulations in article 125. (Quoted in Jiryis, 1976:26)

Another dimension of the legal duality was the establishment of military courts alongside the civilian ones. While the emergency regulations specified the nature of offences which were tried in either of these courts, the military commanders were given discretion in deciding the choice of the court that would deal with any case. The military courts epitomized the arbitrary judicial system which was the essence of the state of emergency.

They were of two types. The first was composed of three officers (who did not necessarily have legal education) who were mandated to deal with any breach of the emergency regulations and to pass any verdict the officers deemed appropriate. The second, of a lower rank, was composed of a single officer who could pass sentences of up to two years' imprisonment and impose fines.

Until 1963, the verdicts of these courts were final. Indeed, many Palestinians passed through this legal system. For example, during March–December 1951, some 2,028 Palestinians stood in these courts (Korn, 1995:668). Another type of military court, the tribunal for the prevention of infiltration, was established on the basis of the Prevention of Infiltration Law, 1954. It consisted of a one-officer court that was authorized to deal with all offences of this law, though an appeal could be filed to request a tribunal of three officers. This type of tribunal operated until 1959, when offences under this law were transferred to civilian courts.

To make these arrangements more effective, the police force acting in the Military Government zones was put under military authority (Korn, 1995:668–9). The implication of this duality, according to Koren, was the criminalization of Palestinians on political grounds:

> Many categories of crime are a clear 'outcome' of the political character of the law and its selective implementation on the Arab population. During the military government ... crime in the Arab population was, to a large extent, a result

> of political control over it ... the political use made of the criminal law, both in respect of its content and the methods of its enforcement, played a central role in 'creating' crime and delinquency among Arabs. ... [Thus] a very broad area of social, economic and political activity was defined as 'crime' and was dealt with by the rhetoric and practices of crime control. (*Ibid.*:659)

Third, intimate surveillance was sought not only through Palestinian collaborators – who passed on information which people made public in social gatherings or while travelling on public transportation (e.g. Cohen, 2006:13) – but also through their operators. The regional representatives of the Military Government were required to live in the area under their supervision in order to obtain first-hand and unfiltered information when necessary and to be in reach of the *mukhtar* and collaborators.

Moreover, they preserved what might be considered a primitive archive, a 'record of sins' in which the names and addresses of offenders and their punishments were recorded (Eyal, 2006:155). More generally, Cohen (2006) maintained that the security agencies paid special attention to the method of face-to-face interview with Palestinians, assuming that the balance of power in such encounters was in their favour as the majority of their interviewees would be anxious and shaken. Moreover, this method enabled them to use ways and means of hearsay, promises or intimidation (*ibid.*:250–1).

The desire for intimate knowledge took two forms: attempts to get in-depth knowledge, which took the shape of psychologism such as the construction of pseudo-psychological profiles for 'leaders and collaborators by the security agencies' (*ibid.*:21), and the opening of a file by the security agencies for any Palestinian who approached any of the state's institutions for any reason: work, license for business, a pass, permit, etc. (Bauml, 2007:246).

I have discussed thus far the structures of power that characterized the Military Government and the ways in which power was deployed to control the Palestinian population. In the following section, I shall look at this form of power through the premise of exceptionalism. This chapter opened with a discussion of the adoption of the emergency regulation and the institution of the Military Government; what follows here explores the impact of this method of governance.

Exceptionalism

Daunting lives

What characterized the state of exception was not only the suspension of the normative law but the awarding of power to officials who would render the law irrelevant and whose behaviour would turn any appeal to justice or rule of law a mockery.[6] Yet, the state of exception was not devoid of laws and regulations, but emergency laws possess different motivations and ends than normal ones.

In this regard, it is worth distinguishing *rule by law* which is characteristic of emergency laws from the normative *rule of law*.

In the first instance, the rules and regulations are not universally applied and they are considered another tool of domination. Therefore, the law loses its 'objective and universal aura'. Thus, its statue is diminished in the eyes of both the dominant and the dominated. In this regard, Jiryis (1981) described Israel's rule in the discussed period as 'domination by law'. Indeed, the Military Government as the embodiment of this regime had the vices which were characteristic of it, mainly the pervasiveness of large-scale abuses. Such abuses had taken many forms, two of which will be discussed in some detail: spectacular punishment and the pleasure of control.

There is hardly any Palestinian community in which stories of spectacular punishment from that period did not exist. The story of one village revolved around Commander Blume:

> He used to patrol the village; and whenever he encountered a man he would ask him: 'Are you married?' If the answer was positive he would beat him up saying: 'Do you want to increase this wicked nation?' If the answer was negative he would say: 'what is a donkey like you lacking? Do you think you are still young?' Then he would beat him up. Once he encountered an elderly man and ordered him to draw a circle and stand inside it. He threatened the man that he would kill him in case he steps outside it. The man stayed inside the circle from the morning till the evening. The commander left him and returned in the evening to check if the man was still standing inside the circle. When he found him standing there he hit him saying: 'what a stupid donkey, why did you not run away?' (Ghanim, 2009:11).

Jiryis (1976) provides several such stories (see 27–30). Probably the one which has stuck in the public imagination more than others is the story of Ahmad Hasan, a man from a tribe which resided close to the village of Arraba.

> [I]n August 1958 ... the military governor ordered him to sit every day for six months, from sunrise to sunset, under a large carob tree which stands to the west of the village of Deir Hanna. The purpose was to prevent him from contacting smugglers. (28–9)

While these forms of spectacular punishment might have been intended to frighten the population and to break its resolve or resistance, there were other forms which represented direct assault on the Palestinians' fundamental beliefs, dignity and what they considered the essence of their humanity.

Among these were the desecration of holy sites or scriptures and the violation of fundamental moral values. For example, a Military Government officer named Avraham Yarkoni and his assistant, a 'Haggai', were accused by the residents of the village of Deir Hanna of extortion, theft and severely beating residents of the village. More ferocious behaviours included 'urinating on residents in public places and taking Avraham's dog to defecate inside the mosque' (Robinson, 2005b:152[7]).

Although such abuses were not exceptional, the manner in which the Military Government managed the daily life of Palestinians was by its nature abusive. For example, the Military Governor of Jaffa was surprised by the brutality of his soldiers, complaining that 'They do not stop beating people' (cited in Pappe, 2006:205). The manner of getting passes was also a humbling experience (see, e.g., Ozacky-Lazar, 2002:109) and was often used as a means of exerting reward or punishment. Jiryis (1976) writes:

> The refusal of a permit to enter or leave a closed area meant that a worker, for example, could not get to his place of work or a peasant to his land. Usually the confinement to a village or a particular area and the consequent inability to go to work continued for an unlimited period. These restrictions were most frequently used against Arabs connected with political organizations or engaged in independent social or cultural activities disapproved of by the military government.
>
> The imposition of the travel restrictions was so frequent in Israel's first years that the military and civilian police made a habit of stopping both public and private traffic, especially on the main roads and sometimes daily, in order to check Arab identity cards. Those without passes, whatever the explanation, were arrested and driven off to prison, and from there they were taken before military court. (*Ibid.*:27–8)

Exceptionalism was also characterized by the absence of relevant knowledge by those who were under surveillance, a state which guaranteed their precarious position. The passes were written in Hebrew, a language that the vast majority of the population could not read (Ozacky-Lazar, 2002:110), and the boundaries of the closed areas were not known to the population.

The Military Government never published the extent of the areas under its control and very rarely disclosed anything about its activities. Anyone wanting to find out which areas he/she could visit without a permit had to go to one of the few Military Government offices or to a police station, which could rarely provide the information. Anyone entering or leaving a closed area without a permit was liable to prosecution for breaking the emergency regulations, despite the fact that he/she did not, or might not, know the boundaries. Ignorance was not a valid excuse before a military court (Jiryis, 1976:23).

The pleasures of control

In contrast to the above-mentioned abusive and restrictive acts, Military Government officials and Jewish employees in Palestinian communities made a habit of inviting themselves to the houses of Palestinian citizens or making sure that Palestinians understood that hospitality was part of the dues they had to pay (Benziman and Mansour, 1992:103; Robinson, 2005b:155–7).

In late 1949, the Military Government sought to tackle this habit by reminding low-level officers and clerks that everyone but the Governors themselves had to follow 'strict orders on gatherings and meals in Arab villages' and should take care 'to undertake visits ... without promis[ing the residents] to take care of anything' (Robinson, 2005b:156).

Such lunches and celebrations were often explained by reference to Palestinians' cultural values of generosity and hospitability. However, in practice, they violated the essence of these values, as hospitability and generosity rested on underlying perceptions of mutuality, reciprocity, goodwill and voluntarism. In this case, it was obvious that they were not supported by any of these perceptions. No mutuality, reciprocity or voluntarism existed; rather, they reflected the existing hierarchy of power and they reinforced the power relationships; in fact, they were a sort of extortion.

Yehoshua Palmon, the first Advisor on Arab Affairs who in 1950 expressed apprehension regarding Palestinians' ability to corrupt his staff had to admit within a year and a half that corruption had become endemic in the state bureaucracy which dealt with Palestinians, not because of the Palestinians but the abuse of authority by state officials.

> In the field there is wide-ranging corruption by most of the staff [who deal with the Arabs]. Bribery is taken in exchange for doing things. This finds expression in ... joint ventures of persons who fulfil official functions in areas on which they are responsible, like quarries, the custodian [for absentees' property] etc. ... [Moreover] in most cases the difference [in the prices paid to Palestinian farmers and the prices in the market] reached 60 per cent instead of 25 per cent as [officially] decided.
>
> We decided to allow a certain number of infiltrators who were in the country during the election, as a result of a law which was passed in the Knesset, to stay. We decided to allow this as goodwill, however in reality this cost the Arabs 50–100 Lira for each identity card; our goodwill was turned into something negative. ... There is corruption among Jews, however, it has limited political implications, the corruption in the relationships between Jews and Arabs gives the Arabs the feeling that this is not corruption but 'Khawa' (extortion). This means an Arab has to pay it because he is an Arab for a Jew because he is a Jew. (The Political Committee, 24 January 1952:5–6/3)

Aestheticizing power

Exceptionalism is usually imposed to confront imminent real or imaginary danger, and it is supported by the covert or overt promise of overcoming the danger and establishing a better state of affairs. But how can those who reject exceptionalism and its false promise impose it themselves? This contradiction has been at the heart of the Israeli leadership's discussions on the aesthetics of power; namely, how can the representation of the exception conceal its nature? Before 1948, Zionist politicians, lawyers and jurists condemned the Mandatory emergency regulations in the strongest language (Jiryis, 1976:12–13); 'Even in Nazi Germany there were no such laws. ... It is mere euphemism to call the military courts "courts". To use the Nazi title, they are no better than "Military Judicial Committees Advising the Generals". ... No government has the right to draw up such laws', declared Yaakov Shimshon Shapira, who after 1948 became the legal advisor to the Israeli government (*ibid.*:12). However, when the state of Israel reintroduced these regulations after 1948 to rule the Palestinians, there seems to have been a need to justify this change. In 1953, Ben-Gurion explained this alteration as follows:

> We opposed this law of the Mandate government because a foreign government, neither elected by us, nor responsible to us, had given itself the right to detain any one of us without trial. In the present instance the law is being applied by the state of Israel, through a government chosen by the people and responsible to them. (Quoted in Peretz, 1991:91)

Ben-Gurion's argument is problematic as the juxtaposition which he made between elected and non-elected government and the right to impose a state of exception is spurious. Imposition of a state of exception had to do with sovereignty rather than legitimacy. This is clear from the opening sentence of Schmitt's *Political Theology*, where he declared: '[S]overeign is he who decides on the exception' (5).

Democratic and non-democratic countries alike, as recent history has shown, have imposed decrees of emergency. The state of emergency should be compared to the juridico-formal point of view (in Agamben's words), or, as Schmitt postulated, exception as the sovereignty of men should be juxtaposed against normalcy as the sovereignty of law.

Given this contradiction in the Israeli imposition of the Mandatory emergency regulations, various sections of the Israeli elite had been uncomfortable with the Military Government, though not with its goals. For example, the left-Zionist party Mapam publicly stood at the forefront of the struggle for the abolition of the Military Government. Yet its leaders did not hesitate to pressure military governors and commanders to confiscate lands of Arab villages – on the basis of these regulations – and transfer them to their settlements (The Arab Affairs' Committee, 30 January 1958:12).

They wanted to keep the Military Government but in a different form. The main question which bothered the opponents of the Military Government was its representation, rather than what it did. For example, in the discussion on the political plan of 1958 (see chapter 2), Michael Assaf, an orientalist and one of Mapai's leaders, suggested playing down this contradiction through obfuscation by 'maintaining the Military Government but changing the name – the Military Government – which has become a monster' (*ibid.*). Assaf's idea was to be repeated on several occasions by other Israeli leaders. For example, Mordechai Namir stated in the discussion on the Military Government on 14 August 1958:

> In general I also claim that we can achieve the same social and economic goals, which adjoin the security issue after ten years of Military Government rule, not under this awful title 'Military Government'. Maybe a change of the name under existing complex circumstances plays a positive role. (The Arab Affairs' Committee, 14 August 1958:18)

He went on to suggest:

> I don't see that others have better methods ... and I don't absolve our party and those who work [on this issue] from looking for ways to add 'lipstick, powder and rouge'. (*Ibid.*:21)

Even the head of the Military Government in 1958, Mishal Shoham, was well aware that his organization was not viewed favourably:

> I want to repeat some of the things I have already said in the ministerial committee. ... Maybe the Military Government is not an aesthetic pot however it contains good wine ... it can be crushed ... however with one stipulation, that the wine be transferred to another appropriate container. (*Ibid.*:24)

Yet, the severity of the Military Government was eased in the 1960s, not due to theories of justice or moral considerations but to two other reasons: first, the fast economic growth which was triggered by the import of capital, particularly from West Germany, following the reparation agreement and consequently the growing demands for workers in the labour market (Sa'di, 1995:432–7); and, second, the political pressure by other Jewish parties from the right and left, who argued that the Military Government was used to coerce Palestinians to vote for Mapai (see, e.g., Jiryis, 1976; Sa'di, 2003a:78; Bauml, 2007:232–45; for thorough discussion, see chapter 7).

Several relaxations were introduced by the early 1960s. In 1963, Prime Minister Levi Eshkol, who succeeded Ben-Gurion, expressed his wish, in line with the colonial vision, that the Military Government would, like Bentham's inspector, 'see without being seen' (quoted in Bauml, 2007:238). That year, most Palestinians were no longer required to acquire specific passes for movements outside the areas of residence, although they were not allowed to enter closed areas.

By 1965, the heads of the security apparatuses in the Central Committee reached the conclusion that the Military Government had run its course and on 1 December 1966, it was abolished. Its responsibilities and authority were transferred to the police and the Shin Bet. However, the emergency regulations remained unchanged, and many of the restrictions imposed on Palestinians were not lifted. Moreover, the new system was no less oppressive than its predecessor.

The Military Government was reinstituted for the week of the Six-Day War and the following week. The abolishment of restrictions on the freedom of movement of Palestinian citizens finally took place on 3 October 1967 (for a discussion on the abolishment of the Military Government, see Bauml, 2007:226–45).

Conclusion

This chapter has attempted to analyse the structures of power through which Israel ruled the Palestinians. Generally speaking, two paradigms were introduced to explain the functioning of these structures, principally the Military Government: the panopticon and the state of exception. The premises of these paradigms are contradictory.

The paradigm of the panopticon, at least as it was employed by Foucault (1991), was meant both to achieve a low-cost (illusion of) total surveillance and normalization of those deemed as deviants. Politically, this would mean an administered integration of unfit citizens to the mainstream of society. This could be achieved through the use of some of the techniques that Bentham (1995) and Foucault (1991) described including the fixing of the subjects, (the illusion of) their subjection to continuous supervision, their quarantining, the documentation of their offences and the application of reward and punishment on the basis of binary divisions and branding, and their division and subdivision to governable units. Indeed, most of these techniques were used by the Military Government. Yet, according to the panopticon paradigm, normalization is carried out by a clear and universal set of rules. In this regard, the Military Government was closer to the premises of the state of exception paradigm, where the governing body was not confined by a set of normative laws and their universal application. Rather, decisionism or the arbitrary exercise of authority was the driving force, where the subjects led a precarious life, they lacked control over their environment and their ability to predict events relating to their lives was radically decreased.

The analysis of the control and surveillance practices that Israel employed shows that both paradigms were concurrently used. While various surveillance methods relating to the panopticon were employed, normalization – as integration – was not sought, and the rule of law did not prevail. Palestinians had lived through a long period under a state of exception. What was the final aim of this combination of surveillance methods? It seems that it was meant to normalize the aspects of life that the state of exception engendered, that is, to condition Palestinians to stop imagining that an autonomous life was possible.

Notes

1 On the Web: http://israellawresourcecenter.org/israellaws/fulltext/lawandadministrationord.htm, *Law and Administration Ordinance* (published 19 May 1948).

2 www.israellawresourcecenter.org/websitematerials/mapsg/mapsg1der1945.html, Also Kirshbaum (n.d.), Jiryis (1976:9–20).

3 Among these films is King Solomon's Mines, which is based on a biblical motif. For example, Agasi asked the cinema department on 29 August 1956 to lend him this film as well as the film Children of the Prairie – Hebrew translation (Agassi, 29 August 1956). 'Letter to the cinema department, Hahaver Arie Brzam, the executive, here' (*The Lavon Archive,* Document No. IV-208-1-8559).

4 In fact, it was mostly used for propaganda as the cultural attaches of various foreign delegations were invited: the French, the Russian, the American and the British.

Barkatt, Reuven (4 September 1956) 'Cultural Secretary, Russian Embassy: Inviting You to the Premiere of Majnun Layla', *The Lavon Archive*, Document No. IV-208-1-8559; 'To Dr. Thomas H. McGrail Cultural Attache, American Embassy: Inviting You to the Premiere of Majnun Layla', *The Lavon Archive*, Document No. IV-208-1-8559; 'To Robert E. Gramble, Second Secretary, British Embassy: Inviting You to the Premiere of Majnun Layla', *The Lavon Archive*, Document No. IV-208-1-8559; (5 September 1956) 'Mlle E. Fischer, Attache Culturel, Ambassade de France: Inviter a Assister a la Premier de'Majnun Layla', *The Lavon Archive*, Document No. IV-208-1-8559. Exchange of letters and invitations were sent among others to Moshe Sharett (on 5 September); M. Namir, the Minister of Labour; and Golda Meir, Foreign Minister. Moreover, exchange of letters was conducted between Mr Kadish of the Military Administration and Michael El-Zur, Political Secretary in the Foreign Ministry. All these correspondences are available in the above-mentioned file.

5 See note 4 but also the Foreign Ministry acquired hundreds of copies, for example, of *Al-ta'awin* (Cooperation), which was published by the Ministry of Employment and included summaries in English (*ibid.*: 2–6).

It is highly likely that this report was composed in the early 1960s (either in 1961 or 1962); a more comprehensive review was composed by The Histadrut's Arab Department (1965).

6 Interestingly, Shimon Peres thought that 'the military government is a small apparatus that does not oppress the Arabs ... [it even] helps them' (quoted in Kafakafi, 1998:360).

7 This information was confirmed by personal communication with an elderly resident of Deir Hanna, who recalled many such stories, several of which were on the desecration of places of worship.

4

Divide et impera

Categorizing citizens

In chapter 2, following Michel Foucault, I argued that an overriding concern of Israel, like all modern states, is the population (bio-politics), although the population at the centre of Israel's concern overlaps neither with those who live within its boundaries nor with those holding its citizenship (see chapters 1 and 2). Nevertheless, it has been energetically engaged since its inception in the collection of data – its storage, classification and categorization – according to various organizing principles. The collected data and its presentation through various statistical measures may be used positively – to address the needs of the population efficiently, to target groups which are in need of special attention and to empower citizens – or negatively, to subjugate or marginalize certain groups. Therefore, the Israeli regime of truth has strived to present the various categories of population as 'natural' and as based on interiorities which set them apart from others. The data and the analysis presented in the previous chapters cast doubt on the naturalness of the official order in which the Palestinians are presented as a mosaic of insular minorities. The aim of this chapter is to deconstruct this order and unveil the role that state power has played, *through deliberate planning and direct action*, in engineering a social order where 'ethnic' categories have been presented as the central or the only form of identification for Palestinians.

This constructed order is premised on two representations of the Palestinians: as non-Jews and as a collection of minorities. This balkanized group structure and identity, besides its political ends, has been an essential tool of surveillance and political control. In the following section, I shall discuss how, through various state practices, the Palestinians were constructed as non-Jews. It will be followed by their construction as an assortment of minorities.

Palestinians as non-Jews

As early as 1952, Israeli leaders began to realize that they might have to rule a Palestinian minority – unwelcome citizens – for many years to come and, maybe, forever (chapter 1). However, their relationship with the Palestinians had a long history. They could thus draw on their historical experiences during the formation of the state of Israel which were ultimately materialized in the building of institutions and the preparation of specialized staff; the emergence of conventions, rules, perceptions and stereotypes; as well as the development of an ideological edifice, to justify prevailing conceptions and dogmas (this is partly discussed in Sa'di, 1997). One fundamental principle of these relationships has been the racial boundary between Jewish settlers and native Palestinians. While the results of the war might have created an opportunity for the establishment of a non-racial order, Israeli leaders preferred to go ahead with the achievement of Zionist goals, which are premised on the dispossession and subordination of Palestinians (chapter 1). Consequently, the Jewish–Arab dichotomy became constitutive of a racialized sociopolitical and legal order (e.g. Sa'di, 2004a).

This settlers–natives binary was followed – as in other colonial settings – by divisions and subdivisions of the natives for the purposes of surveillance and political control (e.g. Guha, 2003). For, as Michel Foucault has argued, '[i]nstead of bending all its subjects into a single uniform mass, it [the regime] separates, analyses, differentiates, carries its procedures of decomposition to the point of necessary and sufficient single units' (Foucault, 1991:170). These processes of categorizing and labelling, particularly when they entail differential treatment, can result in the hardening of identities and the instigation of conflicts (Lyon, 2009:30–8).

In fact, the Jewish–Palestinian division is foundational to Zionism. Racialized boundaries are engrained in the idea of establishing a homeland for European Jews through migration and political and military domination of a country overwhelmingly populated by indigenous Arabs. While the history and implications of the struggle over Palestine have been the subject of much scholarly research, this chapter attends to the particular way in which the separation between Jews and Palestinians was reinforced during the first two decades of the establishment of the state of Israel.

From the start, the state itself has served as a vehicle for the achievement and furthering of national (Jewish) goals. The term 'Israeli' has been used as synonymous with Israeli Jew. For example, Israel's founding father and first Prime Minister, David Ben-Gurion, stated at the twenty-fifth World Zionist Congress held in 1960:

> Here everything is Jewish and universal: the soil we walk upon, the trees whose fruit we eat, the roads on which we travel, the houses we live in, the factories where we work, the schools where our children are educated, the army in which they are trained ... the language we speak and the air we breathe, the landscape we see and the vegetation that surrounds us – *all* of it is Jewish. (Cited in Peretz, 1991:86)

This state–ethnic identification has led to what Yiftachel (2006) calls an 'ethnocracy', or the rule of one ethnic group – and precluded the plausibility of an overarching frame of identification for all citizens. Given this, the state embarked on two parallel projects: the homogenization of the Jewish population and the Judaization of the space. The first embodied a vigorous promotion by the ruling elite of a melting pot policy and the construction of a national character of 'Israeliness' (Kimmerling, 2001). The second project entailed the creation of a sense of exclusive entitlement to the country through ideologically inspired school textbooks and 'scientific' knowledge in archaeology, geography, cartography, history, sociology and political sciences, as well as through the de-Arabization and de-signification of the country's landscape (e.g. Firer, 1985; Falah, 1996; Benvenisti, 2000: Ch.1; Azaryahu and Golan, 2001; Abu El-Haj, 2002). Moreover, this notion of state–ethnic identification was linked to security. As Kretzmer argued:

> The perception of Jewish ownership of land and settlement as essential mechanisms of maintaining the security of the Jewish collective means that security measures which restrict basic liberties of Arab citizens may be employed to facilitate them. (1990:137)

Consequently, the road to ethnically based hierarchy and internal colonization (Zureik, 1979) was short. Indeed, the Jewish–Palestinian dichotomy was translated to a hierarchy of rulers and ruled, as Peretz observed:

> No Arabs were designated as officials in charge of Arab affairs in the various ministries. Rather responsibility for such matters, even in ministries unrelated to security such as social welfare, agriculture, health and education, and the like, were entrusted to Jewish employees. (1991:98)

The level of absurdity this racial hierarchy reached was apparent when a Jew was appointed as the head of the Islamic religious administration; Muslims cynically referred to him as 'Mufti Hirshberg' (*ibid.*:98). This hierarchy also formed a guiding principle for those who ruled the Palestinians directly. For example, Yehoshua (Josh) Palmon, the first Advisor to the Prime Minister on Arab Affairs, stated:

> I opposed the integration of the Arabs into Israeli society. I prefer separate development. ... This separation made it possible to maintain a democratic regime within the Jewish population alone. (*Ibid.*:100)

Palmon's observation seems to go beyond the analysis presented hitherto, as it touches on the relationship between political control and the rule of law – a point which I shall explore later. Yet, it illustrates that the power of categorization of citizens stems not only from their construction and their use by the state's bureaucracy but also from their impact on the social structure and, consequently, on the life chances and experiences of citizens. In the current case, various policies had the impact of translating the Jewish–Palestinian dichotomy into ethno-class relations (Zureik, 1979; Sa'di, 1995). Those in charge of

Arab affairs were already aware in the initial stages of statehood that the massive transfer of Palestinians' lands to state and Jewish bodies would result in 'condemning them [the Palestinians] to a life of perpetual poverty' (Peretz, 1991:94). Indeed, an increasing percentage of the Palestinian workforce had become semi-skilled or unskilled labourers in the state/Jewish companies, thus introducing the ethnic hierarchy into the workplace (Zureik, 1979; Lustick, 1980; Sa'di, 1995).

Moreover, Jewish citizens as collective or specific groups of Jews, such as mayors (e.g. Hushi, Kitron, Surkis), teachers in Arab schools, bureaucrats, Mapai and Histadrut employees and high-profile students associated with Mapai at universities, were conceived by policymakers as potential or active agents in the surveillance and control of Palestinians (see chapter 6). This led the head of the Military Government, Mishal Shoham, to declare in the course of a discussion on the future of this administration held on 14 August 1958:

> In order to abolish the Military Government from half of the Galilee, it must be settled so that half of the residents ought to be Jews. ... I am ready to take Nazareth out of the Military Government [jurisdiction] provided that six Jews and not Communist members sit in the municipality and at least the Jews constitute half of its residents. (The Arab Affairs' Committee, 14 August 1958:25)

Officially, this division was reproduced in the ID cards, where each citizen fell into one of two dichotomous ethnic categories: Jew or Arab (the blurred Druze category added in 1962 will be discussed later). Israel's decision to conduct a census/survey at the end of the 1948 War and grant ID cards to its citizens was not a novel idea in the country's history. A previous attempt was made during the Palestinian revolt of 1936–39. Prior to his departure in 1938, the British General John Drill hoped to introduce identity cards to control the citizens' movement across the frontiers and between districts as a measure for quelling the revolt. Yet, Drill's identity card plan was hampered by Jewish objections to a system that would have helped identify illegal Jewish immigrants (Thomas, 2008:249). The Israeli ID system had aims beyond those of Drill, however. In addition to the goals of stopping movement across borders, that is, preventing the return of refugees and linking Palestinian ID holders to places of residence, it had additional restrictive functions similar to those of Stalinist Russia's internal passport system (Lyon, 2009:26). The ID card includes information that could be used for policing, for determining eligibility for movement in certain areas and for providing a shortcut for affiliating persons to friendly or hostile groups (this will be discussed in the following section). Indeed, Ben-Gurion affirmed the security implications of the national categorization of citizens, stating that '[f]or security reasons we did not abolish the registration of religion or nationality in the identity card' (quoted in Bauml, 2007:77). Realizing the import of identification cards (to use Lyon's, 2009 conceptualization) for surveillance, the Military Government's Arabists advised the Population

Registry Bureau of the Ministry of Interior to include information about hamula (extended family) membership – significant information used for the exercise of control – in the official population registry, next to the regular entries marking each Palestinian citizen's name, date of birth, residence and so on (Eyal, 2006:158). Yet, the import attached to the identification of citizens was not matched by a speedy issuing of ID cards to Palestinians. The granting of ID cards and citizenship to Palestinians was a lengthy process mired in bureaucratic confusion and inefficiency (Robinson, 2005b:46–182). Moreover, it was pursued half-heartedly at best, as the state was interested in decreasing the number of Palestinians. Moreover, the granting of ID cards and citizenship might complicate the transfer operations, although citizenship rights could be easily withdrawn, as happened in the case of Al-Majdal residents who, despite having been awarded ID cards, were deported in the early 1950s. Besides ID cards, other means of identification which would make Palestinians visible were introduced. For example, specific plate numbers for cars owned by Palestinians were issued, and the police were instructed to follow the journeys these cars made and identify their parking places (Bauml, 2007:248).

This division was also pronounced at the institutional level, where two bureaucracies along national lines were established. The official state offices dealt with the Jews, while the Military Government and special departments dealt with the Palestinians. Such departments were established in various ministries, such as in the ministries of education and religious affairs, as well as in the Histadrut after the acceptance of Palestinians to its ranks in 1960. In fact, Palestinians were admitted to the Histadrut following substantial change in the labour market, where unemployment ceased to be a worrying issue. Prior to that, the employment of Palestinians was managed by three organizations: the League of Arab Workers, a Histadrut front organization; the Congress of Arab Workers, a communist party–affiliated trade union; and the Christian Labour Union in Nazareth, an organization which was set up by bishop George Hakim. Not only were the personnel in charge of Arab affairs Jews, but they were connected through and through with the surveillance and control apparatus: the Shin Bet, the Office of the Advisor on Arab Affairs and Mapai's Arab Department (see chapter 6).

The Jewish–Palestinian division found expression in laws or through differential application of laws, as legal discrimination was often veiled by universalistic language. The most obvious discriminatory laws are 'the Law of Return, 1950' and the 'Nationality Law, 1952'. They consider every Jew in the world a potential citizen of Israel (Kretzmer, 1987:35–44). Not only does every Jew have the right to immigrate to Israel and to receive upon his arrival Israeli citizenship and considerable economic inducement, but he also becomes eligible to benefit from the state land, which accounts for 80 per cent of the country's surface, a privilege from which Palestinian citizens are excluded. In contrast, the relatives of Palestinian citizens and Palestinian refugees could not return to Israel under the provisions of these laws. Another set of laws concern the status of Jewish organizations such as the World Zionist Organization (WZO), the Jewish Agency and the Jewish National Fund (JNF) (Kretzmer, 1987:61–9; 90–8). These organizations have operated as subcontractors for the state, received state support and consequently became indirect channels for the pursuance of discrimination. Still further, the JNF has been working in Israel since the state's independence despite the racist nature of some of its articles of association. Not only does the JNF prohibit the sale of land to non-Jews, but it also forbids the leasing or subleasing of land to them (Davis and Lehn, 1983).

Besides the overt legal discrimination, many laws had been tailored to discriminate against the Palestinians although they were stated in universal language. Various scholars have discussed in depth such laws (e.g. Jiryis, 1976, 1981; Kretzmer, 1987). Probably the most obvious ones are the Absentees' Property Law, 1950, which enabled the state to seize the property of Palestinian refugees and citizens who were labelled 'present absentees' (Jiryis, 1981:83–6), and the Land Acquisition Law, 1953, which empowers the Minister of Finance to purchase – with or without the consent of the lawful owners – lands that the state had already expropriated (Jiryis, 1981:90–1). One efficient tactic that has been repeatedly applied is the use of the military service criteria as a basis for discrimination. While the Druze and the few Arabs who served in the army would be beneficiaries, the fact remains that such laws benefit almost all the Jews and proscribe the vast majority of Palestinians. This is clearly illustrated in the Discharged Soldiers Law, 1970, which gives soldiers, veterans and their families substantial economic benefits and offers them improved educational and employment opportunities (Jiryis, 1971:66–7; Kretzmer, 1987). Such laws were frequently passed to supplement the restrictions which had already been put in place by the Emergency Regulations.

The Palestinians as a mosaic of insular minorities

After the affirmation of the basic Jewish–Palestinian binary, the subdivision of the Palestinians ensued. Already in 1920, 'the Intelligence Office' of the Zionist Executive's political department in Palestine laid down a plan to manipulate the differences and stir up conflicts among Palestinians. The document it produced included the following principles:

> 1. Cultivation of the agreement with Haidar Toqan. Toqan, who had served as mayor of Nablus at the end of the Ottoman period and represented the city in the Ottoman parliament after 1912, received EP (English pound) 1,000 from the Zionist leader (Weizmann). In exchange, he promised to organize a pro-Zionist petition in Nablus region and to open a pro-Zionist cultural and political club in the city.

2. Creation of an alliance with the influential emirs on the eastern side of the Jordan based on the assumption that they would be reluctant to support a national movement led by urban elites.

3. Establishment of an alliance with Bedouin sheikhs in southern Palestine, in order to sever the connections that already existed between them and national activists.

4. Purchase of newspapers hostile to Zionism in order to ensure a pro-Zionist editorial policy.

5. Organization and promotion of friendly relations with Arabs, and the opening of cooperation clubs.

6. Provocation and dissension between Christians and Muslims. (Cohen, 2008:17)

It seems that the idea of segmenting the Palestinians comprised a cornerstone in the plans of the Zionist/Israeli leaders from the start. Accentuation of differences, instigation of conflicts and the awarding of benefits of various sorts were conceived as appropriate strategies for achieving Zionist goals against the will of the Palestinian population. Indeed, while the Arab Bureau of the Jewish Agency maintained some informal relations with Palestinians during the Mandate period, the main aim was confined to the gathering of intelligence and 'manoeuvres to split Arab ranks' (Peretz, 1991:88).

Yet, this general scheme would have had limited impact had it not been pursued concretely by collecting and filing data, exploring new subdivisions in light of the new data and creating a specialized body with knowledge of the indigenous population and its customs, language, religions, economy and sociopolitical structures. Indeed, these processes, which had been partly demonstrated in the assemblage of the village files (which will be discussed in the next chapter), had a great impact not only on the Israeli war effort but also on Israel's control of the Palestinians during the 1950s and 1960s. Furthermore, many of those who managed the Palestinians after the establishment of Israel acquired their expertise before 1948. Yet, social categorization is frequently the end result of arduous sociopolitical sorting processes that not only construct the way in which citizens conceive themselves and others but also the ways in which ethnic relations are structured. In the following sections, the division of Palestinians by state bodies into different and occasionally contending groups will be explored.

Druze particularism

Historically, the constitution of the Druze category dates back to a meeting held at the beginning of 1932 between the President of the Jewish National Council (JNC), *Va'ad Le'umi*, Yitzhak Ben-Zvi, and the person in charge of the JNC's political department (responsible for the relationship with the Arabs),

Aharon Chaim Cohen, with Abdullah Khayr, an educated Druze from the village of Abu Snan. Ben-Zvi and Cohen wanted to learn about the attitude of the Druze towards the conflict over the country between Palestinians and Jews. During the course of the meeting, Mr Khayr seems to have suggested that the Druze should organize themselves as an autonomous religious group (i.e. millet) and distinguish themselves from the Muslims. Although Khayr's ideas were born out of factionalism and struggle within the Druze community over leadership and prestige between leading hamulas – principally Khayr, Tarif and Muadi (see Firro, 1999:23–4) – his remarks gave insight to the Zionist leadership with regard to the segmentation of the Palestinians. Thus, Ben-Zvi wrote in a letter addressed to Moshe Sharett, the head of the Jewish Agency's political department, on 2 August 1940:

> In my opinion there are shared interests between us and the Druze more than with any other group in the country and its surroundings. ... Among them [the Druze] there are two trends: A. One which aspires to free itself from the Islamic Sharia court; B. [one] which does not want to free itself from this court. I think by an appropriate deception we can help the trend which seeks to achieve independence from the authority of the Mufti and his representatives. (Quoted in Avivi, 2007:24 [Translated by AHS])

However, the 1948 War was a milestone in the construction of the Druze as a distinct category. Their history and behaviour during this period are fairly clear now (see, e.g., Firro, 1999; 2001; Parsons, 2000; Cohen, 2006; Avivi, 2007). The Druze's war record is mixed, ranging from active collaboration (such as in the case of Shafa'amr) to armed resistance (in the case of the villages of Yanuh and Jat). The defeat of the Druze battalion of Syrian volunteers in April 1948 and the changing of sides by some of its soldiers and officers – which was partly mediated by local Druze dignitaries who collaborated with Zionism (Firro, 1999:50–7) – in addition to the formation in May 1948 of a small contingent of some twenty-five men from the Druze Carmel villages, Daliyat al-Karmel and Isfiya, under Shai's (the intelligence organization of the Haganah) officer Giora Zaid, added another dimension to this mixed picture (Avivi, 2007:72). During the war, the Druze (both locals and Syrians) who were attached to the Israeli army numbered some sixty persons. Although their significance to the war effort was negligible, their symbolic participation was essential (Parsons, 2000:104–6) because, as Palmon put it, 'this act has destroyed all ways of going back for them' (quoted in Firro, 2001:42). After the war, the number of Druze who volunteered to join the newly established 'minorities unit' remained small, reaching no more than 400 (*ibid.*).

Yet, this was enough for Israeli policymakers to engage in the construction of the Druze ethnic category. According to Firro (1999) and Parsons (2000), three external and internal policy considerations led to the pursuit of this undertaking. First, they could be used as a link to the large Druze communities in Syria and Lebanon. Thus, they were viewed as an instrument in furthering Ben-Gurion's strategy of building an alliance of non-Arab or non-Muslim minorities in the Middle East (Parsons, 2000:142). Their role was that of 'a poisoned dagger to stab into the back of Arab unity'[1] (Parsons, 2000:104; also Firro, 2001:42). Indeed, on two occasions, Israel tried to intervene in Syrian affairs through the Druze connection. The first took place in 1954 during the struggle between President Adib Shishakli and his many opponents, including Druze officers. Moshe Dayan, the Chief of Staff, thought that Druze men could be trained and sent in sabotage missions to Syria. Yet, as Sharett unveiled, Dayan's plan did not materialize, as the local Druze leaders failed to mobilize enough volunteers (Avivi, 2007:356–60). The second occasion was following the Six-Day War. On 20 August 1967, the then Minister of Labour, Yigal Allon, wrote a letter to Prime Minister Levi Eshkol, suggesting that Israel should seize the opportunity that had arisen from the struggle between Syrian Alawi and Druze officers to intervene in order to set up a vassal Druze state in the area known as Jabal Al-Druze. This state would constitute a buffer zone between Israel and Syria and block Syria's access to the newly occupied Golan Heights, thus nullifying the Syrian claim to it (Avivi, 2007:363–5).

Second, Israel found the Druze beneficial for propaganda purposes (Parsons, 2000:125). They were to be presented as an example of the fair, human and progressive nature of the Israeli regime as well as the harmonious relations which exist between the *various* ethnic groups.

Third, at the local level, they were viewed through the colonialist prism as '"friendly natives", rather like the Gurkhas in India, whose particularistic nature was encouraged in order to help controlling unfriendly natives' (*ibid.*:127). More importantly, the Israeli leaders' interest in furthering Druze particularism was aimed at stirring up acrimony among Palestinians. In this regard, the head of the Military Government, Mishal Shikhter (Shoham), argued in Mapai's Committee on Arab Affairs on 30 January 1958:

> The Arab minority [and I oppose the concept Arab minority; in my opinion we should say the Arabs in Israel] – are not a unified thing ... we are able to encourage this dissimilarity. If we succeed in making Arabs suspicious of the Druze – and not because they are loyal to us – this would be very important. (The Arab Affairs' Committee, 30 January 1958:30)

Similarly, the Deputy Advisor to the Prime Minister on Arab Affairs, Aharon Layish, contended that '[The conscription of the Druze] intensified the crisis of confidence between the Druze and the members of other communities' (Cohen, 2006:196).

To many Palestinians, the causes for suspicion of the Druze were real, given the tasks entrusted to Druze soldiers. The Druze battalion operated from two bases in the north and the south. In the north, it engaged along the borders in blocking the return of Palestinian refugees, in sweep operations – detention and expulsion of refugees who returned to their villages (officially labelled infiltrators) – and in stopping cross-border commerce. Meanwhile, in the south (the Negev), it engaged in the cleansing (*Tihor*) of Bedouin tribes and other Arabs deemed unfriendly to the state and in stopping cross-border commerce (Firro, 1999:106; Cohen, 2006:196; Avivi, 2007:76).

The highlighting of the Druze distinction had already begun in 1948 with one of the first acts of distinguishing the Druze from the Muslims. In October, Yaakov Shim'oni, the deputy head of the Middle Eastern department at the Foreign Ministry, wrote a letter to the Muslim Department in the Ministry for Religious Affairs to change its name to the Muslim and Druze Department, a change which was implemented by June 1949 (Avivi, 2007:25). However, the complexity of the new categorization was manifested in the Druze's conscription to the army, upon which the whole project pended. By 1949, the military was no longer interested in the Druze unit. For example, Amnon Yanai, the first commander of the minorities' battalion, recalled on 30 January 1958:

> During the first years the struggle was very difficult, mainly of the security services against the army. They confined them [to certain areas] and argued that they shouldn't be trusted. They even confined their operation within the areas in which they live. Within three years, there were at least three orders to terminate this business. (The Arab Affairs' Committee, 30 January 1958:33)

On 20 September 1949, Ben-Gurion held a discussion on the future of this unit with Yaakov Dori, the Chief of Staff, and Chaim Herzog, the head of the Military Intelligence Branch, who wanted to demobilize it. Ben-Gurion and Sharett objected, fearing that such a move would have adverse repercussions on the relationship with the Druze community in Israel as well as on Israeli policy towards the Druze communities in the Arab countries (Avivi, 2007:78). The struggle between the military establishment on the one hand and politicians and those in charge of Arab affairs on the other continued until 1951. Then, the battalion's status was institutionalized and was renamed Battalion 300 (*ibid.*, 78–9). In 1953, the Chief of Staff issued an order to mobilize Druze men who had not joined the Israel Defence Forces (IDF) in order to train and incorporate them into reserve units, known as 'the recruitment joint B' (Firro, 1999:114–15). This move increased the divisions and rivalries within the Druze community and added a new dimension to the competition which had begun in 1951 over the Druze representation in the Knesset. Two camps had emerged by 1951: the first, headed by Salih Khnayfis, included among others Labib Abu-Rukun from Isfiya, Farhan Tarif from Julis and Quftan Halabi from Daliyat al-Karmel; the second was headed by Jaber Dahish Muadi from the village of Yirka and was supported by Sheikh Amin Tarif, the long-standing spiritual leader of the Druze community; Salman Tarif; and Najeeb Mansour from Isfiya (Avivi, 2007:80). Although this division was not around the conscription, the main representatives of the two camps took opposing stands on conscription. While Khnayfis was an ardent supporter of conscription, Sheikh Tarif opposed it (Avivi, 2007:80).

Sheikh Tarif's reservations were explained on the following grounds. Young Druze men who serve in the army are exposed to unacceptable cultural norms, and conscription would tarnish the reputation of Druze communities in the Arab countries. Moreover, in wartime, Druze servicemen might be exposed to disproportionate dangers. Thus, when the registration began, Sheikh Tarif's supporters visited various Druze villages and openly spoke against the conscription (*ibid.*:81). Furthermore, Sheikh Amin himself threatened that young Druze men who served in the army might be deemed inappropriate for marriage, and, in fact, in 1953, he refused to certify the marriage papers of a Druze man who served five years in the army (*ibid.*:82–3). Thus, for some time, the state's policy of stressing Druze particularism by underscoring their religious identity (epitomized by the authority of the Druze spiritual leader) contradicted the policy of conscripting them to the army.

In this conflict, as in future ones, the state had chosen to promote its instrumental goals; the main attempt to make the separation of the Druze irreversible was to be pursued through their conscription. To achieve this, Israel resorted to its favoured tactic of absolving the state of actions through inducing or soliciting unofficial actors to initiate the move it aimed to promote. Indeed, it seemed that Druze dignitaries were persuaded to write letters (probably by the Military Government) asking the state to impose conscription on Druze men. Although such letters were sent from time to time, the bulk of them were sent in one month: December 1955 (Avivi, 2007:87).

Although it was known to state officials that these letters were not in line with Druze public opinion, they nonetheless used them as justification to go ahead with the conscription. Indeed, a report composed by the northern district of the Military Government in January 1956 indicated that the majority of the Druze opposed conscription. Those who signed letters in support of it were afraid to show signs of their support. Moreover, Jaber Muadi – who by then had become an ardent supporter of the draft and sent and signed several such letters – was viewed among the Druze as being motivated by personal interests. Yet, on the basis of these letters, the state decided in January 1956 to impose conscription on Druze men (*ibid.*:88).

This move triggered widespread opposition from the start, which took various forms including petitioning, sending letters of protest to state officials, establishing anti-conscription organizations (the most well-known was the Druze Initiative Committee headed by Sheikh Farhoud Qasim Farhoud), anti-conscription meetings, refusal to report to the conscription bureaus, desertion, appeals to the High Court of Justice (Avivi, 2007:89–90) and physical assaults on supporters of the draft (Cohen, 2006:187). In contrast, very few letters in support of the conscription were sent at this stage (Avivi, 2007:90).

The priority given by the state to conscription in the construction of Druze particularism was revealed during the meeting of the Central Committee (a coordinating body of the Military Government, the Shin Bet, the police and the Office of the Prime Minister's Advisor) on 24 April 1956. A decision was taken that 'until the end of the conscription affairs no act should be taken regarding the status of the [Druze] community or recognition of its [spiritual] leadership' (*ibid.*:94). The bargain was clear: Druze particularism could be pursued only on the basis of conscription. Eventually, the activities of the police combined with the pressure employed on the community's leaders brought about a reasonable conduct of the conscription, although it remained an unsettled issue until 1967.

Contrary to the policy of separating Druze from the rest of the Palestinians in the army, they served until 1962 exclusively in Battalion 300 (the minorities' battalion), which included Bedouins, a few Muslims and Christians, as well as Circassians. The reasons for this were that this unit was designated for specific assignments and that they would only be able to acquire limited military knowhow. In public, however, their service in a separate battalion was explained by their mentality and special educational and cultural needs. Moreover, concentration of Druze servicemen would enhance the cohesion of the Druze community and make it easier to present them in parades to local and international audiences (*ibid.*:118–19). Even after 1962, very few army units – mainly supply units – became accessible to Druze servicemen. Yet, even those who served in such units were to serve their reserve duty in Battalion 300. In order to raise the morale and reduce criticism of this quarantining, three symbolic measures were introduced: changing the battalion's name from minorities' unit to Battalion 300, giving the soldiers new black hats (instead of the khaki ones they had) and training a limited number of outstanding soldiers to parachute once a year and stationing the battalion one month a year in the vicinity of Druze villages. Only in 1967 after the Six-Day War did additional units become accessible to Druze servicemen (*ibid.*:120–22). Moreover, the advancement of Druze soldiers in the army's hierarchy was blocked at certain ranks in order not to expose them to specialized military knowledge (*ibid.*:126).

Exclusivity

The hardening of boundaries of a constructed category seems to hinge on four factors: preferential treatment, reasonable degree of exclusivity, the institution of the constructed categories in the consciousness of the population and obtaining the collaboration of the local elite. These factors will be explored in the following sections with regard to the Druze ethnic category.

Preferential benefits
Druze villages were not uprooted, including the two villages which supported the Arab Rescue Army – Yanuh and Jat. Moreover, the Druze received privileges which were mostly economic in nature. They were allowed to harvest their fields during the war and soon after it, while the Arab villages were prevented from reaping the crops (Firro, 1999:54). They were allowed to bring supplies into their villages, and the families of those who joined the Israeli army were given free medical care (Parsons, 2000:142). Moreover, following conscription to the army, they were awarded improved travel arrangements outside the zone of the Military Government, the ability to enter security areas and the ability to move their residence outside the military-governed area (Avivi, 2007:96). As of 6 July 1956, an annual movement permit within the boundaries of the Military Government area was to be issued to any Druze person who would demand it, provided that security considerations would not block the granting of such a permit (*ibid.*:153). And since 1962, the Druze were allowed to move freely in most of the country's regions without the need for passes (*ibid.*).

In addition, at the symbolic level, certain sections of the Druze were allowed to possess arms. These included persons who received written letters from the founders and commanders of the Druze unit during the war in 1948 (Zaid and Shikhvitz), soldiers and dignitaries who collaborated with the state (*ibid.*:157). Although, the confiscation of weapons from the Druze after 1948 was not all-inclusive, when illegal weapons were used in familial feuds, the state did not hesitate in confiscating the weapons of dignitaries and collaborators (Avivi, 2007:158–60).

Consciousness
The state intended to construct Druze particularism, first of all to the Druze themselves, as a fact of life. Already in 1949, Dr. Chaim Hershberg, the head of the Islamic and Druze Department at the Ministry of Religious Affairs, proposed the establishment of separate schools for the various religious groups. This never materialized, and until 1964, the curriculum for the Druze was the same as for other Arab schools (Avivi, 2007:297). The educational goals were Jewish–Zionist in nature and had very little relevance to Arab pupils. Specific goals for Druze schools were formulated only in 1976 (*ibid.*; Firro, 2001:50).

The share of Druze among the teachers in the Arab educational system, including the Druze, was small. For example, in 1952, the religious composition of the teachers working in the Arab education system (including Druze schools) was as follows: Christians 45 per cent, Muslims 41 per cent, Jews 9 per cent, Druze 4 per cent and Baha'i 1 per cent (Avivi, 2007:298). Needless to say, Arab teachers did not properly promote state policy towards the Druze. Thus, a policy was adopted by Mr Gadish, the head of the Ministry of

Education's Arab Department, of employing Druze teachers and headmasters in Druze schools (The Arab Affairs' Committee, 16 May 1968:6). Army veterans were seen as plausible agents for prompting Druze particularism. Indeed, the state made considerable efforts to increase the number of Druze teachers, particularly from among ex-soldiers. For example, in two years, 1967/1968–1968/1969, sixty-six new Druze teachers were employed, some of them ex-soldiers who were trained in a special programme, and in 1967, the first Druze inspector was hired (regarding these arrangements, see *ibid.*:14–15). However, the increase in the number of Druze teachers had to reflect the emergence of an educated stratum. In this regard, preference was given to Druze over other Palestinians in higher education, which was reflected in the awarding of scholarships and grants even when these came from non-governmental sources (Avivi, 2007:303). Moreover, 'Druze students ... were pressured [channelled] (after the mid-1960s) to study in the department of education at the university in order to educate within 3–4 years educational leadership from teachers to inspectors and directors' (The Arab Affairs' Committee, 16 May 1968:7); these are Abba Hushi's words.

The more far-reaching proposal to affect the Druze's consciousness was laid down by Gadish, who proposed:

> [To] increase the teaching of the Hebrew language, without causing an opposition by Arab nationalist Druze ... if we gradually train teachers not in Arab but in Jewish teacher training colleges, the language which they feel at home with will be Hebrew, thus without [official] declarations the teachers will teach in Hebrew from the first grade, and I think we can help through education in integrating the Druze in Israeli society. (*Ibid.*:16)

Firro (2001) has argued that in addition to education and army service, Druze consciousness had partly been shaped by the type of jobs to which they were drawn. Given the massive confiscation of Druze lands and the absence of other viable productive sectors or developed services, the bulk of Druze men had been absorbed at the lower tiers of the security sector, in jobs where the discipline of the body is essential. These jobs demand 'discipline, identification with the official policies, loyalty and subordination' (Firro, 2001:50). About half a century after the first Druze joined the Israeli army, some 40 per cent of all employed Druze men worked in security-related jobs (*ibid.*:42).

Official and legal boundaries

After the creation of the de facto Druze category, the state proceeded towards its legalization. Although Ben-Gurion initiated a discussion on the recognition of the Druze as a distinct community during the war – and the first meeting in this regard between Sheikh Amin Tarif and the Minister of Religious Affairs took place at the end of 1948 (or early 1949), and other meetings between Druze leaders and state officials occurred thereafter – it was only in 1957, after the end of the conscription affair, that the formalization of Druze particularism began (Avivi, 2007:167).

The same tactic which was applied to conscription was replayed; dignitaries were solicited to send letters of request to state officials asking for recognition of the Druze as an ethnic community. To this end, the Advisor on Arab Affairs, Ziama Divon, met with the leading Druze hamula representatives. And indeed, by early 1957, several such letters by Druze dignitaries were addressed to the Prime Minister, ministers and state officials. The letter which Mr Tarif sent to the Prime Minister was particularly interesting. In it, he made it clear that in various aspects, the religious symbolic power should be retained by the Druze community, embodied in its spiritual leader. Therefore, he set various conditions for the recognition agreement: the spiritual leadership ought to be composed of one person; a special court of appeal on religious matters would be composed of the spiritual leader and two persons of the religious council; the judges in the Druze courts would be selected by the Druze community, according to a law which should be tailored and enacted according to the community's tradition; the spiritual leader would be associated with the Druze religious centre in Hasbia in Lebanon (*ibid.*:173–4).

On 15 April 1957, the Minister of Religious Affairs issued recognition of the Druze community as an independent one (*ibid.*:1975). Yet, various matters remained unsolved, particularly the corpus of substantive laws according to which the Druze religious court would act (The Confined Committee of the Arab Affairs' Committee, 11 November 1960). Eventually, in 1961, the official bodies and Druze leadership agreed to adopt the Lebanese Druze personal status law with two significant amendments: the omission of the reference to the Sharia (Islamic law) and to the Hanafi school of jurisdiction in matters of inheritance. In this way, religious and legal dimensions were added to the formal separation of the Druze from the Muslim community (Avivi, 2007:195–6). In 1962, the formal separation of the Druze from the Muslim community was completed.

A loyal elite

As explained earlier, the Druze elite played a significant role in supporting the state's policy of constructing the Druze as a separate community. Indeed, as Firro (1999) illustrates, no Druze figure could have become a political leader without having one or more Jewish patrons among those in charge of the apparatuses of surveillance and control. Thus, loyalty to the state constituted a precondition for joining this elite group, and indeed, all Druze members of the Knesset (MKs) collaborated with the Yishuv (the Jewish community in Palestine) and were loyal to the state. They were ready, without much questioning, to propagate state policy and to keep silent in cases of infringements of their constituents' rights, such as during land confiscations. Moreover, this elite has been characterized by three features.

First, its members did not come from hamulas or branches of hamulas which had traditionally held leadership roles. Rather, the members of this class in many cases had to push aside the leaders who relied on traditional legitimacy (to use Max Weber's terminology). Thus, for example, Labib Abu-Rukun became the leading figure in Isfiya instead of the long-standing mukhtar Najib Mansur, and Salih Khnayfis became the Druze leader in Shafa'amr after the mukhtar Sa'd Nakad was blocked from assuming a leadership role due to his unacceptable stand towards the state (Firro, 1999:92–3). Meanwhile, Jaber Muadi, although from a leading hamula, came from a less prominent branch.

Second, this new elite rapidly gained wealth through the association with the state. Already, by 1953, members of this elite had accumulated considerable wealth, which distinguished them from their community, by fulfilling all sorts of mediatory functions, such as acting as brokers for Jewish employers (*ibid.*) or by using their access to influential persons in the state to get personal benefits or favours for their associates (e.g. *ibid.*:161). Thus, while this elite acquired its wealth partly through the exploitation of its community, it was dependent on the state for its power, and, in fact, its members acted more like emissaries of the state than representatives of their community.

Third, factionalism and bitter struggle among the members of this elite developed, as shall be described in the following section. Given its structure, the emergent Druze elite could do nothing other than play a subservient role and contribute to the idea of Druze exceptionalism, which was the basis for its wealth and power.

The flimsiness of Druze particularism

In its meeting on 13 August 1966, the Central Committee decided – in line with the 1958 policy plan – on two principles in dealing with the Druze: (A) to encourage the unity and distinctiveness of the Druze community (vis-à-vis other Arabs) and (B) to act against cohesion within the Druze community (Avivi, 2007:31). Yet, it seems that these principles had guided the official policy from the beginning and were only formalized in this meeting. The way in which the first principle was pursued has been explored at length earlier. As to the second, Israel adopted the colonial style of patronage and the instigation of rivalries and competition among local dignitaries in order to prevent the emergence of self-assured elite with bargaining power (Robinson, 1972). The manipulation of the dignitaries was a convenient strategy as Abba Hushi – a leading figure in the control and surveillance apparatuses – declared in 1962: 'Those who think of slowly relinquishing the dignitaries and the sheikhs and supporting the young generation are mistaken. If we line up with the young people and discard the Sheikhs and the elderly we shall fail' (The Arab Affairs' Committee, 4 May 1962:14). In this strategy, Hushi himself played a pivotal role. Conjointly, this strategy also meant the silencing of alternative voices and the suppression of dissent. Indeed, the many attempts by all sorts of groups to promote political, cultural or social demands were thwarted by the security services and various official bodies. They harassed an association which had emerged in the 1960s for the betterment of the socio-economic conditions of demobilized soldiers, the cultural association for the promotion of education in Druze villages, the celebration of *Eid Al-Fitr* – a Muslim feast which was up till then celebrated by the Druze as well – in schools (Firro, 1999:154–6; Avivi, 2007:312–13) and the anti-conscription Druze Initiative Committee headed by Sheikh Farhoud Farhoud, mentioned before. Even groups of young Druze men who identified with the state and the ruling party (Ma'arach, previously Mapai) and demanded direct membership in the party and the promotion of young men to leadership positions were rebuffed (Avivi, 2007:342). Indeed, at two meetings of the Central Committee, held on 28 October and 8 December 1966 to deal with Druze organizations, the Committee decided to continue the official line of encouraging associations at the local level while blocking the establishment of any nationwide organization (*ibid.*:320–1).

Various statements indicate that Israeli leaders and bureaucrats did not hold the Druze leadership in high regard or approve of the road the community had taken. The infighting within the community and the letters of slander sent to Israeli leaders by rival dignitaries and their associates accentuated this attitude. For example, Salih Abu-Rukun wrote a letter to Prime Minister Ben-Gurion in which he detailed a series of crimes and sins which Jaber Muadi had supposedly committed. In response, Ben-Gurion entrusted Hushi to investigate the matter. In detailing the result of his inquiry, Hushi wrote:

> Concerning the letter of Salih Abu-Rukun who called himself the Imam of Isfiya: As far as I could establish from reliable sources, Jabber Mu'addi was subject to the three accusations (a), (b), (c) [all of them cases of murder] of Abu Rukun's letter respectively. Even in these cases he did not commit the crimes but others 'at his inspiration'. However, crimes of this kind have been committed by many other important [figures] notably Druze residents. ... In addition, the motives which led Salih Abu-Rukun to write the letter have nothing to do with conscience and morality, but [are all about] disputes between hamulas etc. (Quoted in Firro, 1999:109–10)

Moreover, a pseudo-psychological profile of Muadi by the Shin Bet stated that he was

> one of the chiefs of Mu'addi family who among the Druze are considered as one of the notable families. ... He has the natural characteristics of the Oriental 'leader', he is crafty, an embroiderer of conspiracies, pursuer of power, and quarrelsome. (*Ibid.*:124)

More revealing is the statement made by Golda Meir on 15 January 1951 in Mapai's meeting. She said that when she sees an Arab swear allegiance to the

State of Israel three times a day, 'I feel bad', the same ill feelings she has when, as a Zionist, she sees an assimilated Jew (Benziman and Mansour, 1992:19).

So far, I have discussed how the Druze category was constructed so as to harden the boundaries between the Druze community and other Palestinians. This category depended on the principle of opposition to others (Arabs) while entailing very little principles of particular interiority; a hollowness which the Druze religion by itself, given its secrecy and accessibility to few individuals only, could not rectify. Yet, habitually, the state's attitude towards the Druze had not been different in essence from its approach to the Palestinian minority at large. This similarity is manifest in three spheres: the identity of bodies which were charged with Druze affairs, the confiscation of land and discrimination in development.

The Druze were managed by the same official bodies which dealt with Arab affairs. The addition of the word Druze to the official names of these departments aimed to emphasize their separation from the Muslims. Thus, the existence of separate bureaucracies for dealing with Jewish and Arab affairs was not affected by the Druze's semi-category: Druze affairs were managed by the Arab departments in the various ministries (e.g. religion and education), their representatives were elected to the Knesset through the Arab list that Mapai organized, the Central Committee which was in charge of the daily running of Arab affairs was also responsible for Druze affairs and their service in the army that was supposed to epitomize Druze particularism took place in the minorities battalion.

Second, the efforts by Zionist organizations and the state of Israel to take over Druze's lands date back to the pre-state period. During the late 1930s, some officials of the Jewish Agency devised a plan to buy lands from Druze villages and transfer the Druze population to Syria (Firro, 1999:26–32). During the 1940s, an endeavour by the JNF aimed to buy Druze lands with the help of Labib Abu-Rukun (Avivi, 2007:216). During the 1950s, the state confiscated large swathes of lands from Palestinian villages, a process that did not spare Druze villages (Firro, 1999:134–43). The lands which were registered as state lands but which were intended for the development of the villages were confiscated in contradiction to the spirit of the law. Considerable portions of the private land owned by Druze villages were confiscated and their expropriation was legalized under the 1953 Land Acquisition Law.

For example, during the first decade, the state confiscated 13,000 dunams of land owned by residents of Beit Jann. The JNF official Nahmani wanted to acquire part of these lands, located in an area called 'Ard al-Khayt', and threatened the titleholders that they would be prevented from working their lands if they refused to sell to him; indeed, since 1949, they have been barred from entering their lands as the area was declared a 'security zone', and the lands were distributed between adjacent Jewish Kibbutzim.

The fact that the Druze served in the army did not matter; one of the proposals put forward by the villagers that only ex-soldiers would work the land was turned down (*ibid.*:136–7; Avivi, 2007:228–38). The point, after all, was not the question of Druze loyalty or the vicinity of these lands to the border; rather, it was part of a logic of control and surveillance, which included segmentation and quarantining of Arab localities along with the establishment of a network of Jewish settlements.

Third, conscription of the Druze did not guarantee them socio-economic integration. Although in some areas Druze received better treatment than other Palestinians, they were not treated as equal to the Jews. Those in charge of the surveillance and control agencies were well aware of this inconsistency and were wary that it might push them back to Palestinian identification. For example, Uri Lubrani stated on 1 February 1962:

> We conscript them for two and half years in the army, impart to them civilized practices, and do not give attention to the reality after the army service where they return to their undeveloped villages, which have remained at a medieval level of development. We don't give them the feeling that after the Army service we do things for them, and this causes bitterness among them. If these young men do not move to cities they turn back to the Arabs. (The Arab Affairs' Committee, 1 February 1962:3)

Following an announcement by Prime Minister Levi Eshkol on 10 October 1967, in which he declared that Druze affairs were to be dealt with by the general bureaucracy (i.e. the one that serves Jews), a special meeting classified as secret was held by the Ma'arach's Arab Department on 1 February 1968. At this meeting, Gadish of the Minorities Department at the Ministry of Education expressed the modernization argument, which Israeli officials often employ:

> When the state was established the Druze lacked the three components of education: students, schools and teachers. They were shepherds and burners of firewood in the Carmel forests. They did not go to schools. They were at the bottom of the scale of the Western part of Eritz Yisrael's [i.e. Mandatory Palestine] Arab population. (The Arab Affairs' Committee, 16 May 1968:13)

He went on to elaborate on the progress which was made in the education of the Druze – the building of schools, the increase in rates of school attendance by Druze children and the training of teachers – yet ended with the note stating that 'we should be realistic, integration [of the Druze] will not be accomplished during our lifetime' (*ibid.*:16).

Abba Hushi too acknowledged: 'I suppose if we sinned to a segment of the non-Jewish population in this country, we erred to the Druze. We said one thing and did something else' (*ibid.*:6). Yet, all the proposals for change revolved around the continuation of activities that had been aimed at strengthening their consciousness of particularism. This included employing Druze teachers and headmasters in Druze schools, increasing the number of educated Druze through special programmes and employing them in secondary schools in Druze villages (*ibid.*:6–7), and encouraging the Druze to reconstruct a particular history. In this regard, Abba Hushi, who played a pivotal role in ensuring that the 'dignitaries' maintain the leadership role, stated:

> The leadership is in the hands of Sheikhs and elderly persons, who are ignorant and we have to do something in this regard. When a book was published in Lebanon that proves they are Arabs, I called first the elders and the students including those who studied in Jerusalem and told them: are you angry at this book? Why doesn't one of you sit down and write a monograph that refutes it and we shall publish it. But there was no one who would do it. Therefore we should begin with education. (*Ibid.*:25)

Other proposals included the transfer of Druze affairs from the Minorities' departments to the official bureaucracy and their acceptance as members in the Ma'arach Party (The Arab Affairs' Committee, 16 May 1968). Yet, the most important proposal was to use Hebrew as the language of instruction from an early age at schools and the training of Druze teachers in Jewish colleges.

A Christian identity?

Given the isolated nature of Druze villages, the localized interests of the Druze communities, their small numbers and their lack of coherent leadership, the Druze were not incorporated in the Palestinian national movement (Parsons, 2000:143), and, therefore, their particularization was possible. In contrast, the Christian community was more cosmopolitan, better educated and, due to its shared religion with Western societies, had the feeling of enjoying the protection of Western powers. This feeling had been nurtured by a long history of European protection – particularly during the long closing phase of the Ottoman Empire – and the ubiquitous presence of missionary institutions and Europeans in the Holy Land.

However, during the 1948 War, the European 'safety net' proved to be unreliable. Moreover, Zionist promotion of a 'minorities' coalition' (Linn, 1999:136–41) which would counter Arab/Muslim domination in the Middle East found more of a hearing among Lebanese Christians – particularly Maronites – than among Palestinian Christians. During the 1948 War, the Zionist strategy of 'minorities' coalition' had no impact on the transfer of Palestinian Christians.

On the other hand, Christians had always been highly represented among the Palestinian political elite, particularly among those who remained. The greater part of the Arab Communist Party's leadership – the only organized political body that was permitted to operate – were Christians, including Tawfiq Tubi, Emile Touma, Emile Habibi and Saliba Khamis. They also formed a substantial part of the small remaining nationalist elite, including Elias Kusa; Jabour Jabour, the mayor of Shafa'amr; and Yani Yani, Kafr Yassif's mayor. They were also highly represented among the younger generation of nationalist activists and leaders, such as Sabri Jiryis and Habib Qahwaji.

Consequently, the control–surveillance apparatuses had to rely on the co-option of individual priests, mainly Arabs, as Israelis have been cautious in their treatment of European clergy. The Egyptian-born bishop George Hakim, the head of the Greek Catholic church (1949–67), had been the most conspicuous figure in supporting the state's policies (Linn, 1999:134). His activities included the establishment of *al-Rabbita*, a publication in which official propaganda was rehearsed, the founding of a collaborationist Catholic scout movement and Christian Labour Union in Nazareth, support for the displacement of Tarshiha's residents (which eventually was not carried out due to popular resistance) and an unsuccessful attempt to persuade Iqrit's inhabitants – who were relocated on 8 November 1948 with an official promise to return after a fortnight – to forego their demand of return (Cohen, 2006:64–70).

Yet, the state's policy of creating a 'Christian identity' similar to that of the Druze had, eventually, to pass through the Army conscription threshold. It was estimated that this would lead the Christians into a one-way road of separation from the Muslims. Various state organs collaborated in an unsuccessful experiment in 1957 to draft Christian men. Amnon Linn (1999) described the chain of events that ended in the experiment's failure, where many ordinary Christian citizens actively challenged those who registered and persuaded their majority to withdraw their names from the draft's list (136–7). On the other hand, the few Christians who joined the army were treated with suspicion and contempt by Israeli officers. Amnon Yanai, the first commander of the minorities' battalion, stated:

> It was decided to draft the Christians, with the aim of treating the Christian community in the same spirit (as the Druze). However, this was spoiled. Today Christian soldiers are second class. There are closed areas, such as Eilat, which they are not allowed to reach. (The Arab Affairs' Committee, 30 January 1958:33)

Overall the Christians were conceived as an unfriendly community by leading figures in the control and surveillance apparatuses. Expressing this attitude, Abba Hushi stated on 16 May 1968: 'I think Christians are the least trustworthy and reliable [community]' (The Arab Affairs' Committee, 16 May 1968:20).

The Bedouins

Unlike the previous two categories of Druze and Christians, identified by the clear marker of religion – which has a bearing on the lives of ordinary peoples and was legally sanctioned – the Bedouins were Muslims like all Palestinian

Muslims. Therefore, they could not be declared a separate community according to the Ottoman millet system that Israel had adopted. Instead, the fuzzy terms of culture or 'nomadic way of life' were employed to distinguish this heterogeneous group.

The Bedouins resided in the Galilee and Negev areas, and in fact, the bulk of this population had already settled, particularly in Galilee, when the state of Israel was established. Moreover, for many Bedouins, the nomadic way of life was history, but in the name of this past, Israel tried to construct them as a distinct community. Furthermore, despite the absence of any affinity or relationships between these two groups of Bedouins which might set them apart from the rest of the Muslim population, they were marked as a category, meant to position them in the official hierarchy of loyalty to the state (Parizot, 2001:102). Indeed, Landau (1993) maintained that 'This is a group generally loyal to the state and ready to integrate into the Israeli circle of identity, so much so that a number of Bedouin have volunteered for service in the defence forces' (quoted in Yonah et al., 2004:393).

The term Bedouin was emphasized to highlight their exotic, traditional or 'primitive' culture (Parizot, 2001:102), a designation which meant to nurture orientalist perceptions and legitimize state policies towards them (e.g. Parizot, 2001; Yonah et al., 2004). This designation would serve the surveillance apparatuses and the official bodies in engineering the intersocietal relations among Bedouins, the wheeling and dealing with sheikhs (Cohen, 2006:210–14) and the confiscation of Bedouin lands, as well as the efforts towards their forcible settlement in planned townships (Falah, 1985).

Thus, the seclusion of the Bedouin population in the Negev and the elevation of individuals who lacked the traditional authority – as was also the case among the Druze – to the status of sheikhs in possession of substantial authority over the tribesmen created a shared interest between this elite and the regime (Cohen, 2006:210–15). Similar to that seen in the newly emerged Druze elite, in many cases, the state-nominated sheikhs were chosen for their collaboration with the Yishuv, such as Ode Abu M'amar, who worked as a guard of the fields of some Jewish settlements (Cohen, 2006:212).

A further reaching tactic was the increase of Bedouin fragmentation. In this regard, existing tribes were split, and new ones, whose sheikhs owed their leadership positions to the surveillance apparatuses, emerged. By 1986, the nineteen tribes which existed in 1948 were split into thirty-seven (Meir, 1988:264; see chapter 7). These divisions were tailored in such a way as to enable the monitoring of their political attitudes and voting patterns (see chapter 7).

The considerable power of the sheikhs did not stem from their traditional authority, but rather from the new conditions which emerged after the establishment of the state of Israel. Not only was the Negev emptied of its Palestinian population, including the town of Beersheba, which constituted the administrative and the economic centre of the region, but the displaced Bedouins were concentrated in the infertile Seig area, which amounted to less than 10 per cent of the Negev district. Consequently, eleven out of the nineteen tribes became landless (Falah, 1985:38). Their placement under the Military Government, their seclusion as well as their economic hardship rendered ordinary Bedouins dependent on the sheikhs who were granted substantial authority.

As the tribe was considered an administrative unit headed by the sheikh, he became responsible for registering the residents with the Interior Ministry – recording births and deaths, validating marriages and signing affidavits. Moreover, he was given the role of gatekeeper, whose endorsement was indispensable for anyone who wished to get employment as a teacher or in the civil service. He was permitted by the state to collect fees for most of these activities, thus increasing his wealth and status (Yonah et al., 2004:395). Furthermore, sheikhs acted as middlemen and whenever a demand for workers emerged, the employers – through the Military Government – approached the sheikhs, who would then decide who got employment (Swirski and Hasson, 2006:87).

The sheikhs acted as middlemen not only in such benign matters but also in security-related issues. In the 1950s, during the years of austerity when foodstuff in Israel was in short supply, they organized, on behalf of the state, smuggling networks which brought to the local markets 'all the goodies of the earth', some of which found their way also to state depots (Swirski and Hasson, 2006:87–8). The most notable was Moshe Dayan's personal involvement with Bedouin sheikhs in organizing contraband livestock networks that brought livestock from countries as far and diverse as Syria, Iraq, Saudi Arabia and Yemen (Parizot, 2001:6).

The Bedouins were not drafted to the IDF (though some Galilean tribes were), although some sheikhs committed their men to fight during the 1948 War alongside the Israeli army. By 1949, the majority of these men were demobilized, yet some sheikhs continued to collaborate with the Israeli army in preventing the return of Bedouins who had been expelled in the course of the war or in its aftermath. In some cases, they even stopped the return of Bedouins who were members of their tribal coalitions (Cohen, 2006:213–14).

Generally speaking, the number of Bedouins who saw regular service with the Israeli army remained very limited throughout the period of study (though some tribes in the Galilee were assigned special functions, particularly as trackers) (Parizot, 2001:4). Yet, as Cohen (2006) revealed, their service to the state took another, no less intimate, collaboration than that of Druze. Some sheikhs organized and operated under the direction of Aman's (an acronym of the Military Intelligence) unit 154 various espionage rings which operated in Jordan and Egypt (see the details of some of these operations in Cohen, 2006:215–22). Moreover, they reported to the police Palestinian teachers from the Triangle and Galilee who worked in the Negev and aired dissent or distributed nonconformist material (*ibid.*:224) (it is important to emphasize that 'dignitaries' from the Triangle, such as MK Faris Hamdan, were also involved in such undertakings).

This categorization of the Palestinians to faith communities and ways of life was the beginning of more intrusive processes of segmentation. Given the breadth of this categorization, more refined ones were needed in order to make the surveillance and control of the Palestinians more efficient. The refinement of the categorization of Palestinians at the locality level and beyond will be explored in the following chapter.

Conclusion

This chapter explored the segmentation of the Palestinians into various groups in an effort to create a political reality wherein one group – Israeli Jews – enjoyed group rights, while the other, the Palestinians, would be considered a collection of groups and would be defined negatively as non-Jews. Various boundaries were constructed to affirm the Jewish–Palestinian polarity: principally, through the establishment of a de jure dual legal system whereby Jews were ruled by civilian laws and Palestinians were largely subjected to Emergency Regulations and the institution of two, almost separate, bureaucracies. While the policy towards the Jewish population was premised on their integration, the policy towards the Palestinians aimed to achieve the opposite.

Thus, the Palestinians were subdivided into faith communities and ways of life. The ensuing religious and social categories were hierarchically arranged and through the appointed chiefs and co-opted leaders, they were turned into subsidiary structures of surveillance, thus walling off Palestinians by their religious and blood affiliation. Segmentation as a component of surveillance was highlighted in the 1958 Plan and then in Tolidano's policy principles. It had also been a guiding principle for state officials who dealt with Palestinians. This notion of segmentation had also guided Israeli social science research on the Palestinians. It had mostly presented as natural the order that the state endeavoured to construct through surveillance practices. Yet, this segmentation did not stop at this level. These categories were too general to allow for a constant and 'deep' supervision and control of the behaviour of individual Palestinians. Further divisions and subdivisions were needed. The processes of further subdivisions are the subject of the next chapter.

Note

1 This statement was made by Yaakov Shim'oni an Arabist and an official in the Foreign Ministry.

5

Subdivisions

The 'naturalness' of social sorting

The division of the Palestinians into four ethnicities, discussed in the previous chapter, created large and hardly manageable collectivities. It did not enable continual supervision of the attitudes and behaviour of individual Palestinians, or induce behavioural changes by the application of reward or punishment. To achieve this, subdivisions of these categories into increasingly smaller units had to be pursued. These ought to proceed, as Foucault (1991) pointed out, to 'the point of necessary and sufficient single units' (170), thus enabling intensification and ramification of power (198). Indeed, a process of subdivisions followed. The second subdivision which the Israeli surveillance and control apparatuses identified as a 'natural category', through which surveillance could be exercised, is the locality. It is a spatially defined unit, fairly manageable, and despite plausible differences among the inhabitants, it is bound by common interests and local institutions. Yet, since many Palestinian communities, particularly those in Galilean villages and 'mixed cities', are multireligious, the 'ethnic' divisions were highlighted, reproduced and reinforced at the local level. An additional subdivision in this chain is the division of the local religious groups into 'organic' units – hamulas/tribes. The hamula has been perceived as a strategic unit. It is large enough to enable manageability but at the same time small and meaningful, through which the attitudes and behaviours of individuals could be influenced. The combination of the broad categories of ethnicities and the smaller ones which resulted from the multiple divisions – into villages, local religious groups and hamulas – would make it possible for the surveillance and control apparatuses to act like 'a machinery that is both immense and minute, which supports, reinforces, multiplies the asymmetry of power' (Foucault, 1991:223).

Similar to the Zionist endeavour to exploit and manipulate the religious and social differences among Palestinians before 1948, the Jewish Agency attempted to back Zionist strategy and policies towards the Palestinians by specialized knowledge on nuances and diversities within Palestinian society at the community level. Thus, a systematic collection of data on Palestinian villages began as early as the 1930s, and by the end of the same decade, an archive was completed. It included '[p]recise details ... about the topographic location of each village, its access roads, quality of land, water springs, main sources of income, its socio-political composition, religious affiliations, names of its mukhtars (local leaders), its relationship with other villages, the age of individual men (sixteen to fifty) and many more. An important category was an index of "hostility" (towards the Zionism)' (Pappe, 2006:19). An aerial photograph was also attached to the file of each village (*ibid.*:18–19). These files were updated several times: in 1940, 1945 and 1947. Shai member Ezra Danin, who concentrated the surveying effort since 1945, revealed that the survey was comprehensive and included more than 1,000 Palestinian localities (Danin, 1987:162–3). The final updates were of specific military applications; they included lists of 'wanted' persons – political and military activists – and targets for destruction. These data were invaluable to the war planning of the Haganah in 1948. Moreover, it gave the Jewish leadership a sense of the organization and military capabilities of the Palestinians at the community level (Danin, 1987:162–3; Pappe, 2006:20–1). Besides the information gathered by undercover intelligence agents – who took various jobs which brought them into contact with Palestinians, such as traders, farmers and shepherds – and informers, a decision was taken as early as 1941 to use even the most casual conversations between Jews and Palestinians to gather information. According to Danin, 'I presume that such activity should be similar to the way the Nazis worked in Denmark, Norway and Holland – touching on every area of life' (quoted in Cohen, 2008:178). Such an activity required special modes of operation. Three such methods were devised: bringing Palestinian collaborators into economic dependency upon the Yishuv, the use of professional young Jewish women who worked in mixed workplaces – for example, governmental offices, hospitals, and medical centres – in gathering information from their Palestinian colleagues and the establishment in many Jewish settlements of 'neighbourly relations committees'. Members of these committees were required to acquire knowledge of the local dialect and local culture as well as to spot potential collaborators (*ibid.*:178–9). The acquired information was not meant to undergird the direct war effort only but also to create mayhem in Arab villages through rumours and provocations. Ezra Danin explains that special courses for the intelligence officers were arranged during the 1940s, which included the Arabic language, the mores and mentality of the 'Ishmaelites' as well as the basics of Islam. They were also instructed how to embroil intrigues (*Fusad*) in Palestinian villages in order to weaken them in periods of conflicts with the Yishuv (Danin, 1987:178–9). Some of these officers became experts in the

'Arab field' – as it was usually referred to in official circles – and through their appointment in various official positions after 1948, they became the executors of the official policy towards the Palestinians.

Subdividing after 1948

In 1955, three years after the Israeli leaders' realization that a Palestinian minority would stay in the country for the foreseeable future, a new assemblage of village files had already been put together, including files for the tiniest villages such as Khirbet Al-Byar in the Triangle whose inhabitants numbered seventy-five persons ('An Evaluation of the Situation: Khirbet Al-Byar', n.d.). The structure of these files was modelled on the old one, but with one addition: the voting results of the citizens in previous elections. A file was prepared for each village or tribe, and a table composed of two sections was affixed in it. The first section included the basic data for surveillance and political control purposes. It contained information regarding the demographic and religious composition of the residents, the names of the local leaders, sources of living, access roads, sources of drinking water, rivalries between hamulas or religious groups, the attitude of the community towards the state (index of hostility) and the major problems facing it. The second section presented a deconstruction of each religious community into hamulas. It included the following variables: the name of the hamula, the name of its head, its size, the results of its voting in previous elections and a projection of its voting results in the forthcoming ones. A column at the end of it labelled annotations under which notes regarding plausible means of influencing the hamula's head were recorded. The following is a randomly chosen file of the Galilean village, Maker. While the files of other villages include different details, the structure is identical.

The second section of the file was tailored for 'hamula politics'. In this case, different methods for influencing the heads of hamulas were noted. These included intervention by Jewish employers, the Histadrut, the military administration, influential friends, relatives or dignitaries. Promises of rewards or threats of punishments were recorded. This village, however, was uncharacteristic of the Arab villages in its voting pattern. While the majority of the votes in the Arab villages went to Mapai and its affiliated Arab lists, a pluralistic voting behaviour prevailed in Al-Maker. Does it reflect its categorization as having an 'unfriendly' attitude towards the state? Beyond the specifics of this case, however, the association between hamula membership and voting behaviour had been a significant field where surveillance and control took place as shall be argued in chapter 7.

Given the significance attributed to the hamula for surveillance, the officials in charge of Arab affairs demanded the addition of the hamula affiliation to the entries of Palestinians' ID cards, as mentioned earlier. This information

Table 5.1 The village of Maker – the details of the village as appeared in the village files

1. BACKGROUND

A. Residents

Number	
Number – total	About 1,000
Eligible to vote	About 360
Structure	
Communities:	
Muslims	850
Greek-Catholics	150
Refugees	400 Muslims from (the destroyed village) Birwa 100 Muslims from (the destroyed village) Manshia
Influential persons:	
Muslims	Naif Saleem Melhem (the village's Mukhtar) Muhamad Ahmad Shehada (The Mukhtar's adversary)
Christians	Elias Francis Badria (the previous Mukhtar) Michael Elias Sossan (the secretary of Pi-Yud) Michael Tanus (the Christians' Mukhtar) Aharon Kishoni (Kfar Misrek [Jewish], Mapam) Yusif Dagan (The Development Authority) Saeed Khayyal Saleem, from Berwa who was affiliated to Pi-Yud, and considers himself to be connected with the Histadrut's executive

The residents' attitude towards the state and the authorities

Attitude of hostility towards Israel

Sources of livelihood

Agriculture and olive groves

Level of employment

There is no lack of employment.

B. Local authority

The Muslims' mukhtar: Naif Saleem Melhem

The Christians' mukhtar: Michael Tanus

C. Social life

Newspapers delivered to the village

Al-Ittihad [the communist party organ], *Al-Mersad* [Mapam's mouthpiece] and *Al-Yom* [semiofficial newspaper managed by the Histadrut and Mapai]

D. Services

Water: There is a fountain fitted with a pump.

Transportation: There is no street connecting the village.

Education: There is a joint [Muslim, Christian] elementary school. Religious lessons are given separately.

Religion: Imam [Muslim clergyman] Ghalib Shikl.

E. Locality's problems

Refugees' rehabilitation

2. BALANCE OF FORCES

Maker								
1	2	3	4	5	6	7	8	9
	Family (hamula)	Head of the family	N	K	M	TS	Unknown	Annotations
1.	Sossan + Tanus	Michael Elias+	30					Michael Elias's cousin Zaki voted in the past for TS

(*continued*)

Table 5.1 (Continued)

2.	Melhim	Zaki As'ad Melhim				15	Pressure should be employed on him by persons [officials] in the field
3.	Melhim	Naif Saleem Melhem The mukhtar				15	
4.	Khatib	Ahmad Muhamad Khatib	15				
5.	Shkil	Shkil Ghalib (Iman)	10				
6.	Kayyal Taha + Awad Ahmad Taha					15	Michael Elias can influence him if he offers him a job
7.	Kayyal – Hujjo	Saeed Muhammad Kayyal, Ahmad Hujjo				20	There is a need for Histadrut's pressure on Saeed Kayyal
8.	Kayyal Taha	Yuesef Taha				15	The son-in-law of Nemir Ma'di leans to TS
9.	Mi'ari	Saeed Mi'ari		6			
10.	Shehadeh	Muhammad Ahmad Shehadeh				10	Has leanings towards the authorities. Attention by the Military Administration is needed
11.	Beit Abu-Dolas	(Refugees from Manshia)			70		
12.	Hajj Hammad +Yasin		20				

13.	Badria	Elias Francis				20		He is angry because he was deposed from the mukhtarship
14.	Badria	Hanna Elias			20			Works as a mechanic in Na'man area Kibbutzim
15.	Nabulsi-Isse	Ibrahim Khalil Yousef Muhammad Abd al-Rahman		20				Influenced by Maki's member Jiryis Hunni
16.	Jiryis Hunni	(Refugees) Jiryis Hunni		60				Active family in Maki
Persons with voting right (expected): 361			75	86	90	20	90	
Overall voted for the second Knesset: 326			83	124	77	25		

Party symbols: N, Progress and Work an Arab list headed by Salih Khnayfis and was affiliated to Mapai in this election; K, the Communist Party; M, left-Zionist Party Mapam; TS (Z), General Zionist Party.

('An Evaluation of the Situation: Maker', n.d.)

was partly gleaned from the old village files and partly provided by the mukhtars or was registered in the course of the census (Eyal, 2006:158). The hamula politics was conceived by those who run Palestinian affairs in a simple and cynical way. Pappe (1995) described its essence as follows:

> All what you have to do according to this group's perception was to find an Arab notable, frighten him or seduce him, and you have the loyalty, or at least the obedience, of the social unit associated with this notable. (642)

This system of patronage was highly effective during the period under discussion, given the state of exception which prevailed. Under the Military Government, the whole system of governance was structured in such a way as to bolster the authority of the 'dignitaries' at the various levels: members of Knesset (MKs), Histadrut employees, mukhtars, heads of hamulas, sheikhs, etc. Only through them could 'favours' like movement permits, work, jobs in the public sector and the like be obtained (Sa'di, 2003a; Eyal, 2006:158). This has not only revived and strengthened this structure but also changed its role. The hamula no longer remained a source of solace or material support for its members. Rather, it was integrated in the surveillance and control system. The blood and affinity which held its members together became the element through which the state controlled their behaviours. Nonconformist behaviour by one of its members would blemish the whole hamula and adversely affect the interests of its members. In this way, the hamula politics walled Palestinians by their blood and social association. In the light of this, those in charge of the surveillance and control apparatus, particularly in the Military Government and the Office of the Advisor to the Prime Minister on Arab Affairs, did their best to strengthen the hamula, rather than allowing its significance to wither as a result of generational, economic or educational changes. As already mentioned in chapter 2, Tolidano identified in his description of the official policy in 1968 the effort to decelerate the disintegration of the hamula as a main principle.

Yet, concerns regarding the sustainability of the hamula were raised following the state's tendency, in line with the 1958 Plan, to establish local councils in Palestinian localities. The question was how to keep up the hamula's role in the light of establishing elected local councils. Yehoshua Palmon, who opposed this development, explained his rejection as follows:

> Democratic elections will only augment family feuds and are not in keeping with the existing conditions in the Arab community. The establishment of local councils is also bound to lead to bloodshed. In the Arab community, one must choose a 'middle road' of not-too-much democracy. (Peretz, 1991:98)

Understandably, Palmon wanted to keep intact the system of patronage through sheikhs and mukhtars which he and his colleagues fostered. His justification, however, was disingenuous as Palmon presided before and after 1948 over systems which relied on tactics of divide and rule. Beyond this, the question is why the state attempted to change the patronage system which ostensibly functioned reasonably well. Paradoxically, a top-secret memorandum from 1959 vindicated the establishment of local councils for the same reason which Palmon indicated to oppose it. The memorandum stated:

> The government's policy ... has sought to divide the Arab population into diverse communities and regions. ... The municipality status of Arab villages and the competitive spirit of local elections deepened the divisions inside the villages. (Quoted in Segev, 1984:78)

Besides augmenting rivalries and conflicts between hamulas over status and benefits which were associated with the control of the local council, local councils gave the regime additional advantages. First, they were used for channelling side benefits to collaborators directly or through them to their associates, particularly so that local councils became a main venue of employment for educated Palestinians (see chapter 2). Through their financing of the local authorities, which were used as a subsidiary arm for surveillance and political control, the Palestinians became participants in their own subjection to political control. Second, through local elections, the surveillance apparatuses had an additional opportunity to monitor the behaviours of Palestinians. The formation of local lists, the participation in election campaigns and the voting results were behavioural indicators which allowed the surveillance apparatuses to periodically measure the attitudes of the Palestinians and identify patterns and trends in their attitudes as well as local tension and conflicts.

Nonetheless, the establishment of elected local councils has remained an uncertain terrain as elections could give rise to unchecked tendencies or unsettling forces. The lack of certainty which is associated with democratic elections remained an issue of concern for those in charge of Arab affairs throughout the 1960s and 1970s. Given this, the Military Government and the Office of the Advisor to the Prime Minister on Arab Affairs persisted in their effort to block or at least slow the pace of establishing Arab local councils (Cohen, 2006:238). Along with that, endeavours to refine the procedures that would maintain or accentuate the hamula politics within the new setting of elected local councils had also continued.

Local-level democracy and patronage

Supplied with the village files, Mapai's Arabists, representatives of the Military Government (who were in most cases also Mapai members), the Office of the Prime Minister's Advisor and Interior Ministry officials (in most cases the District Commissioner) made their decisions whether and when to establish a local council in a given village, its size and the names of its chairperson and members.

In this way, they controlled the foundational moment of the Arab local councils, which seemed to be essential for controlling the community's sociopolitical future. Indeed, a decision was taken on 29 June 1960 by Mapai's Arab Affairs' Committee which indicated that '[local] authorities will not be appointed until lists of candidates are prepared in coordination with the relevant bodies. And the elections will be delayed until appropriate preparations are made' (The Confined Committee of the Arab Affairs' Committee, 29 June 1960).

In line with this decision, elections usually took place a few years after the inauguration of the local council. After the holding of elections, local politicians were supposed to reflect the will of the residents. However, considerable efforts were made by those in charge of the surveillance apparatus to ensure that the election results would not contradict the hamula politics or loosen their grip over the local affairs. Apprehension regarding massive support for nationalist, communist or independent local leaders was expressed on 1 February 1962 by Uri Lubrani, the Advisor to the Prime Minister on Arab Affairs (1957–63). He stated:

> if we don't consider it carefully, we might end up soon with six to seven local authorities like Kafr Yassif, hostile to the state. ... We are afraid of establishing Arab local authorities, as they might fall into the hands of Maki [the Communist Party]. (The Arab Affairs' Committee, 1 February 1962:2)

One issue of grave concern to the Arabists was the changes in the Palestinian society, particularly the generational change. For example, in Mapai's Arab Affairs' Committee meeting on 4 May 1962, Dr. Pollack argued that probably young individuals ought to be co-opted and raised to leadership positions instead of relying on the elders. He maintained:

> Up till now we had been only active among the elders and the dignitaries. Today there is big social revolution in the Arab sector. We were not successful in managing or getting into this. Naturally young people tend to extremism, and therefore extreme parties have better chances of success [among them]. However the Party has to be involved [among the young people]. And among the young Arab people, there are some who think that it is beneficial to be on the side of the rulers, provided that they get help in achieving their personal goals. And I think this is possible. (The Arab Affairs' Committee, 4 May 1962:11–12)

Contrary to Dr. Pollack, Abba Hushi maintained that a change of approach was premature.

> Anyone who thinks that he can become increasingly reserved of the dignitaries and move to [the side] of the young people is mistaken. If we relinquish the elders and the Sheiks and move to the young we shall fail. There is a silent and daring war by the Sheiks ... they are fighting to deny access to the young people. We shouldn't help in this, however we should observe the reality as it is, if we fail to see reality as it is – we shall end up outside the field. (*Ibid.*:14)

In this debate, Abba Hushi won out. The local councils, local politics and the engineering of local social relations continued to be managed by the Arabists through the elders.

Various measures, in addition to those discussed earlier, were taken to preserve the hamula politics. Any endeavour to establish non-hamula lists was suppressed. Representatives of non-hamula lists – in case they managed to get elected – were barred from participating in any coalition (see below). Moreover, the domination of local politics by the biggest hamula or one which has branches in other villages was usually prevented. Those in charge of the surveillance and control apparatuses engineered local politics in such a way as to ensure the establishment of shaky coalitions, in which small hamulas play a decisive role. These arrangements, in which the Shin Bet played a key role, increased the dependency of local politicians on the surveillance apparatuses (Cohen, 2006:239–41; Eyal, 2006:159). Even under these conditions, chairpersons of local authorities who showed signs of independence were punished: either they were removed or the council was disbanded.

The new village files, described earlier, were instrumental in this regard. They seemed to exemplify Foucault's (1991) insight regarding the power that the construction of tables embodies: '[T]hese small techniques of notation, of registration, of constituting files, of arranging facts in columns and tables that are so familiar now, were of decisive importance in the epistemological "thaw" of the sciences of the individual ... [where] the coercion over bodies, gestures and behaviour has its beginnings' (Foucault, 1991:190–1). Soon after their creation, the folders of the village files were filled with letters from local residents asking for all sorts of favours, from collaborators passing on information or asking for favours in exchange for their services, from local politicians asking for personal favours or services to their communities and letters of vilification of opponents, etc. In addition, there were letters of Arabists and officials answering such demands, giving instructions, arranging their visits to villages and scheming against those who refused to capitulate. And, of course, there were the minutes of meetings and results or decisions regarding the sorting out, grouping, regrouping and ungrouping of Palestinians. The ramification of power through the local subdivisions and local politics, the story of which may be found between the covers of these files, will be illustrated through a few cases in the following section (see also next chapter).

Local democracy under a state of exception[1]

Discussions regarding the establishment of local councils usually began without consultation with the local residents, and mostly without their knowledge. Only in the later stages were they asked to take part in a political setting that had already been constructed for them. For example, the discussion regarding the establishment of a local council in the village of Kafr Qasim in the Triangle began on 11 November 1958 in a meeting that was attended by the District Commissioner Gochrnik, the Deputy Military Commander Bloom and the Minorities Officer Lalu. The discussions centred on two points: first, the number of representatives in the council (seven or nine) and the representation of the various hamulas; and, second, the candidates' personalities. The political affiliations of the candidates or their political attitudes were not raised, as collaboration with the state and Mapai was a precondition for candidacy. On 18 May 1959, a local council of nine members was inaugurated with seven of its members forming a coalition while two sat in the opposition. Yet, all of them were loyal to Mapai, and their division into coalition and opposition reflected hamula rivalries. The first local elections were held on 16 August 1960 and were contested by seven hamula-based lists, which were all affiliated to Mapai ('Kafr Qasim, Elections for the Local Council', n.d.). This was a common pattern, where Mapai's Arab Department and the Histadrut organized local hamula electoral lists to run in local elections and mobilize votes for Mapai in the national polls.

However, competition and rivalries between hamulas were not always sought. Sometimes, peace between rival hamulas was in Mapai's best interest. For example, in the Galilean village of Tamra, Mapai's Arabists were eager to bring hamulas, which were antagonistic to the Diab family (whose heads were known for their collaboration with the state) to cooperate with it. While one form of inducement was a promise to nominate their representatives in the local council, the other was the fact that this matter received the attention of the Military government and the Advisor's office ('An Evaluation of the Situation': Tamra, n.d.; Mishal, 14 March 1962). Indeed, local politicians were well aware of the identity of those who held the real power at the community level; yet, in most cases, they willingly continued to fulfil their roles. To illustrate this point, I shall briefly discuss the events which took place in the local council of the village Jat – a small Palestinian village in the Triangle area. Immediately following the formation of the coalition in 1966, the elected chairman invited Amnon Linn, the head of Mapai's Arab Department, to visit the local council for a meeting of acquaintance with all its members and to ask for his endorsement and support for the development projects the council planned to fulfil.

> 12.1.1966
>
> Mr. Amnon Linn:
>
> We were not surprised by your congratulations for the formation of our coalition in the local council, because we know your constant support for all the positive coalitions in the council.
>
> My friends in the coalition and myself are very happy to receive your congratulations, and on their behalf, I wish to thank you for his (your) congratulations.

> On this occasion, I have a request from his honor; to set a date for a meeting with the members of the new coalition for acquaintance, and to discuss the development projects that will be initiated in the village. Therefore, we are inviting his honor as the head of the Arab department of the ruling party; (the party) which can help in the development of the village, to visit us in Jat to see in person the problems of the village.
>
> We are extremely thankful to his honor and hopeful that he will always stand with us in the development of our village – Jat.
>
> Sincerely, on behalf of myself and my friends
>
> Sharif Ghara
> The Head of the council
> (Ghara, 12 January 1966)

This letter is ordinary. There are dozens of such letters in the archives. Yet, it was chosen for two reasons: first, it is representative in content and in style; and second, the developments which surrounded it reveal how the hamula politics disorganized the local communities. While the chairperson was eager to establish close relationships with Mapai's functionaries, his colleagues also had similar intentions. Two days after the writing of the letter, six council members rushed to the office of Mapai's regional officer – Mishal – and presented themselves and their demands. Mishal notified Linn of their visit: *Six members of the coalition have already been in my office and submitted their demands regarding the development of the village,* 14.1.66[2] (*ibid.*). Why did these council members not wait for the meeting with Mr Linn and instead rush to Mapai's regional office? The answer is simple: as the main decisions are taken by Mapai's Arabists, their accountability is first and foremost to these Arabists and then to their clans or at least to the segments which supported them. Moreover, they saw their position as a basis for prestige and as a source for personal benefits and privileges to their relatives. In the case of Jat, the council members might have had another reason. They might have known that Mapai's Arabists were suspicious of the new chairman, who occasionally socialized with 'radical elements'. And indeed, within less than nine months, he was unseated (Mishal, 27 September 1966).

Probably the developments which took place in Tayibe's local council in the Triangle in 1962 are illustrative of how Mapai's Arabists managed the Arab local councils and decided on the projects that were to be carried out. Such projects were given as a reward for good behaviour of the ruling coalition and the chairman of the local authority. In March 1962, the representative of the Communist Party, one of fifteen, was able to cause an upheaval. He supported the opposition, which was also composed of Mapai supporters (Sharoni,

25 March 1962). A new ruling coalition was formed in the local council which rested on the support of the communist representative. This development was unacceptable to those in charge of the surveillance and control apparatuses. The two rival camps rushed to get the support of Mapai's functionaries in the Arab Department (e.g. Abd al-Raziq, 4 March 1962[3]). However, following a series of meetings between Mapai's Arabists, and between them and representatives of the rival parties, a new coalition, without the communist representative, was established. Yet, given the acrimony between the two camps, the package deal had to be comprehensive. In the meeting of Mapai's Arabists on 5 September 1963, three decisions were taken: (A) MK Diab 'Obeid (associated with Mapai) will mediate between the two rival hamulas of Haj Yehia and Abu-'Afif Massarwa, (B) there will be a gradual release of the grants and loans which various ministries were supposed to transfer to the local council, and (C) the Jbara hamula will be compensated ('Summary of the Meeting Regarding Tayibe's Local Council', 15 September 1963[4]).

Despite this, uneasy relations between all the parties concerned continued for some time. In order to bolster the fragile arrangement, another meeting of Mapai's Arabists was held on 2 January 1964 and was attended by Yusif Gadish, the head of the Arab Department in the Ministry of Education, and MK Diab 'Obeid. In the meeting, Gadish promised to give the local authority a loan of 110,000 IL (Israeli Lira) for building a school, of which 35,000 IL would be released within a week. In summarizing the meeting, it was emphasized that this would be achieved only after the exclusion of the communist representative from the coalition (Eini, 2 January 1964).

The case of Tayibe exemplifies a well-known fact about Arab chairmen of local authorities. The fulfilment of development projects, regardless of their nature, had to pass through Mapai's (later Ma'arach's) Arab Department rather than through the official bureaucracy. This practice continued well after the end of the Military Government as the following letter shows. It was sent by a chairman of a Galilean local council who was known for his long-standing collaboration with the state.

> 28.9.1975
>
> To: Ra'anan Cohen, the head of the Arab Department of the Ma'arach.
> Tel-Aviv
>
> Greetings:
> Request for help with the Minister of Communication.
>
> Doubtlessly, the situation of S** (the village) is known to you. Since we face difficult tasks after the establishment of a local council in our village, we ask your honor to help in connecting the village to the telephone line, because of its importance for the residents.

> We sent several letters to the minister of communication, but to no avail. We are very greatly hopeful that you will do your best to connect the village to the telephone line, even if for the time being with a single line.
>
> Sincerely
> 'A. R. Fa
> (Fa. 'A. R., 28 September 1975)

Yet, the management of Arab local councils by the Arabists through elders and dignitaries of hamulas was not successful in all cases. Therefore, it is essential to bring up the case of Kafr Yassif, where this method had failed. Moreover, it could shed light on the specific tactics which were employed to unseat an elected mayor, and in this case a popular one.

The limits of categorizations: the case of Kafr Yassif

Kafr Yassif was an unusual case among Arab villages in one major respect. It was the only village with an elected local authority which continued to exist after the establishment of the State of Israel. Its local authority was established by the Mandatory Government on 1 December 1925. Yani Kustandi Yani served as mayor from 1933 to 1948 (Kafr Yassif, 1 July 1963). The Israeli Government reactivated the local authority on 5 June 1951, after a hiatus of three years. The first elections under Israeli rule were held on 26 January 1954 (The Local Council, Kafr Yassif, n.d.).

Despite the dramatic changes in the political milieu, a coalition between the nationalist list – Kafr Yassif List – and the communist party (hereafter national–communist coalition, NCC) headed by Yani won a majority of seats in the council, thus resulting in Yani's re-election. He was able to maintain a ruling coalition in the council, despite the successive elections and the change in representatives, and to stay in office until his death in 1962 (Kafr Yassif, 1 July 1963). The period of Yani's service was characterized by a fierce struggle not only between the NCC and Mapai but also between two opposing ideologies and conceptions regarding the position of the Palestinian minority in Israel. In order to discuss this conflict, I will begin by describing the NCC's ideology, and then I will go on to present Mapai's fight against the NCC's orientation.

Yani as mayor: the practice of a nationalist vision

NCC, headed by Yani, viewed the Arabs in Israel as part of the Palestinian people. Its struggle was characterized by a high public profile, and its aim was to bolster the political position of the Arabs in Israel. According to the NCC's conception, the Palestinians in Israel should be considered a national minority with an Arab identity and orientation. This attitude found expression in the numerous letters that Yani sent to state officials, in his public statements as well as in his political behaviour. The alliance that Yani established with the representatives of the Communist Party in the local council – the party that Mapai considered its main rival in the Arab sector – was a constant source of irritation to Mapai's Arabists and state officials. More significantly, however, Yani, as head of NCC, considered himself to be a representative of and spokesperson for all Palestinians in Israel.

NCC's political orientation manifested itself most clearly in two areas which were of grave concern to the Palestinian minority during the 1950s and early 1960s: the state's massive confiscation of Arab-owned land and the state's harsh treatment of Arab youths who attempted to flee to neighbouring Arab countries (see chapter 7). For example, on 8 March 1962, Yani sent a letter to the Israeli Prime Minister, with additional copies addressed to the Ministers of Interior, Construction, Agriculture and Finance; the Speaker of the Knesset; all of the parties in the Knesset; and the newspapers, protesting the confiscation of 5,500 dunams owned by residents of the villages of Bi'neh, Dear Al-Assad and Nahef. This land was used to establish the Jewish town of Karme'el (see Jiryis, 1976:109–11). In his letter, he wrote that Kafr Yassif's local authority decided

1. To protest against the decision regarding the confiscation.
2. To support the residents of the three villages, Bi'neh, Dear Al-assad and Nahef, in their struggle to revoke the confiscation decision mentioned above and to call upon the authorities to stop the confiscation of lands owned by the Arabs in Israel.
3. To appeal to the Jewish public [asking them] to support the residents of the three villages so that they could keep their land and their source of livelihood, and to endeavor to abrogate the confiscation decision mentioned above. (Yani, 8 March 1962)

Undeterred by security considerations to which Israel attaches utmost importance and which it covers with a veil of secrecy, Yani raised the issue of Arab youths who attempted to cross the borders and enter the Arab states. For example, following the killing in 1961of five Arab youths – from Haifa, Sakhnin and Um al-Fahim – who were shot dead and whose bodies were presumably mutilated by the Israeli army while they were trying to cross the border into the Gaza Strip (see chapter 7), he sent a letter to the politicians and ministers concerned: the Speaker of the Knesset, the Minister of Defence, the Minister of Police and the Minister of Interior. Among other things, he wrote:

> In its meeting of 26.9.1961, our local council discussed the incident in which five Arab youths were killed. ... We decided to strongly condemn the killing of these five youths, and to express our astonishment at the way in which the killing was carried out. Our council particularly condemns the mutilation of the bodies of these youth,

> if what has been reported is correct. We call for the establishment of a popular (Arab–Jewish) committee of investigation to examine the rumors which surround this incident. ... We call upon the authorities to deal with the problem of illegal border crossing by creating employment opportunities for the workers and the educated, and the abolition of [existing forms of] discrimination and oppression.
>
> Our council condemns all forms of racist incitement ... [particularly those] which have resulted in attacks carried out by Jews against Arab workers in Acre's [central] bus station in the last few days. Our council condemns these attacks and calls upon the authorities to take legal action ... [against the attackers] and to prevent the recurrence of such events. (Yani, 29 September 1961)

A clear articulation of the NCC's political attitude can be found in Yani's public letter to the Prime Minister concerning pronouncements made by Uri Lubrani, the Advisor to the Prime Minister on Arab Affairs. In a press conference held on 30 July 1960, Lubrani accused Arabs in Israel of endeavouring to undermine state security. In his letter, Yani wrote:

> Our council views the statement by Mr. Lubrani, your advisor on Arab Affairs, as constituting a serious blow to the amenable relations between the two peoples of this country, and a means of fomenting hatred and animosity between them. Moreover, it constitutes incitement against a people whose only sin is being Arab, a people who desire to live in freedom and dignity in their homeland. It also aims to justify the policy of oppression and subjugation imposed on the Arabs. (Yani, 15 October 1960)

The tone of this letter is unusual and, in many ways, unique. While the Arab representatives under the Military Government were accustomed to employing all kinds of exaggeration in praise of the state, Yani dared to speak the truth to the ruling power. The concepts of oppression and subjugation and the existence of a dignified people which he invoked were not part of the Arab public discourse at the time.

NCC's defiant attitude also manifested itself in political action. In 1958, the Israeli Government decided to celebrate, in nationwide festivities, the 10th anniversary of the state's independence. The Arab citizens were ordered to take part in the celebrations. The governing coalition of Kafr Yassif's local council nevertheless decided not to participate. In explaining its decision, the council argued that it could not take part in the celebrations while Arabs continued to live under the yoke of the Military Government (see Kusa, 4 April 1958). However, the Kafr Yassif local council's decision was reversed following immense pressure exercised by the state. Yet, the retreat was not total. The letter that Yani sent to the 'Department of Illumination and Enlightenment' reveals that the celebration's programme was kept to a minimum (Yani, n.d.).

Another clear example of NCC's defiance was the local council's decision regarding the employment of teachers that was made at the beginning of the

1960/1961 academic year. Teachers whose employment the Ministry of Education recommended in the local secondary school were rejected. Instead, the council hired Botros Daleh, a graduate of the Hebrew University, who was known for his patriotic stand (*Davar*, 24 October 1960). This decision represented a rejection of the official sorting system of candidates (see the next chapter).

Yani's most direct challenge to the hegemonic discourse and the institutions which articulated it, however, was courageously articulated through his activities as a founding member and chairperson of, and chief spokesperson for, the national group, The Popular Front, which was established on 6 July 1958 (Amnon, 6 July 1958; *Ha'aretz*, 7 July 1958). The intention of the Popular Front was to become a nationwide alliance between the nationalists and the communists, which could then represent the Palestinian minority, rather than having it rely on the Arab MKs affiliated with Zionist parties, dignitaries, mukhtars and elders. The Front was established following the repressive police response to the May First demonstrations held in Nazareth and Um al-Fahim during which some 400 protesters were arrested (Amnon, 6 July 1958; see chapter 7).

The Military Governor tried to prevent the Front's inaugural meeting, which was due to take place in Acre, by imposing movement restrictions on some thirty-seven of the leading public figures (*Ha'aretz*, 7 July 1958; The Popular Front, The Executive Committee, 29 October 1958). Yani was among these leaders and was ordered to appear at police headquarters twice a day for a week. Moreover, he was denied freedom of movement for a month. In his speech, which was read *in absentia*, he reiterated NCC's political vision mentioned earlier: 'Our situation is deteriorating; therefore we must unite in order to ensure a future life of freedom and dignity. The Arabs are willing to establish friendly relations with the Jews' (Amnon, 7 July 1958).

In addition, Yani initiated the establishment of a Front branch in his village – the third such branch, the first two having been established in Acre and Nazareth – to serve the neighbouring villages. In the inaugural ceremony, he urged the participants not to be deterred by the Military Government's restrictions and to act with resoluteness. He also emphasized that the Front represented an independent organization and was not an arm of the Communist Party (Dawood, 23 August 1958).

Countermeasures

The struggle against Kafr Yassif's council headed by Yani took various forms. The first and the obvious one comprised a tireless endeavour to unseat the chairperson and punish his supporters. Already by the mid-1950s, a Mapai Arabist was sent to meet with the deputy mayor, Raja Jiryis. The emissary reported that he had not been successful in establishing common ground with Jiryis, for Jiryis had demanded the abolishment of the Military Government in

Kafr Yassif and substantial reductions in the taxes imposed on the residents (Letter to Yaakov[5]). In October 1958, the Military Government banished three dissidents from Kafr Yassif, sent them to Safad and withdrew the travel permits of all Popular Front members (The Popular Front, Kafr Yassif Branch, n.d.).

In 1957/1958, Mapai joined forces with Mapam in its endeavour to depose the mayor. On 29 April 1957, Mussa Bassal, Mapam's representative in the council, left the coalition and his position as deputy mayor. In his public letter of resignation, he accused the council and the mayor of inefficiency in the levying of taxes and of sluggishness in carrying out development projects (Bassal, 29 April 1957). On 12 October 1958, the representatives of the two parties asked Yani to convene a council meeting in order to vote on their non-confidence motion (Safyiah *et al.*, 12 October 1958). This call came as a result of negotiations that had been under way since May 1957; the goal of these negotiations had been to establish an alternative coalition of Mapai's and Mapam's representatives (The Local Authority in Kafr Yassif, 26 May 1957).[6]

After the 1960 elections, Mapai tried to weaken Yani through its support of council member Fawzi Khuri. Amnon Linn of Mapai's Arab Department persuaded Khuri to file a complaint in the High Court of Justice against Yani (Khuri, 1 May 1960). The court ruled in Yani's favour and ordered Khuri to pay a fine. Amnon Linn wrote to Yaakov Eini, suggesting that Mapai pay the costs (Khuri, n.d.),[7] and indeed Mapai paid the fine of 150 IL (Eini, 16 June 1960). Interestingly, Fawzi Khuri later decided to join the NCC.

Of all the councils Yani served in as mayor, the council that emerged after the 1960 election was the most inconvenient for him. NCC won only four out of the council's nine seats. The representatives of Mapam and Mapai won two and three seats, respectively. Yani was re-elected due to the conflict between his rivals. Mapai's and Mapam's Arabists stepped in and tried to achieve their goals, which had been laid out in an aborted coalition agreement. They had agreed to form a new coalition and that the position of mayor would be filled by rotation between the heads of their lists – each serving one half of the term. Beyond the local and technical issues, Article 10 of the agreement states: 'It is agreed that the council will not deal with national political subjects and will confine its activities to the municipal level.' According to Article 11, the highest authority to adjudicate in cases of disagreement would be the Municipal Section of the Executive Committee of the Histadrut. Article 12 states that the agreement requires the ratification of the parties' representatives, Yaakov Eini of Mapai and Simha Flapan of Mapam (Eini and Falpan, n.d.).

Besides this politics of wheeling and dealing, two additional methods were used. The first was to establish a secondary school in Acre in order 'to attract the young people from Kafr Yassif and the adjacent villages, which will constitute a blow to the secondary school in Kafr Yassif and decrease the influence of the nationalists and the Communists who control it' (The Confined

Committee of Arab Affairs' Committee, 25 October 1960). The second was an incitement of the residents by the Military Government not to pay the local taxes, aiming to drive the municipality to bankruptcy. The refusal of the Druze residents to pay their taxes soon turned into religious tension, an escalation which led to the interference of the security establishment in local affairs (Avivi, 2007:290–1).

The struggle after Yani's death

Yani Yani died on 1 August 1962 without leaving a successor who had leadership qualities and who could successfully mobilize the residents. A power struggle erupted in NCC soon after his death (Eini, 24 July 1962[8]). Thus, Mapai's functionaries had their long-awaited opportunity. Although their supporters were disunited (Linn, 7 November 1963[9]; Tuma, 15 November 1963), they were able to lay down a strategy, which eventually allowed the Mapai-affiliated 'the United Block' (Al-Kutlah Al-Muwahada) to form the governing coalition in Kafr Yassif's local council for the first time. This strategy was coordinated in two meetings of Mapai's Arabists, which were held on 3 November 1963 and 10 February 1964. In the first meeting, they explored the manipulation of the religious identities by establishing an Islamic List, which would exist alongside the United Block. To secure its influence, they decided to obtain a state grant of 1,000 IL in order to build a mosque in the village (Report of the Meeting Regarding the Elections of Kafr Yassif's Local Council, 3 November 1963). In the second meeting, they discussed their relation with the Islamic List, which had been established by this time, and with Mapam. Simha Flapan, Mapam's representative in charge of Arab affairs, promised Mapai's functionaries that after the elections, Mapam would only form a coalition with their party (Report of the Meeting which Took Place on 10 February 1964 for Reviewing the Situation in Kafr Yassif, 10 February 1964).

Meanwhile, the manipulation of the religious sentiments was translated into religious rhetoric. In the 1964 election campaigns of both the Islamic List and the United Block, religious motifs and slogans were predominant. For example, the leaflet of the Islamic List began with the title 'In the Name of God' and was followed by Koranic verses, in which the Muslims were called upon to unite. Moreover, the first two objectives on the List's programme were sectarian. They promised to complete the building of the mosque by acquiring government assistance – which had already been promised by Mapai's Arabists – and to outlaw pig rearing (The Islamic List, Kafr Yassif, n.d.). The United Block followed suit; a poem outlining its platform states: 'This day is the day of liberty, of strong unity against infidelity, faithlessness and Communist anarchy. Today we unite. We promise each other, in the presence of God, to mutually support each other, Muslims and Christians. ... We want progress and construction, streets with light [electricity]' (The United Block, Kafr Yassif, n.d.).

The accentuation of religious differences was also evident in the endeavour to stop pig rearing in the village, as pigs are hateful animals to Muslims. In this regard, Jaber Dahish Muadi, a Druze MK in an Arab list affiliated to Mapai, pursued the issue with the Ministry of Interior. He sent a letter to the Deputy Minister of Interior about the legality of pig rearing in Kafr Yassif and the ways it could be stopped (Falk, 28 April 1964[10]).

Moreover, state officials, Arab public figures known for their collaboration with the state and Mapai, and Jewish functionaries took part in the election campaign of the United Block. Ministers were sent to promise that the public projects the state had refrained from carrying out during the Yani years would now be implemented (The United Block, Kafr Yassif n.d.b.). Both the United Block and the Islamic List raised local issues, such as connecting the village to the national electricity grid, the paving of roads, the building of schools and enlarging the area under the municipality's jurisdiction.

Mapai's triumph and its meaning

The 1964 elections were the first ones to be held after Yani's death. They resulted in substantial gains for Mapai-affiliated lists. The United Block headed by Rafeq Shehadeh won two seats, and so did the Islamic List. Mapam and the list affiliated with the National Religious Party (Mafdal) each won a single seat. NCC won only three seats (Eini, 17 March 1964). Despite these results, it was not easy for the United Block to form a stable coalition. Therefore, Mapai's Arabists had to resort to bribery. They reached an agreement with representatives of the Mafdal (the National Religious Party) which stipulated, among other things, that Mapai would be required to pay a monthly instalment of 300 IL to the Mafdal Representative until a job was found for him. It is worth noting that the local representatives themselves were not part of the agreement. Rather, it was reached and signed by Jewish functionaries of the abovementioned parties, and the agreement was composed entirely in Hebrew (Mapai and Mafdal Representatives, n.d.). The implementation was also dependent upon the signatories. Yaakov Eini sent a letter to Reuven Barkatt informing him of the deal and asking him to make the payments (Eini, 19 May 1964).

Subsequently, Arabists began to make all of the main decisions concerning Kafr Yassif's local affairs. Rafeq Shehadeh, the new mayor, was an old and ailing man. He was aware of the limits of his role. His first 'significant' letter in his capacity as mayor was sent to Reuven Barkatt thanking him for his support. Beyond the courtesy and politeness, which are usually included in such letters, it resonates with an admission of his powerlessness and dependency. Among other things, he wrote:

> With great pleasure I received your letter, in which you congratulate us for our victory and the forming of the new coalition in Kafr Yassif. I am most thankful

> for your efforts in this regard. I became head of this coalition thanks to your efforts and the efforts of our great party, Mapai. I will fulfill my role in this coalition to the best of my ability. I am counting on your goodwill to help me fulfill my duty to develop the village. (Shehadeh, 29 May 1964)

The new mayor basically states here that he owed his position, first and foremost, to Mapai and its functionaries. Moreover, he acknowledges that his success was dependent upon their support. Yani Yani would never have composed such a letter. The legitimacy of his leadership rested on the support of the residents.

After Yani's death, Kafr Yassif was still without various public utilities, such as electricity, roads and a zoning plan. However, under Yani's leadership, the residents were not willing to trade their national consciousness for the developmental needs of their village. The new representatives were aware of this reality. Publicly, they could not ignore the discourse that was dominant during Yani's years. While they were trying to change such rhetoric, from time to time they were forced to employ some of its vocabulary.

An examination of the discussions on the guidelines of the coalition reveals the way in which such rhetoric was utilized and manipulated. These discussions yielded two documents. The first, 'The Program of the Coalition for the Management of Kafr Yassif's Council', is long and detailed. It reflects the main demands and interests of the partners and includes thirty-two articles. The articles are arranged according to decreasing significance. The guidelines begin with the objective of ending pig rearing and then go on to detail other local objectives, such as the building of schools, the paving of new roads and the building of a playground for the children. Article 23 begins to address objectives of a collective nature, that is, it mentions the goal of transferring the decision-making power vis-à-vis Islamic endowments from the state to the Muslim citizens of Israel. Article 24 emphasizes the goal of obliterating the Military Government; Article 26 mentions the struggle for a just solution to the problem of the internal refugees; Article 29 calls for a solution to the Palestinian refugee problem through peaceful negotiations between the parties; and Article 31 mentions the struggle for world peace and for peace in the Middle East. This document illustrates the change in orientation, that is, the demands and objectives were clearly focused on local affairs (Kafr Yassif's Local Council the Coalition, n.d.).

The second document, 'The Political Program of Kafr Yassif's Coalition (Kafr Yassif's Local Council, the Coalition, n.d.b.)', is an abridged version of the first and includes nine broad guidelines. However, the priorities and emphasis are reversed. Only one article deals with local issues; Article 3 states the objective of developing the village and of building public utilities that already existed in other settlements. The rest of the articles deal with issues that had been given a low priority in the first policy statement. These include the struggle for the abolition of the Military Government, the achievement of equality between all citizens of Israel and putting an end to land confiscations. It seems that it was composed to help project a nationalist image for the new coalition; in other words, to pay lip service to the discourse that had prevailed during the Yani years. Indeed, in its meeting of 4 June 1964, the council unanimously decided to demand the abolishment of the Military Government, and the mayor communicated this decision to the Prime Minister (Shehadeh, 13 June 1964). However, to prevent a situation whereby nationalist rhetoric might get out of hand, two guidelines were added at the end of the Political Programme. First, the political principles were not binding for Mapai's representatives; and second, disagreements over any of these articles were not to affect the coalition's composition. However, in fact, the political demands were just lip service. All knew that nothing is going to happen. Indeed, Barkatt, who conducted the negotiation with Mapam, stated: I would have given them a lot, but materially [only]. I'd give them nothing in the political field ... [they would say] for a marginal coalition they [Mapai's leaders] are ready to abolish the Military Government. This would mean that it [the Military Government] is no more than a swindle. On these issues I'd never give in, to give money and more money, I don't mind'. (The Confined Secretariat of the Arab Affairs' Committee, 19 March 1964:13)

Crossroads

Twenty years after the establishment of the state, those in charge of Arab affairs discussed their tactics and achievements throughout a generation. Amnon Linn, who gave a long-winded presentation, thought that the engineering of Palestinians' sociopolitical relations through the hamula politics was successful:

> There are about 44 [Arab] local authorities, and there are villages that do not have such councils. We act along with the Ministry of interior for the establishment of local authorities. In the vast majority of the cases we established family based lists which contest among themselves, except one place where we were not able to do so – Kafr Yassif, and this is the reason for our failure there.
>
> (The Arab Affairs' Committee, 6 June 1968:6)

Yet, his presentation signalled the end of an era. He presented a backward-looking description without being able to offer new ideas. His diagnosis of the Palestinian society and the tools for the rejuvenation of the control methods were a recirculation of old ideas. According to his analysis, Palestinian society was changing but, nevertheless, has remained the same. The generational changes, he argued, reinforced rather than altered existing structures. Perhaps this was a convenient way to convince himself and his colleagues that a change of approach was either unnecessary or not urgent. Thus, he maintained:

> A new Arab generation has grown up in the country; a young and intelligent generation, and this is thanks to our developed and progressive life structure. ... They think in new concepts different from those [which prevailed] when we established the state. However I wouldn't suggest that we ought to mistakenly think that the social and familial structure of the Arab community has entirely changed. If in the past we were aided by heads of families, today the influence in the villages is in the hands of the young men who head these families. If in the past we had to deal with one mukhtar, today we have to deal with young people – the sons of the mukhtars. (*Ibid.*:5)

The new methods Linn thought appropriate to upgrade and develop the surveillance system unveiled the dead end which he and his colleagues had reached. His main suggestion was to revive the neighbourly relations committees which were formed in the 1940s.

> Then the National committee (Va'ad Liumi) and the Jewish Agency directed all Jewish settlements to establish neighbourly relations with the Arab villages. When the state was established, the Hebrew settlements did not consider themselves as obliged or have the right to be partner in the endeavour which various circles do for dialogue ... there ought to be a [party] decision that each Kibbutz, Moshav or city establishes relationships with adjacent Arab localities, and in this way it would become possible to increase the number of those who deal with this [the Arab] issue. (*Ibid.*:7)

The aim of such committees would be the same as in the 1940s: to mobilize Jewish citizens besides those employed by the various official and semi-official organizations to take part – consciously or unknowingly – in the surveillance of Palestinians. According to Linn, an experimental project in which nine Jewish local authorities established 'sisterly relations' with nine Arab councils was under way (*ibid.*:6). Moreover, he mentioned that a group of some 200 party members who work in the bureaucracy and deal with Palestinians were ready to contribute to the party's effort (*ibid.*:7). Yet, it seems that not much has come out of it.

The Hamula politics has not lost its allure after the end of the period under discussion. For example, a handwritten document from 1975 (most likely by Ra'anan Cohen who served between 1975 and 1986 as chairman of the Labour Party's [previously Mapai's] Arab Department) regarding the appropriate strategy for defeating the Communist Party in the local elections in the large Galilean village of Arabba identified the hamula lists as the only way for achieving this goal. Various measures to this end were taken, such as the attempt to reconcile two antagonistic factions of the Kana'aneh hamula and to persuade them to run in one list rather than in two. Moreover, discussions were held with some educated persons to lead such lists. One of them, who was thought of as a particularly attractive candidate, seems to have weighed the offer seriously. 'I want to serve my village', he told his interlocutor (Arabba, (n.d.) [notes on the elections][11]). Cohen (23 March 1975) tried to duplicate this strategy in other villages, and the only major concern in this endeavour seems to have been the availability of funding.

Conclusion

This chapter is a continuation of the previous one. It dealt with the increasing subdivisions of Palestinians into smaller categories. While these categories – large and small – existed before, the meaning attributed to them, their impact on the daily life of ordinary Palestinians, their role in the sociopolitical matrix of power and the role they played in the constitution of Palestinians' identities have changed. These categories, most noticeably the hamula, became central for identification, thus penning Palestinians within their boundaries. The various categories were arranged hierarchically, at the national and the local levels, thus hardening the sectarian and localized identities. Besides epitomizing the components of modern surveillance as identified by Foucault (1991) – namely, continual registration, categorization, hierarchical observation, normalizing judgement and spatial confinement (170–228) – the methods of surveillance and control used by Israel vis-à-vis the Palestinians brought to light the relationships between surveillance and political rights. The discussion in this chapter demonstrates how the tight political control imposed on the Palestinians turned their political rights, at the local level, into a means for disorganizing rather than empowering them. Far from fair and free, the elections became an occasion for accentuating rivalries among hamulas, testing the effectiveness of the control system and monitoring the behaviours of Palestinians.

Yet, the discussion on Kafr Yassif's local council highlights two issues, which have had an adverse impact on surveillance and political control. First, the simple cost–benefit calculation, which lies at the heart of the disciplinary process, did not work. The non-material factors in such calculations seem to have eluded those in charge of Arab affairs. Or maybe they viewed such factors as beyond the pale, as they contradicted the minimal ideology that the regime produced for the Palestinians, according to which their aspirations ought to be confined to personal advancement and the elevation of their hamula's status. Thus, despite oppressive tactics, the residents of Kafr Yassif continued to support the mayor until his death. Second, the politics of categorization might unleash forces that the regime never anticipated. The accentuation of the religious identities, in Kafr Yassif as elsewhere in the Galilee, might have contributed in one way or another to the enhancement of Islamic sentiments and a worldview which Israel would consider later as potentially subversive. In short, this chapter has analysed the expansive and intrusive surveillance Israel has employed to control the Palestinians and its incompleteness.

Notes

1

Table 5.2 The establishment of new Arab local authorities, 1956–75

Year	New localities
1956–60	14
1961–65	13
1966–75	13

(Adopted from Al-Haj and Rosenfeld, 1988:27–9).

2 He added this note in the letter itself.
3 This letter includes details of the eventual meeting of the local council and an explanation of the position he took.
4 This meeting was attended by several Arabists: Sh. Brook, Yaakov Cohen, Yaakov Eini, Amnon Linn, Meir Mishal and Mordechai Surkis.
5 This letter was sent to Yaakov, most likely Yaakov Eini, and the name of the emissary is Avner, probably from the Military Government. As the letters are arranged chronically, it is safe to assume that it dates to 1954 or 1955.
6 This list of notes was probably written by Yaakov Eini.
7 Fawzi Khuri, 'Letter to Hananiah, undated [internal number 29]'. A note scribbled on the letter by an Arabists reveals the attitude, '[y]ou should not give him the feeling that we should do that' (pay the money).
8 Presumably, the correct date of this report is 24 August, as the mayor passed away on 1 August 1962.
9 Copies of this letter were sent to Reuven Barkatt, Rahavam 'Ameer (the Advisor to the Prime Minister on Arab Affairs), Yaakov Cohen of the Histadrut's Arab department and Yaakov Eini.
10 He was the legal advisor of this ministry.
11 A handwritten document on the anticipated voting behaviour according to family affiliation, most likely composed by Ra'anan Cohen.

6

The power of mind over mind: surveillance through education

Education and surveillance

The previous two chapters dealt with surveillance and control methods, which took the shape of splitting, subdividing and arranging the Palestinians into various groups and the ordering of these groups hierarchically to ensure the continuity of the identities that these categories engender. This chapter discusses the practices of surveillance and control at the individual level which aimed to affect the ways through which Palestinians form their views and attitudes through formal education and informal learning. Educational institutions have been widely regarded in modern times as the appropriate settings through which certain ideas could be propagated and become hegemonic by acquiring a status akin to the laws of nature (e.g. Giroux and Purpel, 1984; Althusser, 1984; Apple, 1990). Schools, colleges and, to a large extent, universities are particularly fit to institutionalize certain notions, in the light of their structure and sociopolitical status. Not only do students stay long hours daily in these settings under certain rules and regulations and mostly in an inferior position due to their inability to formulate an intellectually critical and coherent position – but these institutions are also surrounded by well-established myths and rituals which are essential for the success of their social and political role. Such myths, for example, include their imparting of objective knowledge, meritocracy and their function as gateways for future success.

Intellectual captivation of the citizens is considered as the preferred method of control. It is more efficient, benign and enduring. Moreover, it is unlikely to stir up much resistance. Antonio Gramsci (1986) contended that ruling groups achieve a certain degree of hegemony when, in a certain formation, they succeed in translating their interests to widely held and presumably universal notions. However, hegemony cannot be always sought. Israel cannot possibly promulgate Zionism as an ideology for the Palestinians. Moreover, the methods of surveillance and political control it had used were incompatible with notions like meritocracy and universalism. Given this, Israel developed a 'minimal hegemony' for the Palestinians (Sa'di, 2005). It basically lays emphasis on personal success within, rather than beyond, their particularistic group of affiliation (which took the shape of announcements about the first Bedouin doctor, the first Druze diplomat or the appointment of Arab tokens in various positions, etc.).

Meanwhile, the hegemonic order of Israel, which was constructed for the Jewish citizens, was articulated in the goals of education. Through them, the state spilled out the overriding components of the collective identity and the 'national psyche' it aspired to shape. The 1953 Law of State Education specified these goals:

> [They are] to base education on the values of the Jewish culture and the achievements of science, on the love of the homeland and loyalty to the state and the Jewish people, on practice in agricultural work and handicraft, on pioneer training and on striving for a society built on freedom, equality, tolerance, mutual assistance, and love of mankind. (Abu-Saad, 2006:34)

These aims intended to socialize young students according to a mythology of national character that Kimmerling (2001) has called 'Israeliness'. They are also in line with the policy of quarantining the Palestinians. But does the absence of detailed and meaningful goals for the Palestinians mean that Arab education evolved purposelessly? Or maybe this absence meant to clear the way for those in charge of the surveillance apparatuses to introduce their policy guidelines and initiatives stealthily? The following sections unveil various attempts to formalize official strategies regarding Arab education and articulate them formally. Yet, not less significant than the message for those in charge of the surveillance and control of the Palestinians was the identity of the messengers: teachers, headmasters and principals. Before discussing these issues, the following section deals with a basic dilemma that faced those in charge of surveillance: how is education likely to affect the Palestinians?

Whither Arab education?

Education for the Palestinians and its plausible impact generated various debates and gave rise to diverse opinions. The main question was whether education would remind Palestinians of their history and thus stiffen their resistance to the control and surveillance policies, as Professor Ben-Zion Dinor argued in 1952, or whether it would lead to their 'cultural assimilation', as Yitzhak Ben-Zvi thought (see chapter 1). If the first position is accepted, why should the state provide education for the Arabs? Indeed, Uri Lubrani, the third Advisor to the Prime Minister on Arab Affairs, expressed this position forcefully:

> Were there no Arab students perhaps it would be better. If they would remain hewers of wood perhaps it would be easier to control them. But there are things which do not depend on our wish. There is then no escape from this issue, so we must be careful to understand the nature of the problems involved and to devise appropriate strategies. (Lustick, 1980:68)

Lubrani might be right; it could be more difficult to control educated people. However, sometimes the educational outcomes were thought of as bolstering rather than hindering political control. For example, an increase in the educational level of women was considered as a means for decreasing the Palestinian population's natural growth, as the Tolidano report indicates (see chapter 2). Moreover, through the educational system, the sectarian identities – most noticeably the Druze identity – could be buttressed. Unlike Lubrani, Moshe Sharett argued back in 1950 that the state should seize the initiative to mould Palestinians' education as a means of influencing their thinking and attitudes:

> Currently the state doesn't provide secondary education; ... it aspires to provide elementary schooling. ... However there is secondary education; there is a wide network of secondary schools in the country ... there are tens of schools for Jews, but not a single one for the Arabs. And there is no private initiative in this regard. ... *I think the state should establish a secondary school for the Arabs and, if it establishes such a school it will be able to control the Arab intelligentsia which will grow up in Israel.* ... If it doesn't do this it will create deprivation and humiliation and those who will develop by themselves [independently] will not be dependent on the state's secondary schooling. Even after that the percentage of Arabs with secondary education will be small in comparison to Jews with such schooling. (The Secretariat's Meeting with MKs, 18 June 1950:4/4–1/5; italics added)

The plausible contradictory outcomes of Arab education were bluntly stated by Abba Hushi in 1964: '... the state invests large sums of money in Arab education. If we don't find a way according to which the content and the method of education is directed by the [Jewish] in charge persons, we would be investing money in raising snakes' (The Confined Secretariat of the Arab Affairs' Committee, 19 March 1964:11).

But what are the methods by which Palestinians with the 'right' disposition could be raised? Such methods of education and socialization were the subject of lengthy discussions. A committee for youth composed of representatives of the Histadrut, the Advisor's Office and Mapai's Arab Department set out to identify the methods and processes by which Palestinian adolescents – in a crucial period of identity formation – could be influenced. Highlighting the uncertainty and unpredictability of such methods, Dr. Pollack characterized this inquiry as a scientific project, and when these discussions were exhausted, he stated on 28 November 1962:

> We are conducting empirical experiments in the Arab field and we draw results from our proceeding activities. We must act among the Arabs because we have to decrease the emerging tension between the two parts of the country's population and to integrate the Arabs in the country's productive system in a way that they don't become an alien body. It's obvious that the key factor which directs our operation is security. (The Youth's Committee, 28 November 1962:4)

Indeed, in the absence of a hegemonic order and an inclusive citizenship project and in the light of the state of exception which prevailed, 'experiments' were the only tool left to find a way for achieving the anticipated results from the educational system. Yet, these 'experiments' were not conducted in a sociopolitical vacuum. Rather, they took place within, and they were part of the state of exception. Indeed, Pinhas Lavon – a politician who filled several high official positions, including the General Secretary of the Histadrut and the Minister of Defence – stated in 1950: 'What is being implemented is brutal and drastic oppression of the Arabs in the state of Israel ... *the Ministry of education is leaving the handling of the Arabs to persons who are unable to do their jobs [properly] and who employ CID methods*'[1] (The Political Committee, 19 January 1950:8; italics added).

The coercive methods, to which Lavon alluded, focused among other things on screening and tightly supervising and monitoring Palestinians in the educational institutions, particularly the teachers.

Teachers and teacher training colleges

Given the destruction of the majority of the urban centres during the war, the rural communities which remained did not have sufficient teachers to run an educational system. Palestinians who had formal education, though not trained teachers, constituted the natural pool of teachers. Their employment was conducted by those in charge of the surveillance apparatuses through the relations they had with Palestinian collaborators or 'dignitaries' before 1948. This method, besides bolstering the status of dignitaries and collaborators – such as activists in the League of Arab Workers – laid the basis for co-option, which would become the main method of employing Palestinian teachers. The below letter is illustrative. It was sent by a functionary of the Histadrut to the person in charge of the Arab Department in the Ministry of Education.

257/1/AM 21.9.49

To Mr. Benor
The Arab Education Department
The Ministry of Education
Jerusalem

Dear Sir:
Candidates for teaching.

A. Below is a list of candidates for teaching who submitted applications but have not received replies yet. We were asked by the *secretariat of the League of Arab Workers* to recommend their acceptance.

Candidates from Jish

1. Marwan H. Shuli – specially recommended
2. Hanna Y. Sadir
3. Raif F. Dahir
4. Bishara Shaqour

5. Ibrahim Shaqour

From Lydda station

6. Qasim And Al-Aziz

From Lydda

7. Elias Farah Munair

From Tarshiha

8. Jamil Gharzuzi

B. Three forms:

9. Salim Kamil Nahas – Bqee'ah
10. Shukri Nakhleh Jum'a – From Mi'lia. He has already submitted an application but has not received an answer
11. George Yousef Hanna – Rama

Please acknowledge the receipt of our letter.

Sincerely, E. Shulman
(Shulman, 21 September 1949; italics added)

This method worked for two years. In 1950, the surveillance over the educational system was institutionalized. The newly established General Security Services – Shin Bet – assumed the key role in monitoring Palestinians (Cohen, 2006:169–70). Moreover, the division of labour and the coordination between the various components of the surveillance and control apparatuses evolved. Another change in the institutionalization of surveillance was the opening in 1956 of a teacher training college in Jaffa, which was moved to Haifa in 1964. Thus, the screening and monitoring of the candidates for teaching began with their enrolment to the college. The list of students who enrolled was carefully screened by the surveillance services. The small number of candidates, the collaboration of local dignitaries and heads of hamulas, and the classification of candidates according to their hamula affiliation, as explained in chapter 5, decreased the margin of error of accepting 'negative elements' significantly, although it did not eliminate it altogether. With the rise in the number of applications, a problem of misidentification appeared, as the following letter shows. It refers to the acceptance of students who were regarded 'negative' elements by teacher training colleges.

21.9.1967

To MK Amnon Linn
By: Meir Mishal

<u>Hostile [persons] who were accepted to the Arab Seminar in Haifa</u>.

1. <u>Qasim Muhammad Mustafa Qatawi</u> – from Beir Al-Sika village; during his studies at the high school he infiltrated to Jordan, returned to Israel and was jailed in 1964.

2. Farid Abd Al Rahman 'Azam – from the village of Tayibe, graduate of Tayibe high school, the son of a Rakah (Communist) family, he organized a nationalist strike and he is hostile. He also tags to tourists who visit the village.
3. Moreover, arrived to my knowledge that Qasim Qatawi, the above-mentioned, was accepted first to Sde Boker college, but since he was accepted to Haifa college, he dropped the [option] of Sde Boker.
4. For your knowledge.

Comradely Greetings
Meir Mishal
(Mishal, 1967)

However, the new method of selection expanded the impact that the processes of categorizations and subdivisions had on the realm of education, and it compelled many secondary school graduates to succumb to the prevailing sociopolitical order had they planned to get a teaching position, one of the few available white-collar jobs for Palestinians. Moreover, the methods of surveillance which were applied to the Palestinian population at large did not spare the students. They had to have travel passes, and as they quite often passed through several closed areas on their way to the college and back, they had to acquire a travel permit for each one of these areas. The quarantining of the students and the panoptic-style surveillance under which they lived in the college, the self-monitoring and the atmosphere of fear were more severe than those which the Palestinian population at large endured. These measures were described in the memories of an ex-student:

> All of the teachers were Jews who spoke Arabic fluently. The students were cut off from the larger world, not having access to newspapers or radios, and all those who came from villages far from Jaffa were only able to visit their families once a month. (Quoted in Abu-Saad, 2006:29)

He went further to describe the way in which the surveillance methods operated on a daily basis:

> Midway through the course, we were surprised by the expulsion of one of our classmates. No one gave us any explanation as to why he was expelled, so one of my friends and I agreed to raise this issue with the director. ... When the director entered our class, I asked for permission to speak and requested that he tells us the reason for our classmate's expulsion. His response was 'This is the business of the administration; it's not your business'. ... During the next break between classes when the classroom was empty, one of the students returned and wrote on the blackboard, 'Woe to the sheep that can't tell the difference between its butcher and its shepherd'. For the next few days, the course administrators were

> consumed with investigating the incident and discovering who wrote the statement. A few of the students, who were 'the eyes of the administration', were constantly going in and out of the director's office …
>
> Sometime later … I found that our classmate had been expelled because he was associated with the Communist Party. (*Ibid.*)

Given the method of students' screening and the surveillance within colleges, it is hardly surprising that meritocracy was compromised. In some cases, students who failed in their studies were allowed to graduate and get jobs. The following case is illustrative. Two Palestinian students who studied at Wingate College for physical education (sports) and whose fees were paid by the Department of Physical Education at the Ministry of Education failed in their studies. Yet, the Ministry of Education had arranged jobs for them, as the following letter shows:

> Mr. Shulmon from the minority's [i.e. Arab] department at the ministry of education promised Mr. Solmon of the department of physical education that even if they fail he is going to employ them as teachers of physical education. … Hahaver [comrade] Peled *asks you to help by allowing their return to the college and [verifying] that they finish the second year in any [possible] way.* (Mishal, n.d.b.; italics added)

The candidates for teaching positions passed through various selection processes. Screening by the security services began while they were still in college. Then, a comprehensive screening was undertaken by a committee composed of a small number of representatives of the main surveillance bodies: the Office of the Prime Minister's Advisor, the Military Government and Mapai's Arab Department,[2] which classified the candidates according to various criteria – their personal history, hamula, etc. On 29 June 1960, this committee took three important decisions which had had direct bearing on the selection process: 'To find employment for educated collaborators in consultation with the relevant bodies. … Teachers will not be appointed without [a prior] consultation with this forum. This committee will meet on regular basis, at least once a month in order to coordinate the activities of the various bodies' (The Confined Committee of the Araf Affairs' Committee, 29 June 1960).

The recommendations of this body were transferred to the professional selection committee in the Ministry of Education in the form of lists with signs of V or X beside each of the candidates' names. These small strokes of pen determined the candidates' future. Even after the termination of the Military Government, those in charge of Arab affairs in the Ma'arach (previously Mapai) maintained their influence. The list of Appointment and transfer to teachers, cited below, which dates to 1971, is interesting as it contains one exceptional case where a recommended candidate was not employed because of his poor academic attainments.

Jerusalem 1 December 1971

To the Havir Meir Mishal:
The Arab Department
The Headquarter of the Labour Party
Hayarkon St. 110, Tel-Aviv

Answers and Clarifications
For the proper procedure, I am dispatching to you answers to considerable part of your demands [sent] during the last months.[3] Unfortunately only now after the situation has fairly calmed down, I can do so appropriately in writing. For the next year, I suggest that such demands would be combined [and sent] earlier (setting a zero hour after which you do not accept further applications; similar to the way we intend to do) etc. And now to the point:

1. M. F. 'A.	Kafr Manda – appointed, he was invited to the committee on your recommendation – To [in] Tayibe al Marj.
2. K. A. N.	Deir Al-Assad – appointed, he was invited to the committee on your recommendation – To [in] Deir Al-Assad B (school).
3. R. H. Sh.	Jat – appointed in Myssar.
4. B. J. Al-H.	'Arara – dismissed from the seminar [teacher training college] because he failed in his studies. We cannot appoint him.
5. W. T. N.	Qalansawa – invited to the committee, found out to be in advanced pregnancy.
6. 'Abd Al Ja'far Naji Yunis	'Arara – was not appointed for security reasons.
7. J. M. Abd Al-F.	Was transferred on your recommendation.

Sincerely
Zvi Katz
In charge of Educational manpower

Copy to Uri Tahon
Advisor to the deputy Prime Minister and Minister of Education

(Katz, 1 December 1971)

The extraordinary decision of not employing the fourth candidate in the list – B. J. Al-H. – although he was recommended needed an explanation, which the following letter supplies. Interestingly, in his letter Katz, who was the official in charge, asked for the help and understanding of a political party's functionary regarding a decision he took within his realm of authority. This epitomizes the subordination of the official system to the surveillance agencies.

Thus, in his letter, Mr Katz states:

> It was decided following consultation with Mr. U. Tahon not to employ him in teaching in order not to impair the credibility of the college and its decision. It is impossible to appoint as a teacher someone who was deemed by the college teacher inappropriate, since he failed in his studies.

> I hope you understand this position and support us in such cases [in the future].
>
> Sincerely,
> Zvi Katz
> (Katz, 17 November 1971)

The criteria set by the surveillance agencies for the selection of candidates were known to the Palestinian public and graduates. Those who wished to get a teaching position knew what it entails. For example, one candidate, A. S. Tibi, who sent his curriculum vitae to Yaakov Eini, highlighted them. It seems that he was a fairly successful student. After receiving the Bagrut (standardized secondary school examinations) certificate, he pursued and successfully completed his studies at the teacher training college. However, he knew that his scholastic achievements would not by themselves guarantee him a job; thus, he referred to the criteria set by the surveillance agencies, whose representative he approached:

> I completed my studies in the college last year, and since then I am waiting for an appointment as a teacher.
>
> It should be stated that *I am not involved in politics. I have been all the time, and shall stay, a faithful citizen of the state.*
>
> As to *my social connections*: most of the teachers in the village are my friends, with whom I spend most of my (free) time.
>
> The Histadrut's secretary in the village of ... – 'A. R. Abu Rass – is my uncle. My other uncle, A. Abu Rass, is a policeman in the Israeli police. Both of them know me very well.
>
> I have all the documents and the certificates which attest to my excellence in the *studies and behaviour.*
>
> (Tibi, 13 June 1963; italics added)

The criteria for selection which this candidate thought were the main ones are, first, to be apolitical – which is taken as not being critical of the state or its policies. Yet, adoption of the official discourse was not seen as taking a political stand. Second, blood and social relations were weighty in determining the candidate's prospects and thus the reference to his uncles and friends.

Yet, the processes of selection and screening of candidates to the college, the socialization in the college and the selection of candidates for teaching were not seen by those in charge of the surveillance agencies as sufficient to ensure that Palestinian teachers impart the official educational messages. Therefore, surveillance was extended to schools. Informers were recruited among the teachers, pupils (even at a young age), headmasters, inspectors and parents (see the examples given by Cohen, 2006:169–86; Bauml, 2007:212–15; see also some of the cases appearing later in the text). In fact, teachers and principals were the second largest group among *Latam's* (a special police unit) informers in Galilee (Bauml, 2007:247). On various occasions, tables were constructed of the teachers, their addresses, social and blood relations and political leanings, as in the case of Kafr Qasim, in order to routinize their surveillance (Table 6.1).

Many such tables were compiled (e.g. Abu Hijla, 4 January 1966). The table of the teachers in the village of Jaljulia in the Triangle, composed in 1962, is extraordinary in one respect: only the political attitudes of the Jewish teachers who constituted one half of the teachers, including the headmaster and his deputy, were listed. It was also indicated that three teachers were to be transferred. One of them, Omar Khalid Shbeta, who was a communist and interestingly taught Islamic religion, was very popular. His transfer caused unrest in the village, and as an act of solidarity, the majority of the students – 70 per cent of them according to a surveillance report – conducted a one-day strike on Thursday, 1 November 1962 (Mishal, 1 November 1962).

Although I have not researched the period after 1968 methodically, there is strong evidence that such lists continued to be produced in the next decade. For example, one table included the names of all the teachers who taught in the mid-1970s[4] in the Galilean village of 'Arabba and those who were residents of the village but taught in other localities and their political attitudes. The list reveals that only five out of thirty-six teachers (less than 14 per cent) were not Labour Party supporters. Four were supporters of the National Religious Party and one had communist tendencies ('A List of the Teachers in 'Arabba', n.d.).

Despite the continuous surveillance, Palestinian teachers were not trusted. For example, Abba Hushi stated on 11 August 1960: 'Considerable proportion (I don't want to give an estimate) of the teachers are Israel's haters and they educate in this direction' (The Arab Affairs' Committee, 11 August 1960:1). Hushi's views were shared by his colleagues in the surveillance agencies (see, e.g., Bauml, 2007:213). For example, Palmon indicated at the end of 1952 that 10 per cent of Palestinian teachers held anti-Israeli attitudes (Benziman and Mansour, 1992:147). A wide array of actions was taken to prevent Palestinian teachers from transmitting messages deemed unacceptable. Besides the creation of an atmosphere of fear and suspicion, there were the continual processes of selection and screening. Teachers were evaluated on many occasions: when they applied for tenure or later in their careers for promotion, transfer to another school or locality, when they applied for an increase of their teaching hours, etc. Moreover, they were under the constant threat of transfer to faraway localities or dismissal.[5] For example in 1952, 42 out of the 685 Palestinian teachers were dismissed for 'abusing their position' (Abu-Saad, 2006:28–31; Cohen, 2006:169; Bauml,

Table 6.1 The list of teachers at Kafr Qasim's School
A School of fifteen classes including the kindergarten and a preparatory agricultural [class].
No. of pupils 562

No.	Teacher's name	Address	Party leaning	Remarks
1.	Ibraheem 'Abd Al-Kadir Shbeta	Tayibe –Natania	Mapai active	Refugee from the village of Miska near Tira
2.	Zakria Muhamad Amin Sarsur	Kafr Qasim	Mapai	The Mukhtar's nephew
3.	'Ab Al-Rahman Yousef Mohmad	Kafr Qasim	Unknown quiet	His father was killed during Kafr Qasim's operation – his brother is active in Mapam
4.	Omar Muhamad Yunis Bdair	Kafr Qasim	Mapai active	Previously was teacher in [the village of] Zalafa
5.	Sa'd Muhammad Wadi' Sarsur	Kafr Qasim	Mapai active	The Mukhtar's grandson
6.	Hamza Haj 'Ali Mustafa Sarsur	Kafr Qasim	Mapai active	His father was member in the first local council
7.	'Ab Al-Latif Habayib Issa	Kafr Qasim	Mapai active	Close to the mayor
8.	Kamil Haj Mustafa Khatib	Jaljulia [village]	Mapai active	Graduate of kaduri school – agricultural instructor
9.	Omar Khalid Shbeta	Tira [village]	Leftist – unaffiliated to any political party	Has leftist view and is influential among the youth of Tira
10.	Amina 'Abid Al-Nashif	Tiba-Natania	Unidentified	A kindergarten teacher
11.	Taha Said rabi	Jaljulia	Leftist inactive	A relative of Yousef Rabi Jaljulia's mayor
12.	Eliahu Deshit (Iraqi Jew)	Petah-Tikva	T"R	5 years teacher in Kafr Qasim
13.	Zion Darwish Atar (Iraqi Jew)	Mgd	Mapai	6 years teacher in Kafr Qasim
14.	Salim Nakar (Iraqi jew)	Petah-Tikva	Mapai	2 years teacher in Kafr Qasim
15.	Na'ima Shmouel (Iraqi Jew)	Rammat-Gan	?	Kindergarten [teacher]

'A List of Teachers in Kafr Qasim School', September 1960

2007:213–14) – a euphemism for airing opinions that were considered critical of state policies. This precarious existence led some teachers to display over-loyalty (Bauml, 2007:210–11), while others were pushed to collaborate, thus becoming both active subjects and objects of surveillance. The principle of favour for a favour that the surveillance agencies employed in every stage of screening was a powerful tool that kept the wheels of surveillance rolling. The case of Abd Al-A. Q. from the village of Q., who endured harsh work conditions and asked for transfer, is illustrative. On 11 October 1960, he sent the following letter to Yaakov Eini:

> Q. village 11 October 1960
>
> Ha-Havir Yaakov Eini
>
> I work as a teacher in the village of Salim. I am one of the graduates of the teacher training college. Every day I pay 3.600 Lira for transportation. I am working part-time ... and I walk everyday more than 8 km from the bus stop to the school.
>
> Dear Sir, Some of my friends approached you regarding my transfer to a closer village and you promised to help me. Eventually I ask your help with the in-charge persons.
>
> My hope pends on your help.
>
> Sincerely, Abd Al-A. Q.
> (Q. Abd Al-A, 11 October 1960)

This teacher was transferred to his village and became – as shall be described later – an informer. He befriended some dissident teachers (most notably Salih Baransi) and passed on to Mapai's Arab Department information about their plans, activities and thoughts.

A similar case is that of A. M. Kh. from the village of Baqa Al-Gharbia, who worked for six years in a remote school in the Negev desert. When he attempted to return to his village in 1966 and become a principal of a newly established school or one in an adjacent village, the price, it seems, was information. He began to pass on information about teachers in Baqa's school who had 'negative' attitudes and collaborated with or were members of Mapam, such as the deputy principal Nasoh Abu-Mukh (Khaw, 9 March 1966). Another object of his surveillance was the Arabic language teacher Faroq Ibrahim Mawasi, who reportedly read to his students *unauthorized* poetry which highlights 'Arab' virtues of courage and steadfastness (Khaw, 21 June 1966).

Yet, the granting of rewards by the surveillance agencies was not always straightforward or automatic. On some occasions, they postponed the granting of help in order to aggravate the condition of the collaborator in order to increase his collaboration. The following letter was sent by A. A. S. Abu-Mukh from Baqa Al-Gharbia on 25 December 1964. Although his fortunes were not improving, he kept spying and sending information:

> I am A.S. Abu-Mukh from Baqa Al-Gharbia, graduated from the secondary school in 1954/5 ... [then he details the various jobs he undertook in a shop in firemen's station etc. and in 1959 in the health center in Baqa Al-Gharbia], I was fired and in 1961 I submitted an application to the [Arab] department of education to become a drawing [art] teacher, but didn't meet success. I resubmitted my application in December 1964 and I hope I'll be successful and become a drawing teacher.
>
> I worked in the Histadrut's club between 1959 and 1963, and worked during the election in support of the Arab lists associated with Mapai, and I had contacts with the Communist Party mainly to pass on information to the concerned people, such as his honor the military governor. ... I hope you will help me to become a teacher of drawing in an Arab school.
>
> Thankfully Abd. S. Abu-Mukh.
> (Abu-Mukh, 25 December 1964)

A different form of surveillance and control was conducted through the employment of Jewish immigrant teachers from the Arab countries in Arab schools. They were thought of as natural messengers, who would impart the official educational message, a view that was openly stated by Abba Hushi in 1960: '... simply – I want a Jewish teacher to teach loyalty to the state and good citizenship. ... The educator, for example, would be a Jew, while the teacher who teaches other subjects such as mathematics would be an Arab' (The Arab Affairs' Committee, 11 August 1960:2). Indeed, following the arrival of 'Oriental' Jews (principally from Iraq) to Israel, some 360 immigrant teachers who had always taught in Arabic were sent to teach in Arab schools (*ibid.*:10). Yet, their majority left within a few years. By 1962 only sixty-five remained (The Arab Affairs' Committee, 1 February 1962:2), as many of them were discovered to be communists and their dismissal was not carried out without difficulties. According to Uri Lubrani, 'They were worse than non-Jewish teachers' (*ibid.*). Indeed, the tables of surveillance discussed earlier show that Jewish teachers who taught in Arab schools were under surveillance similar to their Palestinian colleagues.

Surveillance and control took a totalizing form as Palestinian teachers were not allowed to show dissent, not only in the messages they transmitted in the classroom and outside it but also with regard to their professional life. Although they were members of the Histadrut-affiliated teachers' union, they were barred from taking part in the industrial actions this union undertook (Bauml, 2007:214). They were quarantined even in the teachers' union, and their affairs were handled by Eliahu Barak, a Mapai functionary. Regarding his management of Palestinian teachers' affairs, he stated:

> [T]hroughout the years of this section's existence [ten years], the minorities did not have any say in the teachers' union, and they have no authority to intervene in their own affairs. ... I receive orders from the general secretary and thus this section is run by Mapai. (The Secretariat of the Arab Affairs' Committee, n.d.)

Moreover, they were allowed neither to establish their own party in the union without hindrance nor to select their representatives freely. Rather, in elections for the teachers' union – as in the general elections – they were pressured to vote for Mapai's affiliated lists. An initiative by some teachers to establish an independent party was harassed by the surveillance agency (*ibid.*:214–15). The following letter by the informer Abd Al-A. Q., mentioned earlier, illustrates the deep surveillance. It is a report on discussions that a group of teachers held on the forthcoming elections for the teachers' union.

> Friday, 2 December 1961. In café Anthropya in Natania during the pre-midday hours at 11:30, some teachers gathered around two tables, including:

1.	Salih Baransi	Resident of Tayibe	
2.	Ahmad 'Ali Dussoqi	"	
3.	'Abd Al-Fatah Mussa	"	Works in Mu'aawia
4.	Ahmad Anqr	"	Works in Qalansawa
5.	Gazi Al-Tibi	"	Works in Baqa
6.	Faisal 'Abd Allah Natour	Resident of Qalansawa	Works in Baqa
7.	Husni Rafiq Natour	"	Works in Musherfa
8.	'Abd Al-Hamid 'Abd Al-Rahman Farouga	"	Works in Faradis

> The conversation revolved around the forthcoming elections for the teachers' union. Salih Baransi was the main figure in the meeting. He asked the participants to be faithful and not betray their Arab nationalism ... and said we must free ourselves of the tails (i.e. collaborators) of Mapai and the [Military] Government.
>
> Salih insinuated that a democratic list might be formed, however, if it does not, [they should vote] for Maki (the communist party) ...
>
> Two teachers: 1. Ahmad 'Ali Dussoqi 2. 'Ab Al-Fatah Musa support Baransi's view which is to vote for Maki.
>
> The teachers: 1. Gazi Al-Tibi 2. Faisal Natour 3. Husni Natour, thought that the list of young teachers headed by 'Abd Al-Latif Habib Mussarwa should be supported. Faisal Natour said: We are also democratic teachers, and similar to Mr. Salih we are against the Military Government and against Mapai. However, we should at first pretend to be Mapai supporters. If our list fails (Habib's list), there will be no option other than supporting Maki.

> The teachers: 1. Gazi Al-Tibi 2. Husni Natour, are in favor of Faisal Natour.
>
> The two teachers: 1. Ahmad Anqar, 2. 'Ab Al-Hamid Farouga, think that there is no alternative to Maki or at least to a democratic list.
>
> When the meeting ended, Salih left accompanied by two teachers: 1. Ahmad 'Ali Dussoqi, 2. 'Ab Al-Fatah Musa
>
> I think they are good friends of Salih.
>
> (Q. Abd Al-A, 22 December 1961)[6]

To stop this grassroots initiative of establishing an Arab list – which took place in 1961–62 – the surveillance and control agencies took various measures. First, they stepped up the collection of information on the actual and potential supporters of the democratic list. And, indeed, various tables of the names of such teachers were compiled. Second, they tried to disqualify it on legal ground. One way to do so was by providing evidence that the list of supporters that it compiled to the election committee was faked. Pressure was employed on teachers who endorsed the democratic list either to withdraw their support or to endorse a Mapai-affiliated Arab list and in this way to invalidate their support to the democratic list.[7] Third, they brought the Mapai-dominated election committee of the teachers' union to vote on disallowing the democratic list from contesting the elections. Yet, this decision was reversed by the court.

Fourth, they established an Arab list affiliated to Mapai. And, indeed, a list named 'fraternity and reform' contested the elections and was headed by Abdullah Latif Habib, Shareif Du'san and 'Abd Al-Ruhman Haj-Yihya, who duly came to Mapai's regional office to express 'their loyalty to the Party [Mapai] ... and their readiness to cooperate with the Arab section [of the teachers' union]' (The Arab Department, 15 June 1962).

Nonetheless, in the elections held in June 1962, the democratic list received 24.5 per cent of Palestinian teachers' votes. Retaliatory measures were taken against its representatives and supporters including dismissal; for example, three of its four elected representatives were dismissed without compensations (Abu-Saad, 2006:31–3). Beyond these immediate measures, reflecting the attitude of the surveillance agencies, Yaakov Eini (1962) wrote:

> It would be misleading to explain these results by the propaganda which focused on one issue '*the abolishment of the Arab teachers' section in the Histadrut*', that Maki and Mapam waged, and their attacks on this section and its chairman Mr. E. Barak.
>
> I suppose the relevant bodies should give expression to their attitude towards this grave development (and it is good that it has been unveiled), to uncover its real causes, to pinpoint the weaknesses and to decide on ways of action, which should form a dam to stop this trend. (Eini, 3 July 1962:5)

Pupils too were under surveillance by some of their peers, teachers – who were obliged to report to the school's headmaster – and headmasters (see, e.g., 'The Eichmann Affair in Jat School', 29 May 1960[8]). Probably the well-known case of Mahmoud Darwish, who later became Palestine's national poet, is illustrative. When he was a 12-year-old elementary school pupil, he wrote a poem on the state's foundation anniversary. The poem depicted the huge gulf that separates the lives of Jewish and Arab children. His poem was addressed to an imaginary Jewish peer and basically said: 'you can play in the sun as you please, and have your toys, but I can't. You have a house, and I have none. You have celebrations, but I have none. Why can't we play together?' Darwish's words reached the military governor, who summoned him and threatened him: 'If you go on writing such poetry, I'll stop your father working in the quarry' (Shehadeh, 2002; Clark, 11 August 2008). This deep surveillance – surveillance that targets the intimate and private thought which is expressed in an atmosphere where trust ought to prevail, such as in the classroom – was publicly exposed by Prime Minister Ben-Gurion, who read from the copybooks of Palestinian pupils, in which they expressed dissent, in the course of his speech in the Knesset on 20 February 1963 (Bauml, 2007:213, 248).

Beyond these measures, a desire always lurked within those in charge of surveillance to formulate an integrative plan of surveillance and control through the educational system.

Towards an integrative plan

Abba Hushi, who served as the chairman of Mapai's Arab department in the 1960s, undertook this assignment. He composed a comprehensive plan on 20 May 1960 to solve myriad aspects of the Palestinian minority's status in Israel, particularly in education. In the section of education, as well as in the amendments introduced to it and the ensuing discussions which were held with those in charge on surveillance, he addressed many of the issues which were discussed previously. His approach, dubbed 'integration', was modelled on the surveillance methods which were employed in mixed settings – such as the teachers' union – namely to integrate Palestinians in a joint Jewish–Arab system in which Jews, including persons who are not officially part of the surveillance apparatuses, would conduct mundane surveillance and control activities. The plan states:

> Substantive but gradual change of the educational system for Arab children and youth.
>
> 1. Substitution of the old textbooks in Arab schools by new ones, which are to be compatible with the textbooks in Jewish schools.
> 2. Gradual change of all inspectors in the educational system in Arab localities.

3. In mixed localities – one unified school should serve all children – from kindergarten through secondary education (special hours will be dedicated for the study of religion for Arab pupils whose parents wish so).
4. In order to raise the educational level in all schools in the Arab localities and to ensure education for good citizenship and loyalty to the state, Jewish and Arab teachers and headmasters with appropriate [educational] standards will be employed in these schools. Moreover, a single curriculum for all schools will be introduced.
5. The teacher training colleges will be mixed (Jewish–Arab) and maintain equivalent standards.
6. All post-elementary schools – agricultural, vocational or general – will be mixed and accessible to all children, Jews and Arabs.
7. Proportional fees will be decided for all secondary school students, with the participation of the Ministry of Education and local authorities. (Various versions of this plan are available. This document was intended for internal discussions; Hushi, 27 May 1960)

The premises and the motives behind this plan were unfolded during the meeting of the Committee on Arab Affairs on 11 August 1960 (The Arab Affairs' Committee, 11 August 1960). In the ensuing discussions, Hushi disclosed that his plan was premised on two principles: first, 'to establish in mixed cities a single Israeli, or as Ben-Gurion maintained, Jewish school' (*ibid.*:1–2). Second, to appoint Jewish teachers in Arab schools to teach for 'loyalty to the state and good citizenship' (*ibid.*:2). Accordingly, Hushi thought 'that the inspectors should be on the whole Jews, [adding that he] did not want to put this in writing' (*ibid.*:4). Haddad – an émigré of Iraqi origin – with a rich experience in education both in Iraq and Israel who worked, then, in the Histadrut brought to light the hidden control agenda of the plan. He argued that 'Our interest is that he [the Palestinian pupil] becomes good Israeli citizen, but remains Arab' (*ibid.*:10). Moreover, he maintained that integration is not possible: 'If we implant in Arab youth a Hebrew consciousness and if their parents agree, wouldn't this contradict the orientation of the state of Israel?' (*ibid.*). Haddad's naive comments might reflect his status as an outsider to the circle of those in charge of the surveillance agencies. Integration has never been envisaged as a state's sponsored programme of citizenship; rather, it meant Palestinians' acceptance of the Zionist discourse and their subordinate status. Indeed, Moshe Dayan, who supported the plan, made this explicit, emphasizing that 'My approach is this is not a bi-national state rather the state of Israel' (*ibid.*:5).

Hushi's plan was daring and its consequences were too risky. Therefore, it was not implemented. Yet, he performed a small-scale experiment in his own town of Haifa. A school – called Ironi Alef – where Jewish and Arab students studied in parallel classes and were taught by Jewish teachers began to operate in 1961. Moreover, the municipality was able to secure a fund for scholarships to the Arab pupils (*Davar*, 30 June 1960). However, it seems that the Palestinian students were alienated (e.g. Halabi, 2006:8) and only a small minority of them embraced 'Israeli patriotism'.[9]

University students

The number of Palestinian students throughout the studied period was small. For example, in 1956/1957, there were no more than forty-six Palestinian students, and in 1962, there were some eighty students. Their share among the general population of students remained negligible throughout the discussed period. In 1971, their proportion was 1.7 per cent (Bauml, 2007:302). The university as an autonomous institution that supposedly upheld a culture of freedom, universalism and meritocracy should have mitigated the surveillance over Palestinian students or at least decreased its intensity or altered its mode. Indeed, the students' dean at the Hebrew University, the largest university in Israel, asserted, in line with these principles, that the university's authorities and bureaucracy are 'nationality blind'; they cannot distinguish between Jewish and Palestinian students (*ibid.*). Yet, the dean's statement is fallacious. Not only did the university's authorities and bureaucracy know the national identity of the students, but they actively collaborated with the surveillance agencies in monitoring Palestinian students. For example, the academic secretary of the university (who sits in the dean's office) used to send to the office of the Prime Minister's Advisor on Arab Affairs the information available to the university on Palestinian students. The table headed Minority students (Arab and Druze) included the following information: The categorization of the students according to faculties. Then in each faculty the following information was provided: student's name, number in the university's registry, academic year of education, subject(s) he or she studied, permanent address and address in Jerusalem (The Academic Secretariat, the Hebrew University, 1964).[10] In later tables, the ID number of each student was added.[11]

The pattern of surveillance that was employed in mixed settings was reinstituted at the campus. In 1958/1959, Palestinian students established their own society – the Arab Students' Committee. As a representative body of Palestinians, it was unfavourably viewed by the surveillance apparatuses. To decrease its lure, Mapai established shortly after that the Jewish–Arab students' forum '*Hoog ha-studentim ha-Yuhidi-Aravi*', which included some twenty to thirty students mostly Palestinians. The forum was headed by a Jewish student – Michael Lindenstrauss – who was in fact an emissary of Yaakov Eini, the chairperson of Mapai's Arab department. Eini had to approve all documents and activities of the forum. For example, on 8 June 1959, Lindenstrauss finished composing the forum's guidelines, and on the same day, he forwarded it to Eini to register his remarks, which were to be incorporated in the document before the 14th of July when it was scheduled for discussion in the forum's assembly (Lindenstrauss, 8 July 1959). Eini asked for the removal of the faint call for the abolishment of the Military Government. Moreover, he emphasized the forum's independence of outside political intervention which, as always, meant the influence of non-Mapai organizations (Bauml, 2007:304, offers a similar interpretation).

The forum offered Palestinian students a package of benefits in return for their good behaviour. The benefits included the granting of passes, income and recommendations for jobs. The following exchange of letters between Lindenstrauss and Eini is illustrative. They revolve around the granting of a travel pass to a Palestinian student who was a member of this forum:

27 March 1959

To
Ha-Havir Yaakov Eini
Mapai Headquarter
Ha Yarkon 110
Tel-Aviv

The Havir (friend/member) Mazin Mahmud Nashif from Tayibe asked us for a recommendation to the Military Government regarding the extension of his permanent [movement] permit No. 20568, and adding to it [its conditions] 'to all [parts of] the country except the security area'.

Ha-Havir Mazin Mahmud Nashif had recently begun his activities in the Jewish–Arab Students' Forum and through us he filed this request for help.

I'll be most grateful if you deal with it.

Comradely regards
Micha Lindenstrauss
The secretariat of the student's cell
(Lindenstrauss, 27 March 1959)

The answer was dispatched four days later:

31 March 1959

To Ha-Havir Micha Lindenstrauss
The Workers' Party of Eritz Yisrael [Mapai]

Jerusalem

Your letter of 27 March 59

We have dealt with the issue and the request will be positively answered.

Comradely regards
Yaakov Eini
(Eini, 31 March 1959)

This exchange shows that within four days, a comprehensive travel permit was approved for a student who was branded as positive.

Moreover, Palestinian members of the forum were to be employed in Hasbara – giving lectures in Palestinian villages – as those in charge of surveillance held the belief that educated natives are more effective in the battle over the hearts and minds of Palestinians than Jewish officials (Lindenstrauss, 19 April 1959). To prepare them for this assignment, several key figures of those who laid down the surveillance and control strategies, such as Sharett and Abba Hushi, were invited to meet with the forum's members and give lectures.

Despite all this, those in charge of the surveillance were not ready to ease their pressure off the Arab Students' Committee, and the measures to derail it persisted. The first strategy was to control it by contesting the Committee's elections with a list of Palestinian students who were members of the forum. Yet, the list that Lindenstrauss had jointly prepared with Eini, which was fashioned on the official categorization of Palestinians and included representatives of the various religious groups (Muslim, Christian and Druze), was not successful, thus highlighting the main issue of contention, which was the definition of Palestinian students: are they a collection of minorities or Palestinian students (Lindenstrauss, 7 December 1959)?

This unsuccessful attempt led to a rethinking of the status of the Palestinian Students' Committees at the universities. In December 1962, a decisive strategy was laid down regarding the handling of Palestinian students. In the meeting between officials of the Advisor's Office and the overarching union of the Israeli students, three decisions were taken: first, non-recognition of the Arab Students' Committees at the universities by the students' unions of the various universities, the authorities of the universities as well as the general union of Israeli students; second, the 'election' of an Arab representative(s) to the union of students who would not be conceived as a traitor, but who would be able to resist calls for his resignation; and third, the appointment of an appropriate student who would 'volunteer' to work in the cultural and the housing committees at the students' union and who will be paid by the Prime Minister's Office. His work in these committees would be a cover for his real job of monitoring and surveillance of Palestinian students (Bauml, 2007:305–6). Indeed, the names of the Arab students who would be 'elected' to the students' union were decided by the surveillance and control agencies in collaboration with the secretaries of the students' union. For example, in July 1971, David Zakharia, the chairman of the Ma'arach (previously Mapai) Arab department, sent a letter to Dani Korin, the General Secretary of the students' union, with the names of Arab students whom he thought ought to be nominated for the forthcoming elections:

> In case my suggestion is reasonable, I suggest that we invite the candidates for a meeting to formally nominate them and discuss with them their future role and status.
>
> Sincerely David Zakharia
>
> *Tel-Aviv University*
> 1. Mustafa Ghanaym — Baqa Al-Gharbia
> 2. Qusai Husni Kabaha — Barta'a
> 3. Arafat Musor [probably Mansour] — Tira
>
> *Bar-Ilan University*
> 1. Galal Abu-Tuma — Baqa Al-Gharbia
> 2. Walid Sabri 'Athamna — Kafr Qari'
> 3. Said Husan Qasim — Tayibe
>
> *Haifa University*
> 1. Gamal Tarabi — Sakhnin
> 2. Muhammad Musa Diab — Tamra
>
> (Zakharia, 24 June 1971)

Although it seems that most students were then involved in students' politics, eventually, this politics is confined to the small domain of the campuses. Yet, the surveillance apparatuses thought otherwise; the methods they employed seem to reflect their view of the reality as what Gramsci has called 'war of positions' – a tenacious struggle over the consciousness of Palestinians where a section of Palestinian academics and the state took opposing positions. Reflecting this attitude, the Arabist Eliyahu Sasson of the Foreign Ministry stated on 1 February 1962: 'The educated – This category includes secondary school graduates and literate people. I'd call them nationalist; we cannot leave this element [group] for itself' (The Arab Affairs' Committee, 1 February 1962:4). The Office of the Prime Minister's Advisor kept records of Palestinian students which were supplied by the universities. They helped the Advisor's Office as well as other surveillance apparatuses in monitoring Palestinian students. In these records, the students were classified according to the binary division of positive/radical. Moreover, these lists allowed them to track the political activists. For example, on 16 March 1972, elections were held for the Arab Students' Committee at Tel-Aviv University. On the 20th, a letter was sent to David Zakharia, the head of the Arab department, which listed Palestinian students at all Israeli universities with the categorization of their attitudes and the names of those elected to the committee. Table 6.2 provides a sample for illustration.

Table 6.2 Students at Tel-Aviv University in 1972 and their categorization as positive/negative

1.	Muhammad Kewan	Um al-Fahim – radical Al-Ard
2.	Nazeer Yunis	'Ara – radical
3.	Saeed 'Atele	Tira, influenced by Muhammad Kewan – radical
4.	Nabil Hanna Ibrahim	Raina – radical
5.	Sami Ka'war	Yafa – radical – Rakah – his father too
6.	R. Y. Jbara	Tayibe – weak – works in the library
7.	Rasmi Bayadsi	Baqa – positive
8.	Husni Bayadsi	Baqa – positive
9.	'Abd Al-Karim Al-Dhahir	Tayibe – positive
10.	'Adnan 'Amsha	Tayibe – positive
11.	George Qara	Jaffa – positive – law second year

Meir Mishal'
(Mishal, 20 March 1972; see another list by Dan-Gur, 29 June 1971[12])

The classification of Palestinian students to the negative/positive binary bore particular significance with regard to the awarding of scholarships where the surveillance apparatuses exercised direct influence as well as when they entered the labour market. Already since the mid-1950s, those in charge of the surveillance agencies thought that unemployment among educated Palestinians could lead to the radicalization of the Palestinian community as a whole, particularly given the role of political and moral leadership they attributed to the 'intelligentsia' (see chapter 2). To insure the awarding of jobs for the 'positive elements', and to prevent misidentification due to the multiplicity of the surveillance agencies, the minister Bechor Sheetrit proposed in 1960 to establish a 'multiple-entry [data base], with all these name [of educated Arabs], and it is important that this data base is reviewed occasionally. If a person is rejected for any reason, his name should be removed from the data base. The same procedure would also apply when we add a new person' (The Arab Affairs' Committee, 4 May 1962:9–10).

Indeed, the majority of the students, in these tables, who were classified as positive occupied or continue to occupy prestigious positions. Meanwhile, those who gave expression to their 'radicalism' were punished, such as in the cases of Husan Amun and Ahmad Renawi. Amun's case occurred amidst a campaign by Palestinian students and graduates of boycotting the chairman of Histadrut's Arab departments, Nahum Yahlom, on the grounds of their employment difficulties. Yahlom decided to change the format of his meetings with Palestinians (Haro'veni, 9 August 1960). Instead of mass meetings with Palestinians which were usually attended by Military Government officials and Mapai politicians, he planned to hold a series of small meetings. In the meeting of 11 August 1960, held in Rama area in Galilee, Amun – a student of medicine – pointed to the discrimination against Palestinians in the provision of health services and generally criticized the attitude of the Histadrut's Arab department towards Palestinian citizens. Amun's comments led to unwelcome lively debates, which on the whole showed that Yahlom was not doing properly what he regarded as his job. This meeting spurred strong anti-Palestinian statements by Uri Lubrani, the Advisor to the Prime Minister on Arab Affairs, as well as an order by Mr Yihushua Wrabin, the Northern district military governor, of banishing Amun not only from his village of Deir Al-Asad but from the entire Rama area for an unlimited period (Kardosh, September 1960; see also *Al-Mussawar*, 9 October 1960).

The case of Renawi occurred two months later. His offense was the authoring of an introduction to a book by Faraj Nur Salman entitled *Innocents and Executioners*. The book, a collection of short stories, details the mundane life of the Palestinians under the military rule. Renawi was studying medicine and the developments of his affair are not entirely clear. Yet, a report by Meir Mishal, a functionary in Mapai's Arab department, composed almost two years later, shed some light on it. An order was issued to prevent his father from enlarging his house. This order was linked to the introduction he authored:

> Tawfiq Said Bsool Id number 2/73939
>
> Married and father to 12 children
>
> Occupation: Farmer (and popular poet/singer) [who performs in weddings]. He lives in [a house composed of] two rooms ... (With a solid roof).
>
> Party tendency: Mapai – he is active during election campaigns except the campaign for the fifth Knesset (he claimed). His son Ahmad Tawfiq Al-Renawi studied medicine at the University of Jerusalem. Today he is doing his training at the Hospital of 'Afula Ilit. A radical nationalist (participated with Faraj Nur Salman in publishing the book *Innocents and Executioners*).
>
> Tawfiq Bsool began to build a house without permit and when the bases were laid down he was ordered to halt the construction work. This person is known to Yaakov Eini from a travel together to Turkey.
>
> (Mishal, 3 July 1962)

This report is puzzling. Why should a farmer and a father of twelve children travel to Turkey with an influential person in the surveillance apparatus? How could he travel abroad when the majority of the Palestinians were unable to move beyond the borders of their localities? And, most importantly, is there any relation between the son's ideological leanings and the order the father received to halt the construction of his house? Interestingly, the father did not appeal against the order to the Military Government, but rather, he pleaded with Mapai's Arab department which was headed by Eini (*ibid.*).

The surveillance organizations have also influenced the acceptance of Palestinian students to universities. Their impact on universities, however, was less direct and overbearing than on Arab teacher training colleges. Still, they tried to influence universities' decision by using the rationale of surveillance, which implies that rewards should be given to 'positive elements' as suggested by the following letter which was sent to a high-up person in the administration of Tel-Aviv University:

> 11.3.1973
>
> To Mr. Amnon Golan
> The legal advisor of Tel-Aviv University
>
> Dear Sir:
>
> Mr. Fan. Abd Allah M. M. A. from the village of Kafr Qar'i in the Triangle ID.5xxxxx02 submitted an application to study sociology and law. The Fan. family is known to us as loyal and positive and we are interested in helping this person to be accepted to Tel-Aviv University.
>
> I'll be grateful if you help in this matter.
>
> David Zakharia
> Head of the Arab department
> (Zakharia, 11 March 1973)

Yet, by the late 1970s and 1980s, the Ma'arach lost its hegemonic status in Israel, and it no longer controlled the surveillance and control apparatuses. The rewards they could offer were through personal ties that their leaders and activists had established with influential persons in various state or public institutions. Such rewards were mostly bribes given to people in exchange for voting and persuading their associates to vote for the Ma'arach. For example, a note scribbled on a small sheet of paper written in 1981 exemplifies this exchange. It indicates that 'R. A. 'A ID 5xxxxx7 from the village of Tira wishes to study humanities and biology at Tel-Aviv University. His Bagrut marks are high' (to be dealt with by Aharon Shoush). Another note included the names of persons who wished to study in the teacher training college 'Na'im, Dawoud, Faroq'. These demands were to be submitted to 'Abd Al-Kareem (most likely 'Abd Al-Kareem Al-Dahir, the head of the Arab teacher training college at Beit Berl; these notes are found in the file 26/16/22 in the Labour Party's Archive).

Messages

Almost since the beginning of the existence of official Zionist organizations in Palestine, they engaged in the battle of ideas and tried to influence Palestinians' public opinion. In the Palestine's office of the World Zionist Organization which Dr. Ruppin established in 1908, one of the junior staff, Nissim Malul, was employed in monitoring and translating articles which appeared in the Arabic press on Zionism (Ro'i, 1968:200). Since 1911, they not only monitored articles and sent rebuttals but also endeavoured to buy off Palestinian newspaper owners, editors, columnists, journalists and men of letters (Cohen, 2004:30–3). In March 1937, the Histadrut began publishing the Arabic weekly *Haqiqat Al-Amr* (The Truth of the Matter). It was distributed free of charge in various official venues and Jewish settlements and was mailed to Palestinian teachers. Its publication continued until the 1960s (Lockman, 1996:253–7; Yu and Cohen, 2009:191).

The belief that the Zionist leadership had in the role that the intelligentsia, newspapers and books played in the evolvement of Palestinian nationalism continued to influence its policies after 1948. Already in May 1949, a committee which investigated the Military Government's functioning recommended the omission from the curriculum of educational subjects which might stir up national sentiments and substituted them by general or Hebrew (i.e. Jewish) ones. Moreover, it recommended the imposition of the curriculum used in Jewish education on the Arab one, the teaching of Hebrew language in Arab schools and the preparation of new adequate books. It also recommended the employment of Jewish teachers in Arab schools (Benziman and Mansour, 1992:146). In a similar vein, Ben-Zvi indicated in the second meeting of members of Knesset (MKs) and the Secretariat of Mapai on 9 July 1950 that '....We must impose the Hebrew language on the Arabs. ... We want a state whose language and culture are Hebrew for the citizen and for the stranger who lives with us, for the Jew and for the non-Jew' (The Secretariat's Meeting with MKs, 9 July 1950:5/1). Obviously, the language had been conceived as more than a means of communication. The imparting of Hebrew was thought of as a tool for creating an intellectual and cognitive milieu through which control could smoothly proceed.

At the same meeting, Emanuel Moor of the Military Government thought that assimilation was not possible unless it is done by 'drastic measures':

> Until today, two years following our dealing with this subject, schools are still using the book *Fa-aqoom Li-Filisteen* (I stand for Palestine). This means that there are no textbooks composed by us, this means that the teachers are the same from the Mandatory period and we are not inspecting enough what they teach. (*Ibid.*:5/3)

Moor highlighted the issue of 'appropriate' textbooks, which would be discussed in various forums for many years thereafter. One of the idioms that were invoked was 'good citizenship stems from three sources: home, school and textbooks' (e.g. used by Haddad mentioned earlier). Yet, interestingly, not much was done during the first decade, probably because of the assumption that Palestinians will be transferred. By 1953, only one new book was published (Jiryis, 1976:207), and until 1960, four new books in natural sciences and a book of citizenship education were issued (The Arab Affairs' Committee, 11 August 1960:9). The unsurprising result was confusion among educators and pupils. Only in 1966, when the Military Government was terminated, were all the books for the elementary level (classes one to eight) available (Jiryis, 1976:207).

While the surveillance apparatuses were able to impose certain books on Palestinian pupils, they were not able to do so for the wider readership due to the publication of Arabic books by other Zionist groups (principally Mapam) and the Communist Party. For example, Mapam began since the late 1950s reissuing and marketing books that were published in Egypt. These books were seen by the Histadrut's functionaries as conveying 'provocative' messages, and it was reported that they sold nicely (The Arab Affairs' Committee, 11 August 1960:9). To counter this, a wide-ranging plan regarding cultural activity was prepared. Some of the funds for the plan were to be raised from Arab workers. Additional funds were to be supplied by the Histadrut and the Hasbara department (The Arab Affairs' Committee, 12 September 1957:15–16). Eliahu Agassi of the Histadrut's Arab department was asked to undertake various steps to regain Mapai's lead in this field. He was entrusted to import books and to inquire, with Sharett, regarding the publication of Arabic books by the Histadrut's publishing house Am-Oved (The Confined Committee of the Arab Affairs' Committee, 30 March 1958:2).

In 1960, the Ministry of Education allotted a substantial fund of 30,000 IL for the translation of books from Hebrew to Arabic (The Arab Affairs' Committee, 11 August 1960:9). And, indeed, a considerable number of books were translated. For example, by 1964, 75 books were written or translated in Israel, and by 1971, 128 such books were available (Jiryis, 1976:207).

Yet, books were not the only medium for the publication of literary works and the propagation of ideas. Television, which arrived in Palestinian localities in the early 1960s, and newspapers and periodicals comprised the main sources. By means of the TV, Palestinians were reconnected to the outside world through Arab TV stations, particularly Egyptian channels. Moreover, they were exposed to news, ideas and representations which very often were at odds with the official Israeli version. In this regard, Yaakov Cohen of the Histadrut's Arab department stated:

> A probe ought to be conducted with regard to the existence of the Television in Um Al-Fahim, where for 50 *Prota* [penny] Arabs can watch Nassir, and they watch Lebanese TV stations. ... The Arabs acquire their consciousness from venues which are not associated with us. (The Arab Affairs' Committee, 1 February 1962:7)

The other sources were newspapers and periodicals, particularly those which were published by the Communist Party and Mapam. However, these were Israeli publications, which existed within the Israeli context and were subjected to censorship. Still, their criticism of the state's policies troubled those in charge of the surveillance agencies. One innovative solution to this was the organization since May 1962 of groups of what came to be known as talk-backers among 'positive' Palestinians. Thus, Agassi stated that 'in the last weeks we decided to establish a debate section in the cities of Nazareth and Acre and the village of Kafr Yassif' (The Arab Affairs' Committee, 4 May 1962:12). These were supposed to discuss the critical articles which appear in *Al-Mirsad* (of Mapam) and *Al-Ittihad* (of the Communist Party) and propose answers, which would be published in a special section in *Al-Yom* (*ibid.*). However, Moshe Dayan was suspicious regarding this tactical solution. Witty answers do not, after all, comprise a substitution for a strategy, thus stating:

> The question is, whether it is a Jewish newspaper for the Arabs or an Arabic newspaper that ought to give expression to the Arabs. ... These are two different things. One thing is to publish a newspaper in Arabic for the Arabs, which explain our viewpoint to the Arabs. Yet, another thing, an Arab newspaper that deals with Arab issues, with anti-Nassir position, but deals with their affairs, from their sectarian perspective. (*Ibid.*:15)

Of course Dayan knew that *Al-Yom* was a mouthpiece of the surveillance apparatuses. Therefore, unsurprisingly, along with the changes in the surveillance strategies, *Al-Yom* and similar publications declined. After the termination of the Military Government in 1966, it was only a matter of time until *Al-Yom* lost its raison d'être. On 6 June 1968, Tolidano expressed a negative appraisal of the newspaper:

> This is not a newspaper. It is a disgrace. ... Three quarters of the newspaper are dedicated for notifications. There is no information. There are only the headlines which are broadcasted in the radio. The articles are not directed by a single person (*he means there is no editorial line*) it sells poorly. In the village of Tayibe only a single copy is sold and in Israel and the [Occupied] Territories only 2500 copies are sold. In short this is a bad newspaper and its circulation is limited. (The Arab Affairs' Committee, 6 June 1968:2)

Al-Yom was followed by *Al-Anbaa* (The News), which was published between 1968 and 1985. The *Al-Anbaa* editor, during its heydays – that is, the early 1970s – when it projected a liberal pluralistic stance, summed up its strategy as conducting a psychological warfare:

> Do you want the newspaper to follow the lead of the government's TV and radio broadcasts in Arabic? This is not the proper place to lecture you on the essentials of psychological warfare, but suffice to say that the major rule of psychological warfare is: to give the listener or the viewer whatever you want to give, in small

> pieces, nicely concealing the target. This is what we are doing in the newspaper. *In other words we are washing the brains according to the theory of psychological warfare.* (Quoted in Yu and Cohen, 2009:199; emphasis in the origin).

The eventual collapse of such organs occurred well after the period studied here, and it is plausible to argue that by the late 1960s, the surveillance agencies reached a crossroads in their struggle over Palestinians' consciousness.

Linn's plan

Amnon Linn, the chairperson of Mapai's Arab department in 1965–69, presented on 1 May 1968 a plan entitled 'From victory in the election to the struggle on the embedding of Israeli Arab Consciousness'.[13] Linn's main argument was that the Palestinians, particularly the youth, have a 'divided soul'. Their modernization was not accompanied by an educational process which should have brought them to complete identification with Israel as Jewish and as Zionist state. Although Linn argued that his thoughts were triggered by the emerging reality following the occupation of the West Bank and Gaza, in fact, his point of reference was the debates which took place in the early 1950s regarding the loyalty of the minority, in some of which he participated. In the meeting of the Mapai's Political Committee on 24 January 1952, he stated:

> there were ideas about the establishment of a pure Arab movement, we explored this issue and we thought that it might entail serious dangers, since we will not be able to direct it, and it would become an opposition to us. It is obvious that Arabs are not to be accepted to Mapai. ... We view the Arabs in Israel as an instrument for our activity in the Orient, particularly we think that if the Arabs are accepted to Mapai this activity across the borders might lose its appeal. (6–7/2)

Indeed, on 1 December 1951, he sent a request to Mapai's leadership to establish a '*Movement for peace and Unity of the East*'. Ben-Gurion, who was irritated by Linn's ideas, cut him short in the meeting of 24 January 1952 and stopped him from elaborating his thesis (*ibid.*:7/2).

Linn argued that the main 'educational' failing of the state was its failure to provide the 'faithful' elements (positive Arabs) 'with a logical, clear and written manifesto which vindicates their position' (Linn, 1968:76). However, he was aware that a change of identity requires more than the propagation of ideas and propaganda. Therefore, he linked the change of identity with the material conditions of the Palestinians. Those who identify with the state – in practice – should be given equal rights. Hence, the policy of reward and punishment should become clear and official, and there should be no room for those who lay on the fence – who identify with the state at the declarative level only. Rather, the distinction between the 'faithful' and the 'negative' elements should become unambiguous. Although in his presentation, Linn does not explain the policy towards the 'negative' elements, yet he hints that eventually they have to leave the country.

The implanting of the Israeli Arab consciousness, according to Linn, should start at an early age: '[w]e have to rouse at the heart of [Arab young men] the consciousness of his complete identification with the state' (*ibid.*:81). Various settings should tune their activities for achieving this goal including the educational system and shared Jewish–Arab settings at all levels which should be established or revived including the neighbourly relations committees. Put simply, Linn argued that Zionism should be the ideology of both Jews and Palestinians. Although it does not relate to Palestinians' history and national aspirations, it comprises a gateway for their continual residence in the country and their achievement of material benefits. It is highly likely that Linn had read Ze'ev Jabotinsky's (1923/1937) famous article 'The Iron Wall', in which he argues that no living nation would accept such conditions. Only after total submission, the Palestinians would accept such terms. Linn might have thought that after eighteen years of military rule and the defeat of the Arab states in the Six-Day War, the Palestinians' spirit was broken.

Conclusion

This chapter detailed the surveillance and control methods which had been employed to affect the ways in which Palestinians form their views, particularly through the educational system and the media. The surveillance narrowing focus in terms of both the space and the size of the supervised category – from the large groups of ethnicities to Hamula and then to the individual – created an accumulative effect; its ramification and intensification were for many educators and students overpowering. Added to that, the frequency at which each educator was screened throughout his/her career and the reward or punishment that accompanied the screening heightened his/her fear and distress. These screenings were not only a vivid reminder to each teacher regarding the flimsiness of his/her economic security but also a method to keep his/her dependency on the chain of collaboration. Furthermore, these screening events were occasionally used to draw teachers to collaborate or to provide certain information. Added to that, the use of informers in the schools including headmasters, teachers, pupils and parents besides the conveyed educational messages converted the Arab educational system to something analogous to a panopticon within a panopticon, where watchful eyes and eavesdropping ears that might see or hear dissent were imagined everywhere.

Meanwhile, the supervision of students at the universities was routinization, where various actors including some Jewish students took part in all sorts of mundane surveillance activities. The collaboration of universities made this surveillance possible but at the same time less visible than in schools and teacher training colleges although not less grave.

Abba Hushi thought of extending the model of surveillance which prevailed in mixed settings, such as the one that existed at the universities, to the whole educational system by giving Jewish teachers and supervisors an important role of supervision and control. Besides dictating the educational messages, Hushi's plan was tailored to implant Israeli patriotism within young Palestinians. However, given the dramatic change it required, Hushi's plan was not implemented on a large scale, and only a small experiment was carried out in Haifa. More than a decade and a half later, Amon Linn, Abba Hushi's son-in-law and his successor in the Ma'arach, previously [Mapai] Arab department, proposed a plan which went one step further. Acceptance of Zionism by the Palestinians was to be linked to their material conditions and even to their very existence in the country.

Besides the tight surveillance which prevailed in the formal settings, sustained efforts were made to dominate the media discourse and to regulate the books which were available to the general public. Considerable funds were allocated to this end. However, some new technologies, particularly television, which became available in increasing numbers in the villages, opened a window for new ideas and information that the regime found hard to suppress. Yet, despite the tremendous changes which took place after 1968, the endeavour to control the Arab educational system including by some of the methods described in this chapter – particularly screening and tight surveillance – has not lost its vigour.

Notes

1 The Criminal Investigation Department (CID) was a branch of the mandatory police force which used plain clothes.
2 Tables of teachers and candidates for the teacher training college are available in *LPA*, Files 3/1.
3 Some of the cases are omitted from this list, because they follow the same pattern and there is no point in copying the whole list.
4 It is highly likely that this list was compiled along with other lists such as the list of the hamulas in the run for the local elections in 1975.
5 Such tables are available in *LPA*, Files 3/1.
6 Although the informer did not write his name clearly on this report, he added the name of his village and his signature. Moreover, the writing and the style are similar to his previous letter. There is no doubt that the two letters were authored by the same man.
7 Amnon Linn sent a note to Yaakov (most likely Eini) asking him to call Mr Eliahu Barak – the head of the Arab section in the teachers' union – and request Palestinian teachers who supported the democratic list to sign their names in support of

Mapai's affiliated lists, thus nullifying their endorsement of the democratic list. This note was written in a list of teachers who were either activists or supporters of the lists of Arab teachers for the 1962 elections – the democratic list and the list of reform 'Islah' ('Teachers: The Democratic and Islah Lists', 25 May 1962).

8 An anonymous detailed report on 'the attitudes of teachers and pupils towards the Eichmann Affair', *LPA*, Files 26/7/10.

9 The author studied at this school, and the shared memory he had with his peers is of marginalization and an unconcealed goal of the school of fostering Arabs with a 'captive mind', just as European colonial powers did in the colonies.

10 This list was stamped by the Office of the Advisor to the Prime Minister on Arab Affairs on 23 November 1964.

11 The Hebrew University 'Minority Students who are studying at the Hebrew University'; there are various lists which are available in *LPA*, Files 26/13/15.

12 There are several such lists of classification of students.

13 The plan is available in two versions: a short version and a detailed one; both are available in the Labour Party's archive. I quote from the longer version.

7

Political rights under a military rule

Irreconcilable conceptualization?

Citizenship, as a bundle of rights and as experience, is regarded in the political thought as a safeguard for the citizens against excesses by the state or by powerful groups (e.g. Marshall, 1950). Among these, political rights have been associated with highly esteemed notions such as the sovereignty of the people. However, what could the meaning of political rights be under a state of exception, where the basic rights, which enable citizens to participate in the political democratic processes, are curtailed?

This contradiction lies at the heart of Palestinians' experience of citizenship under the Military Government. While they were granted the right to vote and to be elected, their basic rights, which enable and give meaning to the practising of political rights, including freedom of movement, freedom of speech and association, fair trial and participation in political processes free of compulsion, were denied. Although Foucault (2004:239–64) demonstrates that democracies employ various forms of surveillance and population management, this however is not carried out in a flagrant breach of their citizens' rights. Meanwhile the disciplinary measures and the sovereign power which are embodied in the emergency regulations and which were practised by the Military Government are at odds with the notion of citizenship rights.

Unmindful of this contradiction in the political experience of the Palestinian minority, many social scientists have classified Israel, since its foundation, as democracy (e.g. Dahl, 1971; Powell, 1982; Lijphart, 1984, 1994; Dowty, 1999; Gavison, 1999) by referring to procedural issues, mainly the carrying out of multiparty elections on regular bases. The fact that the preconditions for a democracy did not exist for the national minority seems to have no effect on their definition of democracy.

Meanwhile, in chapter 5, I described how the local democratic process was turned into means of control, where the elections became an occasion for the practising of surveillance and the deployment of hamula politics. Had the national politics taken a different form?

To answer this question I shall deconstruct the contradiction between political right on the one hand and the policies of surveillance and control, which were enabled by the state of exception, on the other, to a series of queries regarding structures, procedures and processes. Thus, I shall explore the venues of political participation which became available to the Palestinians, the mobilization of Arab members of Knesset, their representativeness and their impact on national politics. Moreover, I shall discuss alternative modes of political participation through the formal channels and political contestation that Palestinians had undertaken. Overall, the discussion in this chapter aims to clarify the relationships between Israeli goals of political control and population management and the political rights which were granted to the Palestinians.

Officially sanctioned venues of participation

Although the Palestinians who had nominally become citizens of Israel (the nationality law would pass three years later) were permitted to participate in the first elections as voters and as candidates, questions regarding the content and seriousness of their political rights were raised from the beginning. One of these questions revolved around the venues of their participation. Until 1952, it was not entirely clear to those in charge of the surveillance agencies how the Palestinians would be politically organized. Therefore, various initiatives by all sorts of groups and parties emerged. For example, in late 1949, some 300 Palestinians from Lydda expressed their willingness to join Mapai. Besides that, the Communist Party renewed its activity among the Palestinians, particularly given that its Arab leaders either remained in the country or some of those who became refugees were allowed to return (The Political Committee, 19 January 1950:7). Moreover, the left-Zionist Mapam party began its activities among Palestinian intelligentsia and established an Arab party. In the meeting of Mapai's political committee held on 19 January 1950, member of Knesset (MK) and Chairman of Foreign Affairs and Defence Committee, Zalman Aran stated:

> Our party is outside this issue [organizing the Palestinians politically]. ... The issue of an Arab socialist party is still on the table. With the passage of time, this will become a serious matter. The question is who among our comrades can deal with this project, which demands knowledge of the language and an [appropriate] approach. I think there is a solution to the Arab question. The Arabs must go to the same places to which the other Arabs went; I've always been supporter of transfer. As long as they continue to live in the country, we have to give them equal rights. ... I think we have to establish a socialist party among them. ... The truth is that the Party [i.e. Mapai] is not psychologically ready for this. (*Ibid.*)

Yet, it was clear to the Arabists that an Arab party affiliated to Mapai would not give expression to the demands and aspirations of the Palestinian minority. In the course of a meeting of Mapai's secretariat with the party's MKs, Reuven Barkatt maintained:

> Ha-Havir Moshe [Sharett] knows that I have always objected to the establishment of an Arab party, and my reasons in short are as follow.
>
> I thought that the establishment of an Arab party constitutes a public deceit. An Arab party that will not have a plan or slogan, which does not know the government's policy line, it will be a 'party of emissaries' and it will not constitute an influential factor in the Arab public. Moreover, I said that there are no [Arab] personalities which might comprise a basis of progressive party. ... I think, there is a need today to consider, in the light of the activities of Maki [the Communist Party] and Mapam among the Arab community, the plausibility of trusting various elements [persons], with the assignment of laying down a sincere program in order to establish a party, by which our party [Mapai] would be aided. (The Secretariat's Meeting with MKs, 9 July 1950:6/2)

In the same meeting, MK Shlomo Lavi thought that this option was unworkable: 'I don't think that we can organize an Arab social democratic party, this is a mistake' (*ibid.*:6).

Thus, those in charge of surveillance continued a search for an Arab leader who would be held in high regard by Palestinians and at the same time be subservient to Mapai. But can such a leader exist? MK Aran thought that the expectations of finding such a leader were unrealistic:

> Which Arab who has self-respect would like to associate himself with us; only an Arab who can be bought up by money. I'd distain Arabs who would ally themselves with us under this policy ... we are cheating ourselves and we are cheating the world's nations. Whoever investigates this profoundly will not accept it. (*Ibid.*:3–4)

The array of political action was summed up by MK Yona Kesse, who stated:

> According to one approach there is a need to establish a socialist party (Mapai) among the Arabs. According to another, the Arabs are still incapable of establishing a political party by themselves, and we have to act among them by a way of deception. We need to bring some Arab leaders from abroad (refugees), who are influential among the Arabs and who can control them by oppression. ... The two Arab Knesset members have no popular support and we cannot count on them. (The Political Committee, 19 January 1950:9)

Indeed, on the eve of the elections for the second Knesset – held on 30 July 1951 – there was a feeling among Arabists that Nimer Hawari could fill the function of an Arab leader. His history as a nationalist figure seemed promising. After the end of the Second World War, he established a quasi-military scout movement known as Al-Najada (auxiliary corps), which numbered some 2,000 members on the eve of the 1948 War (see, e.g., Morris, 2004:59). Although Al-Hawari allied himself with the Palestinian national leadership before this war, the sincerity of his political stand remained questionable. According to Morris (2004), 'Hawari ... may have been a HIS [Haganah Intelligence Service] agent' (111). And the statement by Barkatt, mentioned in chapter 1 '[t]here was someone in the name of Nemri who was supposed to fill in the role of leader, he betrayed us, then he returned, in the meanwhile, however, it became clear that he is worthless in the Arab community' (The Political Committee, 24 January 1952:10/2) – seems to support Morris's assumption. Moreover, his return to Israel in 1949 could not have occurred had he not been in close collaboration with top Israeli Arabists and security agents. However, within less than two years, it became clear that he was not the anticipated leader, and his political saga was short-lived (see Cohen, 2010:53–9).

Yet, the growing realization among the Israeli leadership and those in charge of the surveillance apparatuses during 1952 that the Palestinian minority would stay in Israel for a longer period than what they anticipated (see chapter 1), along with the failed attempt to appoint Al-Hawari as a leader, highlighted the need for a strategy to organize the Palestinians. In the meeting of Mapai's Political Committee on 24 January 1952, Ben-Gurion laid down the principles for the future organization of the Palestinians, stating that 'they cannot join the party [Mapai], because our party is a Zionist party, similar to the state of Israel, which is a Zionist state. ... Therefore, the League of Arab Workers exists [a front trade union governed by the Histadrut], which is composed of Arabs only. ... [T]here is a need for an instrument for Jews and Arabs, a league, club, etc.' (The Political Committee, 24 January 1952:4). Ben-Gurion's verdict against the establishment of Arab parties reflected a wide consensus not only among those in charge of the surveillance agencies but also among the Jewish political class as a whole.

Consequently, no independent Arab party – or even an independent nationwide framework which could constitute a basis for such a party – was allowed to operate not only during the Military Government era but also in the following two decades. While Ben-Gurion's decree regarding the prohibition of the establishment of an independent Arab party became a cornerstone of the political control policy – as the various policy principles and political plans described in chapter 2 illustrate – his idea of creating a joint club for 'positive' Arabs and Jews associated with Mapai, which might constitute a veneer of amenability, had never taken off. A decade after Ben-Gurion's suggestion, Barkatt tried to make sense of it; thus, he stated on 1 February 1962: 'I am referring to a suggestion by Abba Hushi proposed 3–4 years ago regarding the establishment of Party [Mapai] clubs in Arab localities; a club does not mean party membership, rather a mediating body between the Arabs and the party ... [whose aim would be] bringing closer and educating' (The Arab Affairs' Committee, 1 February 1962:9). Similarly, an idea by Sharett of establishing a movement among the Palestinians that would give them an illusion of having a political–ideological project had proven to be unworkable (The Political Committee, 24 January 1952:2/2).

If the Palestinians were barred from establishing their parties and at the same time were denied membership in the main Jewish parties (except Mapam), how could they practise their political right? The main officially sanctioned outlet for Palestinians' participation therefore had become Mapai's affiliated Arab lists. These lists were put together before each election by those in charge of the surveillance agencies without any input by Palestinians, not even by the candidates who appeared on them. The Arabists decided on all the matters concerning these lists including the identity of the candidates, their ranking, the names of the lists, their symbols and their campaign strategies.

For example, in the run for the fourth Knesset elections, Yaakov Eini (23 February 1959) composed a document entitled 'Towards the Elections for the Fourth Knesset: A Review and Suggestions', in which he laid out three plausible compositions of the Arab lists along with an appraisal of the popularity of the various candidates. The first alternative included the following lists and candidates: (A) the list which gets the votes from Nazareth and its adjacent villages, which would be represented by (1) Yousef Fahum, (2) a Catholic, (3) a Muslim from Al-Zaydna family and (4) Ra'if Al-Zu'bi (a supervisor in the Ministry of Education); (B) the list of Progress and Work, which would be represented by Sheikh Salih Khnayfis and Yousef Abdullah – instead of Sheikh Salih Salim, 'whom [Eini thought] it is pointless to re-nominate'; and (C) the Triangle list, which would include (1) Mahmoud Nashif or Faris Hamdan, (2) Sheikh Jaber Dahish Muadi and (3) Hassan Abdullah.

According to Eini, this option would leave the ethnic composition of the Arab MKs unchanged: two Muslims, two Druze and one Catholic. Eini estimated that each of the lists A and C would achieve two seats in the Knesset, while list B would gain a single seat. This alternative would entail personal changes, but it did not meet – what he considered to be – the demands of the Muslims for more equitable representation (they numbered 150,000, while the Druze who numbered 20,000 were represented by the same number of MKs) nor the demands of the Christian Orthodox who did not have any representative in the Knesset. Then Eini brought a second suggestion for the composition of these lists and analysed its drawbacks, followed by a third option and its appraisal. These alternatives were discussed in detail by those in charge of the surveillance agencies, including representatives of the Office of the Advisor to the Prime Minister and the Military Government.

On 18 August, the lists were prepared. Less than three months before the elections, invitations were issued to the successful Arab candidates for meetings with the Arabists. The candidates were expected to express their gratitude and readiness to perform the required tasks. Thus, in the meeting of Mapai's election headquarters, it was decided on the schedule of the meetings:

> Yousef Fahum will be invited [to meet with] Shetreet, Ziama Divon and Yaakov Eini to get his final answer; Eini will arrange the meeting. [It will take place] [o]n Wednesday 19.8.59; consultation will take place in Haifa to decide on an alternative name. On Friday the 21.8.59 a decision will be taken.
>
> Salih Salim: He will be invited to Shetreet. Eini will make the arrangements. (1)
>
> Salih Khnayfis: Will be invited for a new meeting with Barkatt on Wednesday 13–13:30.
>
> The list of Sheik Labib: [The meeting with its representatives will take place] [o]n Wednesday 19.8.59, an exploration will be made whether it is possible to place Suleiman Qutran in the third place. (The Confined Committee of the Arab Affairs' Committee, 18 August 1959:2)

This schedule shows that Al-Fahum was considered an important candidate, as he was invited to meet three central figures: a minister, the Advisor on Arab Affairs and a prominent Arabist. The import assigned to Al-Fahum might shed light on the sources of power he had, and which were highly valued by the Arabists. His power according to the Arabists had to do with his ethnic and family origin as well as his past political behaviour. He was a Muslim and member of a large hamula. Therefore, he was conceived as an apt substitute to Saif Al-Deen Al-Zu'bi, the leading candidate in the Arab lists – to whom I shall refer later – who took temporary leave from national politics. Second, he was a well-known local leader who before 1948 opposed the leadership of the Haj al-Hussyni and served as the mayor of Nazareth during and following its occupation. Third, some of his close relatives were active in Mapam and the Popular Front – an Arab nationalist movement. General Shoham, the head of the Military Government, highlighted these characteristics in Mapai's Arab Affairs' Committee meeting on 24 February 1959:

> As to the Fahum family, it is a respected family in Nazareth and its surrounding. ... We succeeded in making Fahum leave the [the Popular] Front; this is for the possibility of enhancing the status of the family. We should visit him [Yousef] regularly and, in a way, prepare him not to yield to pressure by others. (The Arab Affairs' Committee, 24 February 1959:24)

It is not clear whether Tahir Al-Fahoum, a key figure in the nationalist movement, the Popular Front, was persuaded by his older relative Yousef to stop his activity in the Popular Front or not. It is obvious that the surveillance agencies saw in Yousef a figure who could block the growing support of Al-Fahoum hamula to Mapam, particularly that two of its members Abd Al-Aziz – who would later become the first Arab deputy minister – and Abd Al-Majid were chief Mapam activists among the Palestinian minority (Eini, 23 February 1959:3–4). Unexpectedly, Yousef Al-Fahoum turned down the offer, telling his interlocutor (most probably the Minister Shetreet) that he would not like to be treated like a lemon: squeezed to the last drop and then thrown into the dustbin (Benziman and Mansour, 1992:202; Linn, 1999:80–1). Nevertheless, on 7 September 1959, less than two months before the elections, all the arrangements were made and Barkatt presented to his colleagues the final results:

> As agreed, *we have to give our final approval of the three lists which are associated with the Party [Mapai]. We have to approve the first five names of each list*, which are as follows:
>
> The Nazareth List
>
> 1. Ahmad Kamel 2. Elias Nakhleh 3. 'Awad Ibrahim Abdullah 4. Abdo Kardish 5. Abdullah Younis
>
> The Western Galilee List
>
> 1. Labib Abu-Rukon 2. Yousef Abdullah Diab 3. Salim Jubran. 4. Muhamad Ibrahim Zubidat. 5. Indrawis Karkabi
>
> The Triangle List
>
> 1. Mahmoud Al-Nashif 2. Shiek Jaber Muadi 3. Tawfiq 'Asalia 4. 'Adel Younis 5. Kanj Qubalan
>
> The closing names of the lists. The Galilee list – Sharif Mamlock or Nadim Batheesh. The List of Nazareth – Sheik Salih Salim. The Triangle list – Faris Hamdan.
>
> Names and Signs of the Lists
>
> The following names and signs were decided upon.
>
> The Triangle list – Agriculture and development – 'A.
>
> The Nazareth List – Progress and development – RA
>
> The Galilee list – cooperation and fraternity – Youd, A.
>
> (The Confined Secretariat of the Arab Affairs' Committee, 7 September 1959)

Thus, all the issues which in free elections comprise arenas of contention – the forming of political parties, the elaboration of ideologies and the management of election campaigns – were summed up by an Arabist in one half of a page. Yet, they were clearly tuned in various ways with the surveillance and control discourse. They reaffirmed in the political sphere the categorizations and the hierarchies on national and ethnic grounds: they embodied the reproduction of the Jewish–Palestinian hierarchy and the definition of the Palestinians both as non-Jews and as a collection of minorities. The ethnic representation of the various ethnicities meant enhancing and solidifying the constructed ethnic identities at the expense of the more inclusive Palestinian affinity. Additionally, the elections had become an essential behavioural dimension of the binary indices according to which Palestinians were appraised as positive/moderates or negative/radicals. Those who voted for Mapai or its Arab affiliated lists were branded as positive, and those who voted for other parties, particularly the Communist party, were labelled radicals and subsequently punished.

Free elections?

It is obvious by now that the officially sanctioned venue for Palestinians' political participation allowed only for a phantasm of democracy. Why did Palestinians go along with that? Did their voting patterns reflect the system of patronage which existed before 1948 and was reproduced under the new conditions of Israel's democracy, or were they coerced to do so? Put differently, did the voting patterns of Palestinians reflect the social structure of their society – the ethnic and hamula affiliation – or the state of exception? The debate regarding this question which took place among scholars is largely academic. Those who employed the argument regarding the role of the 'traditional social structures' tended to essentialize them (e.g. Cohen, 1965; Abu-Ghosh, 1972; Stendel, 1973; see also critical reviews by Asad, 1975 and Zureik, 1979:93–4, 99–101). By doing so, they disregarded the role that state power had played in solidifying and reconstructing them and eventually turning them into vehicles for official strategies of control (see chapters 4 and 5). Indeed, the coagulation of these structures, principally the hamula and the tribe, was identified by Shmouel Tolidano – the long-standing Advisor to the Prime Minister on Arab Affairs – as a main policy principle during the 1950s and 1960s (see chapter 2).

Yet, instead of sweeping generalizations, there is a need to look at the tactics which those in charge of the surveillance apparatuses planned to deploy or employed. These tactics relied on binary classifications and the use of reward and punishment. For example, in the course of the discussions in Mapai's Arab Affairs' Committee held on 5 May 1961 on the forthcoming elections, Persmann of the Military Government employed a phrase connoting godlike authority – 'the righteous prosper and the wicked suffer' – emphasizing that the Military Government and the Histadrut have worked hand in hand in implementing this policy all along (The Arab Affairs' Committee, 5 May 1961:10). Similarly, MK David HaCohen stated that although 'It is true that there is disrespect and unfulfilled promises (for the Arab population) ... we ought to employ force when dealing with them. This means if you don't vote for us, we shall not support you and we shall bully you ... they understand this language' (*ibid.*:8). This approach was discussed in detail with regard to

Um Al-Fahim, the large village in the Triangle, where in the previous elections, held in 1959, only 45 per cent of the voters cast their votes for Mapai and its affiliated Arab lists. Thus, it was decided (1) to threaten to disturb the supply of water to the village and (2) to promise some people with jobs: 'The lack of sources of livelihood [in the village] is a fertile soil for a large-scale purchase of votes', the document indicated (quoted in Bauml, 2007:257). The role of the Military Government and other state apparatuses in ensuring Palestinians' vote for Mapai was clear to those in charge of the surveillance apparatuses. For example, Yehoshua Habushi, an Arabist, ex-Shai member and the head of the Ministry of Labour's Arab department, explained in the course of the discussion in Mapai's committee on Arab Affairs on 24 February 1959 that 'there are Arabs who are influenced by the Military Government, and we shouldn't undermine the position of the Military Government. ... Since we receive there 80 per cent of the votes [in the areas under this regime]' (The Arab Affairs' Committee, 24 February 1959:18). Habushi was, in fact, alluding to the system of patronage that the Military Government created through the hamula politics (see chapter 5). Habushi's argument regarding the vital role played by the Military Government in enlisting Arab votes for Mapai was supported by Uri Lubrani, who stated: '...The Party relies in this matter on offices and bodies – including the Military Government – who are active in this field [among the Palestinians]' (*ibid.*:18). Indeed, the village files comprised an essential tool for soliciting Palestinians to vote for Mapai, as explained in chapter 5. The Military Government in collaboration with the Shin Bet, the Advisor's Office, the Histadrut, Jewish employers and the various ministries employed reward and punishment in accordance with the voting results of villages and hamulas.

Although the conditions of free elections were superficially guaranteed, in reality, those in charge of the surveillance apparatuses could identify and subsequently punish the 'negative elements'. Study days were organized before the elections regarding how to bring the voters to the polling centre and at the end of Election Day how to identify the voting results of each hamula or family (Bauml, 2007:257). The most obvious way for identifying the voting behaviour of Palestinians was the placing of the polling centres according to the residency of the various hamulas (neighbourhoods). In this way, the heads of the hamulas were held responsible for the voting results of their kin. In places where the neighbourhood did not overlap with hamula/tribe identification, the hamulas or tribes were split, heads for the new units were appointed and polling stations were rearranged accordingly.

For example, a steady decline in the participation rates among the Negev Bedouins for the Knesset elections from 80 per cent in 1955 to 68.8 per cent in 1969 was identified by an internal Ma'arach memorandum. This decrease was attributed to two factors: the size of the tribe, which was found negatively associated with the participation rates in the elections, and the contacts between

Bedouins in the Negev and other Palestinians, particularly teachers. Consequently, it was recommended to increase the surveillance over the teachers ('The Election for the Knesset Among the Negev Bedouins', n.d.[1]) and to split the large tribes into smaller ones according to geographical criteria. In this regard, David Zakharia, the chairperson of Ha-Ma'arach's Arab Department, suggested, for example, the splitting of the Abu-Raqiq tribe into five small tribes: Abu-Raqiq, Abu-Kuff, Hawashleh, Turshan and Al-Sayeed. And, instead of one voting centre, a polling station was opened in each of these subtribes (Stevisky, 30 January 1967; Zakharia, 29 November 1970). Such subdivisions were believed to strengthen Mapai's and subsequently Ma'arach's grip over the Bedouins. Thus, the political rights became an additional factor for the fragmentation of the minority and the increase of the surveillance over it.

Occasionally, direct and intimidating tactics were employed. Mapai's Arab department used to collect the ID cards of Arab voters on the eve of the elections and returned them before Election Day with Mapai's ballot, making it obvious to them which party they were ordered to vote for (Bauml, 2007:257).

In short, the discussion presented so far suggests that the political rights were used as a means of control: to survey the attitudes of the Palestinians regularly, to monitor the trends of their attitudes, to divide and subdivide them into manageable units, to rank them hierarchically, to strengthen their parochial identities and to create a state of affairs where a discourse of patronage rather than one of rights would prevail.

Yet, could some sections of the co-opted Arab elite, despite all this, establish an autonomous basis of power and influence the national politics? Put differently, what are the methods which the regime used to maintain the flimsiness of this elite's position?

Mapai's affiliated Arab lists

Leadership?

Although elevated to their position by those in charge of the surveillance apparatuses, Palestinian MKs of these lists were referred to as the representatives of the Arab minority. On the whole, they were drawn from two groups: long-standing collaborators and dignitaries. The first and the largest group consisted of long-standing collaborators including Saif Al-Deen Al-Zu'bi, Jaber Dahish Muadi, Salih Khnayfis, Labib Abu-Rukun, Faris Hamdan and Diab Obeid, whose biographies I shall succinctly describe and highlight the reasons for their selection to this position.

Saif Al-Deen, who served as MK for some 20 years – between the first Knesset (beginning in 1949) and the ninth (ending his service in 1979 with interruptions in the middle) – was according to his Knesset web page 'active in

Haganah [and for that] received the Fighter of the State Decoration'.[2] That is, he worked as an informer for Shai (the intelligence branch of the Haganah) and was also a *simsar* (land dealer) who bought land for the Jewish institutions, an act that was considered by Palestinians a national treason before 1948 (Jiryis, 1976:166; Cohen, 2006:35–6).

Jaber Dahish Muadi also worked for Shai before 1948 for a monthly salary of 40 pounds and helped the Israeli forces to occupy a number of Druze villages in the Galilee in the 1948 War. As a result, he was nominated for the Israel Independence Medal but was found wanting following suspicion regarding his murky past (Jiryis, 1976:166–7; see also chapter 4). Palmon suspected that Muadi participated in the 1936–39 Palestinian revolt, but changed sides during the 1940s (Cohen, 2004:254–5).

Salih Khnayfis had had long relationships with Shai which dated back to the 1930s. During the 1948 War, he was active in enlisting Druze men to the Haganah and helped the Israeli army in the occupation of various Galilean villages and the town of Acre (Jiryis, 1976:167; Cohen, 2004:254–5; also his Knesset web page[3]). Although, like Muadi, he did not receive the Fighter of the State Decoration, he was nonetheless awarded various symbols of 'honour' such as a Bren machine gun and seven rifles (Cohen, 2006:43). In 1942, he had a spat with Abba Hushi, where he accused Hushi of fiddling with money that Shai sent to him (see Firro, 1999:31). Unforgiving Hushi promoted his protégé Labib Abu-Rukun at the end of the 1950s at the expense of Khnayfis. Consequently, Khnayfis was excluded from the list of Arab candidates for the fourth Knesset that Mapai arranged.

The last Druze MK of this generation, Labib Abu-Rukun, was the least prominent of the three Druze leaders and served the shortest period in the Knesset; he served in the fourth Knesset only (30 November 1959–54 September 1961) (see Avivi, 2007:338). Yet, he too was a long-standing collaborator and *simsar* (see chapter 4). His relations with Abba Hushi and the Haganah dated back to the 1930s, and during the 1948 War, he was active, like his two colleagues, in recruiting Druze volunteers to the Israel Defence Forces (IDF) (see his Knesset web page[4]).

Similarly, the two MKs who represented the Triangle during the bulk of the discussed period, Faris Hamdan and Diab Obeid, were long-standing collaborators. Hamdan, however, differed from his colleagues in this category by having various sources of power. He was educated in terms of his time, as he finished high school and, in 1944, was elected head of the local council of his village.[5] Moreover, he came from a wealthy landed family. During the Mandate period, he appeared to have contradictory loyalties. While showing loyalty to the Palestinian National Movement headed by Haj Amin al-Hussyni, Zionism's arch enemy, he collaborated with the Zionists. In the post-1948 era, he was awarded both political power and economic resources. Besides his involvement in local and national politics, he was permitted by the Israeli security agencies to conduct, along with his espionage activities, extensive border-crossing smuggling trade in which high-ranking officials in the Jordanian security establishment and dignitaries were involved (Cohen, 2006:41–2). In return, he was asked to set an example to other landowners in his village by accepting the state's inadequate compensation for his expropriated land (Hamdan, 14 May 1965).

Meanwhile, Diab Obeid had secondary school education, but unlike Hamdan, he allied himself since the mid-1930s with the Zionist movement and worked according to Shai's instructions against the Arab boycott in the 1930s as well as in espionage. His undercover activity continued after 1948 in the West Bank, until his apprehension in late 1949 by the Jordanian authorities and his eventual return to Israel in the same year (Cohen, 2006:79–80).

The second group was composed of dignitaries: heads of large hamulas, representatives of religious communities and big landowners, whom the leaders of the Zionist movement derogatorily referred to as effendis before 1948. The first MK in this group was Amin Jurjora, a well-known local leader in Nazareth. During the Ottoman and the Mandate eras, he held various positions: teacher at the Russian School in Nazareth, lecturer at El-Rashidia College in Jerusalem and lawyer in Haifa and Nazareth. In the first elections, he headed the Mapai-affiliated Democratic List of Nazareth (see his Knesset web page[6]). However, his political career was cut short as he belonged to the Christian Orthodox sect.

Those in charge of the control and surveillance agencies appointed Christian MKs in coordination with the bishop Hakim, who was instrumental in advancing their strategies. Thus, the two other Christian MKs who served during the discussed period, Massad Qassis and Elias Nakhleh, were Greek Catholics (Stendel, 1973; Linn, 1999:79). Qassis from a landed family was active before 1948 in organizing Palestinian farmers, an assignment he continued after the establishment of Israel. His sociopolitical commitments – which would take a clear political direction in the 1970s – might not have been welcomed by those in charge of the surveillance and control apparatuses and his patron, Hakim. For example, in 1954, the Regional Committee – a body which represented the various security and surveillance apparatuses – decided that a cold shoulder would be turned to Qassis, although 'no special [disciplinary] measures against him would be taken' (Cohen, 2006:242). After two terms in the Knesset, he was substituted by Elias Nakhleh (Stendel, 1973:112).

Similar to Qassis, Nakhleh came from a wealthy landed family. Prior to his placement in a Mapai-affiliated slate, he was associated with the General Zionist Party (Jiryis, 1976:167). Yet, unlike Qassis, he accepted his role within the structure of control and surveillance, as shall be illustrated later. The ability of Nakhleh to get the support of Hakim until his departure from the country secured him a seat in the Knesset for some 14 years, from the fourth to the seventh Knesset (see his Knesset web page[7]).

Other dignitaries in this category, who received some public visibility, include Mahmoud Nashif and Ahmad Kamil Al-Dahir. Nashif was chosen as a substitute for Faris Hamdan for his good appearance, his ability to gain the trust of a largely disillusioned Palestinian population and his affiliation to Achdut Ha'avoda, where his defection was thought to comprise a blow to this party among the Palestinians (Eini, 23 February 1959:4). Yet, within a short period, these hopes were dashed (The Arab Affairs' Committee, 5 May 1961:7), and after one term, he was substituted by Diab Obeid, who served three terms in the Knesset, between 1961 and 1974. The last Arab MK of this group is Ahmad Kamil Al-Dahir. He was chosen for being the representative of the third largest hamula in Nazareth and served two terms in the Knesset – the fourth and the fifth Knesset, 30 November 1959–2 November 1965 (Linn, 1999:81).

Those in charge of the surveillance agencies were well aware of the spuriousness of this 'democratic' process. Josh Palmon, the first Advisor to the Prime Minister on Arab Affairs, who pioneered these arrangements (Bauml, 2007:255), described them later on candidly:

> ... the Arab members of the Knesset were not in fact chosen by the Arab community; and the Arab members of the Knesset and the Arab lists were not independent agents. ... It is also true that the Israeli [Jewish] parties are not prepared to give up this state of affairs. (Quoted in Jiryis, 1976:166)

Their status and performance

The initial goal for having Arab MKs was to maintain a presentation of the Israeli political system as democratic, yet other functions, principally the consolidation of the control system, were added later on. In the thrust of daily life, however, they were considered as an 'unnecessary burden' (see chapter 1). As such, their experience was humbling. About a year and a half after the first elections, their marginalization and embarrassing position in the Knesset became difficult to conceal. In the meeting of Mapai's Secretariat with the Party's MKs held on 9 July 1950, Yitzhak Ben-Zvi described the chastening existence of the two Arab MKs in Mapai's affiliated list, Saif Al-Deen Al-Zu'bi and Amin Jurjora, as follows:

> The two Arab [MKs] of our Democratic List, who were elected by 30,000 voters, are tense and bitter: no one approaches them, no one greets them, no one answers their greetings and they are not invited to meetings. A year ago they received invitations, but no longer. They suspect that they [their bosses] are dissatisfied [with them] and have other candidates. (2/1). They said they were ready to resign and I didn't know whether to advise them to quit or not. (The Secretariat's Meeting with MKs, 9 July 1950:2/1–3/1)

This reality persisted throughout the discussed period. In a discussion held on 4 May 1962, Abba Hushi maintained:

> As to the Arab MKs, there are four. They do not receive attention. ... They complain that when they go to the Knesset refectory MKs from different parties approach them, except members of the Party [Mapai]. Some explain this by the linguistic barrier. ... I think we should nominate someone, [but] I don't know whom ... there is a need for someone from the Knesset [i.e. among Mapai's MKs] [who would communicate with them regularly]. (The Arab Affairs' Committee, 4 May 1962:3)

MK Beba Idelson objected saying that 'it is not true that others approach them. They sit lonely. When there is voting they are approached. And this gives bad impression' (*ibid.*:6). Similarly, the minister Sheetrit maintained that 'it is true that they feel miserable. ... They are approached only when they are needed to vote or regarding other matters. In general they do not receive attention. ... They shouldn't always get orders: do this and do that. If we want to increase their influence in the Arab sector, we ought to listen to them and help them' (*ibid.*:8). Summarizing this discussion, Dr. Pollak maintained that 'one of the claims of Arab members of the Knesset and in the Arab sector is that the Arab MKs are machine for raising hands [for voting in the Knesset]. Unfortunately this is true. And had it been possible to maintain this, from the Party's [Mapai's] viewpoint, for a long time, it would be marvellous' (*ibid.*:10).

This attitude continued, and soon after this debate, the Arab MKs were summoned on the day of their feast *Al-Adha* – the Muslim feast – to the Knesset to vote against a motion of no-confidence (The Arab Department, 15 May 1962), despite the existence of various procedures which would have allowed their absence without affecting the voting results.

The sidelining of these MKs usually began prior to their entering the Knesset. Before each election, they were left guessing in the dark whether they would be included in the lists or not, until the last moment. For example, in the run for the fourth Knesset elections, Mishal Shoham, the head of the Military Government, stated in the meeting of the Arab Affairs' Committee on 24 February 1959 that '... We should make visits without making commitment (to anyone). I think this would not hurt the current five Arab Knesset members, because no one has told them that they will not appear in the lists [although all of them were to be substituted]. We should visit them as well as other persons' (The Arabs Affairs' Committee, 24 February 1959:23). In the same meeting, Mr Habushi – the head of the Ministry of Labour's Arab department – emphasized that 'the lists of candidates should be kept in an iron drawer until the last minute before the finalization of the lists' (*ibid.*:16).

Given this, some of the candidates tried to get hints or answers from their patrons, but most often to no avail. In the meeting of the Arab Affairs' Committee which discussed the election campaign for the fifth Knesset, the

Arabist, David HaCohen, informed his colleagues that 'I did not see Salih Khnayfis ... since I was abroad and suddenly, two weeks ago, he arrived to my house, and five days ago Sheikh Jaber came – they, for sure feel that their day [of judgment] has arrived' (The Arab Affairs' Committee, 5 May 1961:7).

After entering the Knesset, they followed Mapai's line; they voted with the government and did not rebel even when the government opposed various motions which called for the revoking of the Military Government. The voting of Arab MKs of Mapai's affiliated lists, on 20 February 1963, for the continuation of the Military Government accentuated the prevalent public impression that they were emissaries of the regime and had neither the support nor the respect of the audiences they supposedly represented. This event was particularly significant as a large coalition of political and civil organizations put together an orchestrated effort to end the Military Government. This coalition included various political parties from the right and the left of the political spectrum including Herut (headed by Menachem Begin), Mapam, the Communist Party, the Liberal Party and Achdut Ha'avoda Party (a split-off party from Mapai). Moreover, it included various groups and organizations of the civil society including the Jewish–Arab coalition for the abolishment of the Military Government, the Popular Committee, the Committee of the Arab Students at the Hebrew University and public figures including 100 lecturers from the Hebrew University who signed a petition to this effect. One of the motions was voted down by one vote – 57 to 56 – because Jaber Muadi and Diab Obeid voted with the government against the motion, while the other two, Elias Nakhleh and Ahmad Al-Dahir, played a trick by which one would abstain while the other would support each of the various motions, knowing that in this way the motions would be defeated (Sa'di, 2003a:78–9) (Figure 7.1).

This event illustrates the inherent contradiction in the position that these dignitaries held and the impossibility of their success. Various face-saving measures, which those in charge of the surveillance apparatuses devised, were not effectual enough to rectify this incongruity. Those in charge of the surveillance apparatuses discussed on various occasions the political basis of these MKs and always reached the same conclusion that they were unpopular. For example, in Mapai's Arab Affairs' Committee held on 24 February 1959 to discuss the strategy for the forthcoming elections, Yaakov Eini began his opening presentation by indicating that 'some Arab Knesset members lacked popularity' (The Arab Affairs' Committee, 24 February 1959:13), an understatement that prompted protests by other participants. Yaakov Cohen of the Histadrut's Arab department boldly stated:

> It was mentioned here that some of the serving Knesset Members are liked. As far as I know the field – and I talked to [Arabs] people at the local level – I can say that all of them are unpopular. ... These people got the votes mainly due to our support and not for their personalities. (*Ibid.*:24)

Figure 7.1 Resistance, surveillance, collaboration and control

This clandestine leaflet was composed and distributed by Arab Students at the Hebrew University and by young activists. It includes a condemnation of the Arab MKs who voted with the government on 20 February 1963 against various motions to end the Military Government. The cartoon on the top of the leaflet shows Prime Minister Ben-Gurion riding a donkey and waving with his right hand a stick symbolizing the Military Government, while he seems to offer in his left hand a carrot to the two donkeys which represent the Arab MKs (Jaber Muadi and Diab Obeid) who voted with the government. The carrot symbolizes a promise to these MKs that they will be included in the Arab lists for the sixth Knesset. On the top is the information given by the collaborator who passed on the leaflet. It includes the names of the persons who authored, typed and distributed it.

Although all the Arab MKs were substituted by new ones in the fourth Knesset (1959–61), the popularity of the new MKs did not increase. In the preparation for the next election campaign, David HaCohen stated, as if he were continuing the discussions on the previous one:

> I am in total agreement ... regarding Shikh Jaber or Nashif ... what counts is the import of the person in the field rather than in the Knesset. ... I don't know the difference Between Labib and Nashif; and I am not sure if we change 'horses' Labib wouldn't make troubles as Salih did. (The Arab Affairs' Committee, 5 May 1961:7)

The Arab MKs were well aware of their reality. Their senior, Saif Al-Deen Al-Zu'bi, described their experience as follows: '[T]he Arabs in Israel are right to criticize us, since [Mapai's members] show little respect for the Arab Knesset members: they interfere with us, insult us, and play games with us' (quoted in Jiryis, 1976:176).

Indeed, these cooped MKs walked on thin ice, and those who challenged the Arabists found themselves in a perilous position. MKs Salih Khnayfis and Faris Hamdan did not accept what they considered unjustified treatment to which they were subjected. Khnayfis was not included in Mapai's affiliated Arab lists for the fourth Knesset. Therefore, he decided to contest the elections in an independent list. Go'el Levitzki, who previously served as the northern district's (Galilee) military governor but in 1959 was in charge of income tax collection from Palestinians, presented Khnayfis with a huge bill which he could not pay. Consequently, an injunction was issued on his herds. Although the ex-military governor claimed that his action was not politically motivated, its political consequences should not be underestimated (Benziman and Mansour, 1992:202). Khnayfis ran several times to the Knesset in an independent list without success. Yet, in one of the leaflets entitled 'Beware of those who have no self-respect ... My Arab bother ... This is your enemy ... Beware ... Oh my brother beware'[8] that his party distributed, he renounced his long history of collaboration. Regardless of his sincerity, it is interesting to note the slogans he thought that Palestinians wanted to hear:

> There is a need for attentiveness against our segmentation to ethnic groups, parties, factions and minorities within minorities. We awaked and realized the huge void and the net that was brutally laid down against us, and the conspiracies which are schemed against our future.
>
> ... [T]hy are trying to deceive us [by claiming] that they will stop the robbery of our lands, they will remove the burden of the Military Government, they will abolish the emergency regulations which threaten our lives and through which they subjugate us like slaves to the interests of their masters; and who doesn't anticipate these results from the association with Mapai?
>
> ... We tried the game of Mapai and abandoned it! We don't claim to be among the best people of the Arabs, but we say that we are sincere regarding the public interest and we shall do our best to protect our rights. (Progress and Work, n.d.)

Hamdan also faced financial ruin. According to several letters he sent to the Prime Minister, ministers and Arabists, he was advised by the Minister of Trade and Industry to enter a joint venture with a Jewish partner in a stuffed food factory. The bankruptcy of the business – after a single season – led creditors to impose an injunction on his land and bank accounts, and his furniture was auctioned, although his partner was not harmed (Hamdan, 14 May 1965). The relationship between these cases might be circumstantial, yet it is interesting that those who toed the line were not persecuted.

Given all this, the main function which remained for these Arab MKs was to act as gatekeepers, a channel through which Palestinians submitted their demands to those in charge of the surveillance and control apparatuses (see, e.g., Muadi, 14 December 1960[9]). Although this practice constituted a veneer of representativeness, it was in fact part and parcel of the control system. Even then, the main function of this practice did not elude many commentators and ordinary citizens. For example, *Ha'aretz* wrote the following about the activities of MK Diab Obeid (1961–65):

> All his activity, and the source of his pride, lies within the narrow scope of influencing the appointment of a school teacher, or having him transferred from a distant school to one nearer his home; or arranging meetings at the Mandelbaum Gate in Jerusalem between Arab citizens and their relatives living in Jordan; or speeding the grant of a loan. In a democratic society, an ordinary citizen may expect to attain such things without having to appeal to a member of parliament. (Quoted in Jiryis, 1976:169)

However, there was an alternative for voters other than these dignitaries – the Communist Party. Why did the state allow it to operate? What was its relation to the control and surveillance apparatuses?

The Communist Party

The Israeli Communist Party (ICP) occupied a unique position in Israeli politics. It was a Jewish–Arab party, though unlike other Jewish–Arab settings such as municipalities of mixed cities, student unions or the Histadrut, it was not dominated by Mapai, and within it, the Palestinians were not secluded. Its Arab leaders were the only group of the Palestinian political elite who were permitted to stay in the country and to resume their political activity even before the end of the 1948 War. The Communist Party had shown an ardent support for the state, as shall be illustrated later, but was opposed to Mapai's policies. It had also been embroiled in the complex relations that Israel had with the Communist Bloc countries, but had conducted its struggle firmly within the realm of the law, even when the legality was the Emergency Regulations (Jiryis, 1976, 1981). Moreover, the Communist Party was principally active among the Palestinians and its impact on the Jewish community had been trivial all along. As some of these assertions might be contested, I shall discuss them succinctly before tackling the role of the Communist Party in the state policy of surveillance and political control.

Unlike Palestinian political organizations which could have been easily suppressed as a result of charges relating to security or loyalty, the Jewish communists have supported Zionism since the late 1930s and played a major role in arming the main Zionist militia in Palestine – the Haganah – as well as in using their good services with various governments in the Eastern bloc to train Jewish men, particularly among the partisans, and send them to fight in Palestine. For example, they played a significant role in the contacts for the Czech arms deals[10] (signed in December 1947 and May 1948) between the Jewish Agency (and later Israel) and the communist government of Czechoslovakia, which gave the Haganah an edge in the firepower over the Arab armies (Pappe, 2006:144).

Additionally, communist leaders secured the establishment of training camps for Jewish field officers in Poland, before their arrival at Palestine to participate in the actual fighting in 1948. These Jewish officers were vital for the Haganah's performance as it suffered from shortage of such trained officers (Pinkus, 2007:191–9).

Jewish Communist Party members took part in the fighting alongside other members of the Zionist parties. Moreover, in 1948, Shmuel Mikunis – the ICP's secretary – was member of the Provisional State Council of the newly created Israeli state. Mikunis was also an 'emissary of the Communist Party to Communist countries to obtain weapons for the 1948 War'.[11]

The following letter of complaint about the situation in Haifa sent two weeks after the occupation of the city by the central committee of ICP reveals complete identification of the Communist Party with the Zionist mission:

> We see as our obligation to bring before you the situation in Haifa following the occupation of the Arab parts of the city by the Haganah. We reveal before you the main facts – facts which are gloomy and disturbing and should worry every righteous Jew.
>
> Now we are in the third week after the liberation of Haifa from the gangs, *we took part in this victory of the Yishuv's security forces*. ... After the agents of imperialism and gangs' members succeeded in the creation of panic among the peaceful Arabs who ran away in their masses. ...

The letter ends as follows:

> The national institutions should ensure *the purity of arms of our military* ... we should spoil the plots of the enemy of our independence, the imperialism and its agents the Arab reactionaries. (The Central Committee of the Eretz-Yisrael Communist Party, 14 May 1948)

Furthermore, the Communist Party's statement on the occasion of the declaration of Israel's independence reaffirms this identification:

> On our side stands the whole Jewish people. ... The whole *Yishuv* must be united to fight for freedom [against the invading Arab armies]. ... Long live the Jewish State! Long live our independent democratic state! Glory to the defenders and fighters for independence! Justice is with us! Victory will be ours! (Quoted in Beinen, 1977:15)

Israel's declaration of independence was signed by Meir Vilner, the representative of the Communist Party, although he was well aware of the exclusionary nature of the state which was envisioned in the document (Davis and Lehn, 1983:145–6).

Moreover, while communist Jews were engaged during the war in fighting and securing arms for the Yishuv and later on for Israel, the majority of the Arab communist leaders were engrossed in the dissemination of pro-Zionist propaganda. Two leaflets, dated July 1948, were signed by the organization of Arab communists, National Liberation League (NLL). The longer one was entitled 'To the soldiers: soldiers of Egypt and the brotherly Arab states, go home and direct your fire to the chests of the imperialists and their lackeys'.[12] Moreover, Jamal Musa,[13] Emile Habibi and Zahi Karkabi – representing the Arab communists in Palestine – helped in October 1948 in composing a leaflet by four Arab communist parties: the Iraqi, the Syrian and the Lebanese in addition to the NLL, attacking the Arab regimes and the Arab League for rejecting the UN partition resolution and for sending troops to Palestine.

After 1948, the leadership of the Communist Party has maintained its deep commitment to the state, along with an allegiance to the Communist Bloc. With regard to the Palestinian minority, the Communist Party preached for their accommodation (Israelization). In one of his first interventions in the Knesset in early September 1949, Tawfiq Tubi condemned the expulsion of Palestinian citizens who were considered unwanted by military commanders or *mukhtars* at a time when the state was allowing the return of some Palestinians who themselves or one of their immediate relatives fought alongside the Arab Rescue Army or incited against the 1947 partition plan (Robinson, 2005b:69). Moreover, he criticized the law draft of conscription to the Israeli army which was debated in the Knesset in 1950 for excluding the Palestinians from the military service, arguing that the law draft contradicts 'the efforts to obtain the friendship of the Arab masses' (Avivi, 2007:85; also Benziman and Mansour, 1992:117). Furthermore, it seems that unlike the bulk of the Palestinians who were disoriented and overwhelmed in the new state, the Communists felt part of it. Already by 4 August 1948 (before the end of the war), Tawfiq Tubi submitted an application for the publication of a newspaper, and on 2 September, Shmuel Mikunis submitted an inquiry to the Minister of Interior regarding the reason of delay in granting the license (Jiryis, 1976:181).

Yet, those in charge of surveillance apparatuses suspected that the ICP's activity could entail subversive potentials. The Arab rank and file of the party was thought to be driven by nationalist, rather than socialist, sentiments. In this regard, Issar Harel argued in 1952: 'We ought to know that communism gives national outlet to the Arabs' feelings of existing discrimination and injustice against them' (The Political Committee, 24 January 1952:1/3). Similarly, following the elections for the fifth Knesset held in September 1961 which revealed a growing support for Maki, Yaakov Eini stated:

> Maki [ICP] received far more votes than what we predicted – in many cases the support for it increased by 150%–300%. They [the Arabs] have anti-Israeli sentiments, and this is the reason that they vote for Maki. It became known that a majority of the youth who benefited for the first time from the right of voting – went to Maki. We thought that if we educate them, they will distant themselves from nationalism, in fact however the opposite occurred. ... The impact of the nationalist circles is increasing; therefore we should inquire whether we should continue in the same way. (The Arab Affairs' Committee, 1 February 1962:8)

Thus, a clear distinction was made between the leadership of the ICP and its supporters. Already in 1948, Ben-Gurion thought that there is a need to prevent the ICP from having an effect on the Palestinians: 'Margovski was appointed head of the Military Government in the Galilee. ... I gave him two instructions: to prevent the infiltration of Arabs to the Galilee and to block the Communists from influencing the Arabs', he wrote in his diary (Ozacky-Lazar, 2002:107).

Besides this adverse impact, the Communists' allegiance to the Soviet bloc brought Mapai to treat the ICP, on various occasions, as a chip in tit-for-tat moves when Israel's relation with the Communist Bloc deteriorated. For example, an initial decision was taken, following the trial of Jewish doctors accused of conspiring against Stalin, to expel Maki from the Histadrut. However, following a change in the Jewish doctors' affairs, Mapai's Political Bureau discussed on 10 June 1953 a strategy of how not to put the expulsion decision into effect without disclosing the association between these two affairs. In the course of the discussion, Namir stated:

> There is the question of Maki. The decision we took, was taken in specific circumstances. ... this was the right decision, against which only Maki protested. There was an atmosphere where a body that doesn't have a national obligation cannot be part of the Histadrut. ... I don't know if the decision is still binding or not. ... The doctor's trial which caused our decision is no longer relevant ... however the need to withdraw from our position is a complicated matter, because it would be difficult to explain abroad. (The Political Committee, 10 June 1953:1–2)

Moreover, Ben-Gurion wanted to outlaw the ICP for the potentials entailed in its activity among the Palestinians as well as for its international allegiances. In this regard, Namir stated:

> The Prime Minister wants something to be done against the communist party, and he conducted talks with the [political] parties in Israel. He did not mean that a danger was posed to the Jewish community by its Jewish members. ... He meant the international dimension; they can travel abroad with diplomatic passports and denounce the state. Ben-Gurion's negotiation with the Jewish parties to

> make a limit, in this context, failed. ... I think we should raise anew the problem regarding the constitutional status of the communist party which constitutes a cancer in the state's body. We should initiate talks with the [Jewish] parties and assure them that they will not be harmed. (The Arab Affairs' Committee, 30 January 1958:17)

However, this approach was contested by some of Mapai's leaders. MK Yona Kesse thought that such a move would be unhelpful: 'We shall not achieve any political benefit because we shall not get the consent of the other factors (i.e. parties) in Knesset. ... This means, legislation is not a precondition for an effective surveillance. ... We can make a dramatic shift in the consciousness of the Jews in the country and the awareness of other parties in case of a valid justification for such an action' (*ibid.*:21).

Indeed, the Arab members and supporters of the ICP were subjected to tight surveillance and oppression. They were branded as negative/radical elements and consequently subjected to all sorts of punishment: their barring from official posts including teaching, withholding of travel passes from them or relegating them to the end of the line, the imposition of restrictions on their activities and the banishment of activists. Moreover, the party itself was put under constant surveillance and was infiltrated by informers (e.g. Cohen, 2006:55–62, also Mapai's Arab department files, 3/14/17).[14]

Yet, ICP was not outlawed. Issar Harel, the powerful head of the Shin Bet and the Mossad, who objected to the banning of the ICP, argued in 1958 that it ought to be incorporated at the periphery of the surveillance and control system. Such incorporation was possible given the party's history, ideology and mixed composition. He thought that the Arab leaders of the party represent a substitute for a national Arab leadership. They would collaborate, despite some tension, with their Jewish colleagues, particularly that their majority does not have serious reservation towards Zionism and the Jewish state (Bauml, 2007:262). According to Harel, the terms of an unwritten deal, which permitted the ICP to pursue its activities were: (A) the ICP would struggle against the state's policy towards the Arab minority within the margin of freedom that the state creates; (B) the ICP would be unofficially recognized as the organized political expression of the Arab minority; and (C) The ICP would struggle against the emergence of Arab nationalist leadership with 'extremist platform', such as the Al-Arad group (see the next section) (Bauml, 2007:262–3). In this regard, '*the ICP's role was to "act against extraordinary [Palestinian] nationalist discontent and for calming down the situation*' (*ibid.*:262). In other words, the ICP was thought of as a manageable safety valve through which Palestinians' discontent would be aired. Thus, even the ICP, whose members and supporters were harassed and suppressed, was eventually incorporated in the surveillance and control system. Besides such understanding, various methods of surveillance including the collection of information on the party and its supporters were used.

Resistance, criminalization and control

Some Palestinians resisted not only their normalization but also the premises of the control system: they rejected the state-sanctioned venues of political participation (Mapai-affiliated Arab lists, the Communist Party and Mapam), their categorization, the hamula politics and their quarantining. They did so through various means, three of which will be briefly discussed hereafter: opting out, 'weapons of the weak' and social protest, and autonomous organization.

Opting out

During the 1950s and 1960s, very often the newspapers reported on young Palestinians who attempted to flee to the neighbouring Arab countries. Such attempts were perilous, as they quite often ended in apprehension or death before the crossing of the borders. In cases of success, they ended in detention by the host country – particularly in the case of Jordan and Lebanon – and later on were deported to Israel where interrogation and imprisonment ensued. The young men who fled were from all the 'ethnicities' and regions.

For example, during two months, August–September 1960, thirty-seven young Palestinian men 14–25 years old from twenty Arab localities fled the country to Lebanon and Jordan (*Davar*, 20 November 1960). Despite the dangers, some tried to do so several times. For example, on 15 January 1961, *Al-Yom* newspaper reported that five young Palestinian men – Khalid Hassan Mahagneh from Um al-Fahim, 18 years old; Salim Saleh Musa Jamal from Nazareth, 18 years old; Ibrahim 'Awad Muhammad Zubedat from Sakhnin, 21 years old; Munir George Huwa from Kababir, 17 years old; and Nimer Fuad Nimer Wakim from Haifa, 20 years old – were sentenced to two months imprisonment or the payment of fine of IL 100, for attempting to flee to Gaza. It was also reported that this was not the first attempt by some of them. All the convicts went to prison as they could not afford to pay the fine (*Al-Yom*, 15 January 1961).

Some young Druze men fled the country to evade the draft, such as Amin Shaheen – 22 years old – who after several unsuccessful attempts to cross the borders to Syria and Lebanon arrived at Gaza (*Al-Yom*, 12 December 1960; Darwish, 30 December 1960; *Davar*, 12 December 1960).

This way of resisting clearly points to the dispiriting and precarious lives of the Palestinians under the control system. Indeed, in a note left by two young Druze men, 30 years old from Isfyia, who fled the country in early January 1960, they stated: 'we are fed up. Therefore we decided to leave the country and look for a [better] future and happiness in the neighbouring Arab countries' (Darwish, 12 January 1961).

The establishment of the Fatah movement for the liberation of Palestine in 1959 amidst a feverish atmosphere of anticolonial struggle and Third-Worldism added another incentive for young Palestinians to flee. The tables compiled by the Arabists show that young educated Palestinians were particularly lured by this option, such as the people who appeared in the following list of *hostile* persons in the Triangle.

Um al-Fahim: Hassan Qassim Mahameed, secondary school pupil (his brother is a Communist Party representative in the local council). Ghassan Fawzi 'Abdallah, Wahab Agbaria (secondary school in Nazareth)

Sandalah: Abdullah Jafa 'Aomari – pupil, secondary school, Nazareth

Qafr Qari'a: Hashim Muhammad Jubir – pupil, secondary school, Nazareth. His father is a policeman in 'Ara. His uncle Suleiman Jabir works in the workers' union (Histadrut)

'Ara: Hasan Abu 'Ailah, 30 years old. Suleiman Khalid Yunis – Mapam, works in the ministry of health, jailed for fifteen days, suspected of sheltering his son who had fled to Damascus. His other son Khalid who is pursuing his studies at Tel-Aviv University (social sciences) received a big grant, following a recommendation by the Arab department (of the Histadrut), contrary to our recommendation. His daughter received support from the working women's union and was appointed as a teacher for handcraft

Saeed Khalid Yunis, Mapam. His brother is radical and inimical

Ya'aqob Masoud Gizmawi, Mapam, second-year student in economics and Arabic language in the Hebrew University of Jerusalem, was accused of infiltration to Syria establishing links with the Syrian intelligence services and then returning. He was detained

Yama: the son of Masoud Mustafa Daqa was accused of driving the members of Fatah cell to a place where they conducted an operation that caused the injury of some people. His brother is known to be a member of Al-Ard. Two years ago, this family was about to get irrigation water for two farm units

Tayibe: detained for fifteen days – Salih Baransi, Omar Baransi (he was convicted in membership in Fatah) and Othman Baransi. Muhammad Khalil Dasuqi – member in Achdut Ha' avoda – was accused of membership in Fatah. Abdullah Halim Nashif was accused of membership in Fatah (Mishal, n.d.)

The list shows that the endeavour of controlling the Palestinians by their blood and social affiliation was self-limited. Young educated Palestinians aspired to move beyond these structures, to develop wide affinities, to choose idealistic goals and to explore liberating potentials.

Weapons of the weak and social protest

Following Scott (1985, 1992), weapons of the weak refers to subversive acts carried out by individuals who cannot defy the system of domination openly. Such acts aim to minimize the impact of the domination rather than challenging its foundations. One such method that Palestinians widely used was the spraying of Graffiti nationalist slogans at night. For example, on 8 October 1962, various such slogans were sprayed on the walls in Um al-Fahim. They included names of martyrs who died for Palestine such as the mythical martyrs Izz al-Deen al-Qassam and Abd al-Qadir al-Hussayni and the local martyr Hassan al-Saeed. They also included threats to land dealers, *samaserah*. Local dignitaries and Communist leaders were quick in expressing their condemnation (Mishal, 15 October 1962). Moreover, state flags which were raised in public buildings were occasionally torn or removed. For example, in 1962, seventeen flags in the village of Tira were either spoiled or removed. Similar acts, though on a limited scale, occurred in several other villages (Robinson, 2005b:276–7).

Other noticeable acts included the airing of nationalist views by public figures such as teachers, poets and leaders. The surveillance methods used in schools and colleges to suppress dissent were discussed in chapter 6, yet I will bring the case of one teacher, 'Ali Saeed Wahba, twenty years old, from the village of 'Akbara in the Galilee, which received some publicity. He was accused of tearing the picture of Herzl – the founder of the Zionist movement – in the classroom in front of his pupils. Ten days after the event, he was fired and legal action was taken against him. As the law did not oblige the citizens to show respect for Zionist figures, the court ordered him to pay a fine of IL 10 for the destruction of school property (*Davar*, 28 December 1960; *Maariv*, 10 January 1960).

During the discussed period, there were several renowned poets who gave aesthetic expression to the grievances and aspirations of the Palestinians, most notably Mahmoud Darwish – who later became Palestine's national poet – Samih Al-Qassim and Rashid Hussein. Yet, they were affiliated to and published their work in sanctioned venues of political activity. The first two were affiliated to the Communist Party, while the latter worked as editor for various Mapam's publications.

The other method in this category of resistance is social protest. It is different from the previous one by its collective nature; it was carried out by a group of people who had similar motivations or grievances. Such outbursts were mostly spontaneous or sporadic. The control and surveillance system, particularly through the regime of quarantining and travel permits, was effective in obstructing the development of an organized protest movement as will be discussed later. However, two mass demonstrations are worth referring to: the 1958 mass demonstrations in Nazareth and Um al-Fahim and a demonstration in Haifa in 1961. They reflected, in some ways, the beginning and pinnacle of a remarkable wave of a nationalist challenge to the control system.

The 1958 demonstrations erupted unexpectedly as a result of a window of opportunity for protest that was opened. The tenth anniversary of Israel's independence, which occurred then, was seen by state leaders as an opportunity to project an image of Israel as an enlightened, egalitarian and young democratic state. Palestinians' participation was essential for the credibility of the planned spectacles. Palestinian mayors, chairpersons of local authorities and dignitaries received orders to put on shows and conduct celebrations according to a comprehensive plan (Sa'di, 2001; Robinson, 2005b:263–74; Cohen, 2006:248–50). Along with that, various preventive measures such as detention were taken against potential 'troublemakers' (Bauml, 2007:274–6). However, on the 1 May march in Nazareth, Palestinians began to demonstrate and chant slogans against the various manifestations of the system of control: the Military Government, the quarantining, the regime of passes, the high unemployment, the prevalent discrimination, etc. Two days later, a similar protest took place in Um al-Fahim. The state reacted by suppression: wholesale arrests and show and use of force. Some 400 Palestinians were arrested and were put on trial before military courts. This event led Palestinian leaders, nationalists and communists to establish an organization to defend the detainees, as will be detailed in the following section (Amnon, 6 July 1958; Nakdimon, 11 August 1958; Jiryis, 1976:185–7).

The mass demonstrations in Haifa and several other localities, principally Um al-Fahim and Sakhnin, ensued from the killing and apparently the mutilation of the bodies of five young men who attempted to flee the country on 17 September 1961 (Asadi, 1999:6–9; Sa'di, 2001:35; Linn, 1999:164–6). This event, similar to the previous one, led to the emergence of an organization which called for the formation of a legal investigative committee, yet not much was achieved (The Committee of the Victims, Haifa, 30 September 1961).

The Popular Front and Al-Ard

After the 1958 demonstrations, a 'popular committee for the defence of the detainees and the banished persons' was established. Its aim was to offer various forms of assistance – principally legal – to those who were affected by the state's reprisals. The committee included nationalist leaders and Arab leaders of ICP. Committee members thought of formalizing this cooperation and creating a permanent forum, which they called 'the Arab Front'. The state was not ready to allow the formation of an organized Arab political group. It reacted by using a wide array of bureaucratic and legal means as well as decisionism to suppress this initiative, particularly to prevent Arab nationalists from having any political role. Indeed, state oppression was overwhelming from the start.

The inaugural meeting was scheduled to be held in Acre at a local restaurant – Abu Christo restaurant – on 6 July 1958, and an invitation was issued by Yani Yani, the chairperson of Kafr Yassif's local council. The state reacted by banning many invitees from arriving to the meeting and by preventing the meeting from taking place at the designated venue. Orders of travel restrictions along with the obligation to report at the local police station were issued against 40 leaders including the clergymen Yousef Stephan Susan and Najib Khuri and the chairpersons of Shafa'amr and Kafr Yassif local authorities, Jabour Jabour and Yani Yani (*Ha'aretz*, 7 July 1958). Moreover, the restaurant owner was pressurized to disallow the meeting from taking place at his premises (Nakdimon, 11 August 1958).

Despite that, the meeting took place in a new venue, at the local Communist Party club, with the participation of some 120 communist and non-communist delegates. At the end of the meeting, police photographers accompanied by policemen in uniform photographed the participants (Ha'aretz, 7 July 1958). After the inauguration, the law required that the association notify the Ministry of Interior of its goals and activities. However, the Ministry rejected the application of the Arab Front citing an Ottoman law dating to 1909, which prohibits the establishment of national associations (Jiryis, 1976:186; Zvi, 21 January 1959). Then the term 'Arab' was substituted for 'popular'; thus, the name was changed to the Popular Front.

Having passed the first hurdle, the Front began to expand, and state oppression against it concurrently increased. Within less than two months, two branches were opened in Nazareth and Kafr Yassif in addition to the Acre branch, and a call to open branches in other Arab localities was aired (Dawood, 23 August 1958). Indeed, by the end of 1958, six branches were active (Jiryis, 1976:186). Moreover, the Front listed the political, social-economic and legal demands of the Palestinian minority. These were presented to the Jewish public by leaflets composed in Hebrew as well as by a press conference which was held on 10 August 1958 at the Sokolov house in Tel-Aviv (*Davar*, 11 August 1958). The representatives of the front who participated in this press conference came from various political trends, including a supporter of the General Zionist Party. Moreover, the Front pinpointed with clarity and precision the demands of the Arab population and offered practical solutions to these requests in various booklets (The Popular Front, n.d.). The Front's aim of presenting the Palestinians as a national community and as citizens with rights negated the principles and suppositions of the control system and the official policy guidelines.

The state reacted by gathering information and extensive use of the emergency regulations. For example, the minutes of the inaugural meeting of Kafr Yassif's branch were sent to the surveillance apparatuses (Dawood, 23 August 1958). It seems that informers used to collect all the public material that the Front published and hand it over to Yaakov Eini of Mapai's Arab department (see, e.g., The Arab Front, 17 September 1958).

Besides information gathering, severe restrictions on the movement of the Front's leaders were imposed. These restrictions aimed to prevent them from meeting and affecting their economic or professional activities. For example, orders of movement confinement were issued to the founders of the front:

Yani Yani the chairperson of Kafr Yassif local council, Jabour Jabour the mayor of Shafa'amr, Tahir Al-Fahoum from Nazareth and Dr. Yousef Haddad and Dr. Atallah Sheban, both physicians who as part of their work visited adjacent villages.

As the Front grew, so did the cancellation of the movement permits to its members. Thus, the passes of Abdulhamied Abu Atiya, a member of the executive committee of Tayibe's branch, as well as the passes of the many active members in Kafr Yassif's branch – Salim Saeed, Ahmad Shihade, Hanna Daleh, Salim Dawood, Yousef Shihade, Hassan Sha'ir, Muhammad Haj, Nicola Daowd, Elias Daleh, Nimer Morqos and Raja Jiryis – were revoked. Additionally, members of Acre branch's executive – Mahmoud Sruji and Ramzi Khuri – were barred from visiting the Galilee, and the Front's members who lived in Haifa, attorney Hanna Naqara, Shukri Khazin, Habib Qahwaji and 'Issam 'Abasi, were banned from visiting Nazareth and Kafr Yassif (The Popular Front, The Executive Committee, 29 October 1958). Tougher actions were taken against some active members. Zuhir Halaq and Ghassan Habib were put under administrative detention without any explanation, and Mbada Farhat, Jamil Shihade and Gabriel Shihade from Kafr Yassif were banished to Safad without any arrangements being made to supply them with shelter or food (*ibid.*). Added to that, threats of physical violence were voiced by officials in the Military Government against activists (*ibid.*). These actions were accompanied by a wide-ranging campaign to delegitimize the front by leading state figures including the Prime Minister, the Advisor on Arab Affairs and leading police officers (Dawood, 23 August 1958; Jiryis, 1976:187; Bauml, 2007:278–80).

The Front's disintegration began in early January 1959 in a series of resignations by nationalist leaders. This was the result of different agendas and an ideological rift between the communists and the nationalists. The communists wanted to use the Front to garner support for their party in the forthcoming elections which were due on 3 November 1959. Nationalist leaders objected to the use of the Front for election purposes, particularly because many of them viewed the participation in the national politics under the Military Government and the extensive employment of the emergency regulations as futile. Additionally, both sides took opposite stands on the rift between the nationalists in the Arab World headed by Egypt's President Nassir and the USSR and its Arab supporters (*Jerusalem Post*, 19 January 1959; Zvi, 21 January 1959; Jiryis, 1976:187).

The surveillance and control apparatuses learnt their lesson. As described in the previous section – on the Communist Party – these apparatuses sought to allow the functioning of the ICP and keeping it as a safety valve. Thus, effectively, the ICP became an auxiliary instrument of control and surveillance; while its supporters were tagged as 'negative/radical' elements, the party was allowed to operate and was entrusted to oppose any nationalist surge among the Palestinians.

Some nationalist leaders, particularly those who composed *Usrat Al-Arad* (the land's family), endeavoured to politicize and mobilize the Arab public through various means, yet they did not stand much chance. At first, they tried to do so through the publication of a newspaper. However, their application was met by an overlong delay. Consequently, they began to air their views in a weekly, which, in order to abide by the letter of the law, was marked as a single issue. However, all the titles included the term Al-Arad (the land). All the journal's issues were collected by Mapai's Arab department, and the articles were translated and summarized by Yaakov Eini – a leading Arabist (they are found in the Labour Party's archives[15]).

Although all the published material was submitted to the censure prior to its publication, the publication of two issues by the same editorial group was regarded as a criminal offence. The police raided the headquarters of the journal as well as the flat of two students at the Hebrew University and confiscated considerable material including unsold copies of the last (the thirteenth) issue. Criminal charges of violating journalism and emergency regulations were pressed against six of the editors (*Davar*, 24 February 1960).

Al-Arad's application to publish a journal was turned down on technical grounds, and after fulfilling all the requirements, a new application was submitted. This time, the district commissioner, in line with a decision that was taken by those in charge of surveillance apparatuses (Bauml, 2007:290–3), rejected the new application without listing the reasons for his decision, and an appeal to the Supreme Court by Al-Ard was also turned down. The judges argued that the commissioner's discretion was unbounded (Jiryis, 1976:189).

Al-Ard's application to form a political party was also rejected by the district commissioner. Although his role in such matters was to ensure adherence to the procedures, he justified his decision by the unacceptable ideology of the movement. His fuzzy interpretation of Al-Ard's articles of association was reaffirmed by the majority of the Supreme Court's judges (Jiryis, 1976:190–2; Kretzmer, 1990:24–6). By following the sequence of events in this case, Bauml (2007) raises the plausibility that the government might have hinted to the court regarding the required verdict (294–5).

Even prior to the verdict, the government decided to suppress Al-Ard once and for all. Yet, as Al-Ard declared intent to contest the elections as a political party, the government decided to suspend its move in order to allow for a veneer of due process (*ibid.*; Jiryis, 1976:190–2). Two days after the court's ruling, three of Al-Ard's leaders were arrested; the declared reason was that a group of agents from Arab countries who were on a mission to meet these leaders was apprehended. The Minister of Defence, using the authorities entrusted to him by the emergency regulations, outlawed Al-Ard, declared the seizure of its assets and announced that any attempt to renew its activities would be punishable with ten years' imprisonment (Jiryis, 1976:102–3). The final round in this saga was the establishment of a political party – the Socialist List – by Al-Ard to contest the elections for the sixth Knesset in 1965. Again the suppression began with the declaration of the movement's intention. The military governor banished four out of the ten party's candidates, and orders of house confinement were issued to many activists. Furthermore, considerable pressure was employed on those who condoned the list. The Central Elections Committee, which had a procedural role, disqualified the party, a decision that was upheld by the Supreme Court (Jiryis, 1976:193–4; Kretzmer, 1990:24–6).

Al-Ard's episode highlighted the role that decisionism had played in suppressing Palestinian dissent and drew the margins of the limited space within which they can practise their political rights. Meanwhile, the old nationalist leaders passed away. Describing their departure, Ori Stendel, who worked for many years in the Advisor's office, stated with a sign of relief:

> None of the three is still alive. Yani Yani died in 1962. Jabour Jabour died later. On June 21, 1971, the last of the three Elias Ni'matallah Kusa died in Haifa. These three personalities of the older generation were fanatically radical Arab nationalists. The world of the communist party was alien to them, but they saw it as an ally in their struggle against the state of Israel. (Stendel, 1973:122)

The leaders of the younger generation either left the country, like Sabri Jiryis and Habib Qahwaji, or were silenced like Mansour Kardosh. Others like Salih Baransi tried to find other channels for their activism but were contained.

Following the end of Al-Ard's episode, the surveillance agencies continued, without a worthwhile organized challenge, to operate the system of patronage and maintained their methods of dividing, categorizing, labelling and arranging Palestinians hierarchically according to clan and ethnic identities. Moreover, they continued their nominations of collaborators and dignitaries to represent the Palestinian community. The Communist Party also continued to perform its role as a sanctioned venue for dissent and as an outlet for the discontented sections of the community, performing an auxiliary function of surveillance. Thus, a veneer of democracy alongside a state of exception prevailed even after the cancellation of the Military Government.

A forum of chairpersons of local authorities

During the six years (1959–65) in which the Al-Ard affair was unravelling, various developments occurred. One of these was an attempt in early 1962 to establish a framework for the elected chairpersons of the Arab local authorities. This initiative was started by the mayor of Shafa'amr Jabour Jabour and was supported by Yani Yani and Hanna Mwais, who became the chairperson of Rama's local council in 1959. Jabour and his associates tried to get the support of their colleagues by raising issues of concern to the Palestinian society at large. These, according to surveillance reports, included:

1. The prices of the olive oil paid for Palestinian farmers.
2. The amounts of state loans to Arab local authorities in the light of the currency devaluation.
3. The salary and advancement scales of the employees in the Arab local authorities.
4. The state grants for building schools for primary and secondary education.
5. The granting of pensions to secondary school teachers (The Arab Department, 15 March 1962).

Despite the apolitical nature of the issues raised, Mapai's Arab department employed immense pressure on Arab chairpersons to shun this initiative (e.g. The Arab Department, 24 March 1962), which was eventually thwarted. Moreover a conference on Arab education, to which they called, was cancelled. Summarizing this episode, a report by Mapai's Arab department indicated:

> The meeting of the chairpersons of Arab localities, called for by Yani Yani, Jabour Jabour and Hanna Mwais, will not take place due to lack of participation by chairpersons of [Arab] local authorities [who refrained] *following our request*. (The Arab Department, 25 March 1962; my emphasis)

Conclusion

The expansion of the surveillance and control practices to the political sphere meant the abrogation of the Palestinians' political rights. Thus, the democratic process among the Palestinians served ends which contradict the democratic principles. Contrary to what is expected in democracy, free and fair elections among parties which compete to represent the interests of the Palestinians did not exist. The officially recognized 'Arab leaders' were chosen by Arabists rather than by the Palestinians, and they were emissaries of an oppressive regime. These leaders, who were mostly long-standing collaborators, representatives of a collaborator or 'dignitaries', were part of a spectacle of cynicism and oppression and had to endure a humbling experience where they were dehumanized and turned into 'machines for raising hands'.

This deformed process of political participation where subordinates were compelled to vote for emissaries of the regime meant the bolstering of a cruel system of patronage and the reinforcement of the power of categorization that the regime created.

Palestinians' endeavours to resist this reality took various forms – including opting out, the employment of 'weapons of the weak', organizing social protest and establishing autonomous political organizations – all of which were met by actions that emanated from the state of exception and the practices of control. This includes extensive reliance on the emergency regulations and decisions that military governors or bureaucrats made. Public dissent was not allowed and those who defied the control system were either pushed out of the country or were silenced, and few were co-opted.

Only a small margin for supervised protest was allowed through the Communist Party. Yet, this was more of a manageable safety valve than a sound venue for free expression of opinions, particularly given the genesis of this party which is non-accommodative to free public debate and pluralism and its incorporation at the periphery of the control system. Thus, while the ICP leadership was incorporated into the political system, the party's rank and file were put under surveillance and were harassed.

As to the young men who tried to flee the country or to join the Al-Fatah movement, their affair was contained through a combination of stiff measures and the creation of new opportunities. These included the passing of the Prevention of Infiltration Law, 1954, on whose basis a special type of military courts were established (Korn, 1995:668–9; see the discussion in chapter 3), and the placing of pressure through intimate social structures including families and hamulas by holding them accountable for the acts that such youth undertook (e.g. *Al-Yom*'s editorial, 18 November 1960). Meanwhile, new employment and educational opportunities became available to Arab men. In a meeting on 25 November 1960 which dealt with the flight of Arab youth and was attended by some senior Arabists – Hushi, Yahlom (of the Histadrut's Arab department), Lubrani and Eini – a decision regarding the opening of such opportunities was taken including the creation of training courses for lower clerical professions such as typists, the publishing in *Al-Yom* newspaper of a section for occupational guidance whereby youth are advised on the needed professions in the labour market and the exploration with the Hebrew University of enabling some youth to study medical-related subjects (The Confined Committee of the Arab Affairs' Committee, 25 November 1960).

In retrospect, it is startling how this system has been presented as a democracy, and how despite the state of exception which prevailed and the violation of every principle of democracy, very few social scientists and commentators have appraised it critically or tried to demystify it. In this chapter not only was this edifice deconstructed but its dark side, as a method which contributed to the accumulation of control and surveillance, was also described.

Notes

1 A Mapai's internal Memo, the author is unknown.
2 www.knesset.gov.il/mk/eng/mk_eng.asp?mk_individual_id_t=251.
3 www.knesset.gov.il/mk/eng/mk_eng.asp?mk_individual_id_t=422.

4 www.knesset.gov.il/mk/eng/mk_eng.asp?mk_individual_id_t=233.

5 The Knesset webpage of Mr Hamdan: www.knesset.gov.il/mk/eng/mk_eng.asp?mk_individual_id_t=420.

6 www.knesset.gov.il/mk/eng/mk_eng.asp?mk_individual_id_t=345.

7 www.knesset.gov.il/mk/eng/mk_eng.asp?mk_individual_id_t=520.

8 This leaflet was distributed by Khnayfis' party 'Progress and Work'. The reference is to the Hebrew translation of the leaflet found in Khnayfis' file in the Labour Party Archive. This leaflet is not dated but most likely was distributed in the election campaign of 1959 or 1961.

9 Lists of demands to official bodies were quite often submitted through dignitaries. For example, on 14 December 1960, a long list of persons who applied to visit the holy places in the West Bank, then part of Jordan, was submitted to the Advisor on Arab Affairs Uri Lubrani via KM Mudai. Interestingly, Lubrani forwarded it to Yaakov Eini.

10 According to Yigal Eilam (2002), this arms deal had significantly affected the end result of the war and the fate of hundreds of thousands of Palestinians:

> In this respect, the Israeli narrative that states the Czech weapons we received, with Russian backing, were critical to the war effort is correct.
>
> We also received additional, smuggled weapons from American and European sources. But the Czech weapons were critical – light arms and planes, the basis for the small Israeli air force. We also acquired tanks and even ships. The Czech assistance was already a factor during the first phase, when 5,000 rifles arrived on the eve of Operation Nachshon [during which Israel successfully engaged in the battles for the Jerusalem Corridor, the battle of Mishmar Ha'emek, Ramat Yohanan, the occupation of Arab Tiberias and Arab Haifa]. The embargo hurt the Arab side more than it hurt the Jews. It worked in Israel's favor, because it prevented the Arab armies from replenishing their equipment.

11 See his public activities on the Knesset website: www.knesset.gov.il/mk/eng/mk_eng.asp?mk_individual_id_t=507.

12 Regarding this point, see Sa'di (2010).

13 Jamal Musa was described as the secretary of the Arab camp workers in the 1940s.

14 Most of the parties' leaflets and many deliberations can be found in Mapai's Arab department files, *LPA*, Files 3/14/17.

15 See Mapai's Arab department files.

Concluding remarks

Reflections on Israeli policies

Israeli policies of population management, surveillance and political control described in this book had not been entirely known before. Scholars who previously wrote on state–minority relations were largely guessing in the dark; thus, their assumptions and biases might have found their ways to the models or narratives they composed. Two widely held theses in Israeli social sciences were disproved in the current study: the absence of a clear state policy towards the minority and the major role that personal dispositions of politicians and Arabists had supposedly played in moulding the official attitudes towards the minority.

However, the archival documents on which this book relies show that a deeply seated understanding regarding state objectives vis-à-vis the minority had existed all along. An extensive debate – *birour* – took place among leading politicians and Arabists during the war and continued intermittently during the first four years. These deliberations could be divided into two periods. The first, until 1951, was marked by the belief that an opportunity for driving out the remaining Palestinians would arise soon, and therefore the debates revolved around a simple question: How to manage their lives during the transitory period? However, a growing realization, since then, that this minority might stay for a long time led to an exploration of methods through which they would be governed, yet without abandoning the transfer option. The subsequent devised methods of governance can be subsumed under three topics: population management strategies, identity alteration and conduct moulding through structural determinants and disciplinary practices.

In 1958, a decade after the state's establishment, a comprehensive plan of governance was laid down. Its principles continued, with some elaborations and insertions, to constitute the basis of Israeli policy towards the Palestinian minority during and after the discussed period. These guidelines were reiterated in 1968 and seem to have acquired a long life, as they might have persisted until 1991.

While the question regarding the reasons for the failure of many scholars who researched 'the ethnic relations in Israel' and the Israeli political system in identifying a pattern of state governance of the Palestinian minority might be rhetorical, some of their empirical findings could be of unexpected significance. Given state policy guidelines described in this book, some findings of existing research might shed light on areas of success and failure of this policy at a certain point in time. One readily available example is the research on the identity of the Palestinians. The major part of this research explored the self-categorization of Palestinian citizens. Typically, interviewees were asked to choose among a list of labels the most appropriate social construction that describes their identity. The lists usually included images: Arab, Israeli, religious affiliations, Israeli Arab and Palestinian. The findings were interpreted as indicating Israelization versus Palestinization or radicalization versus moderation. On the basis of the state policy plan of dividing the Palestinians into ethnic groups with insular identities, these findings could be reinterpreted as pointing to the degree to which this policy had succeeded (see Sa'di, 1992, 2004b).

In the main, the evolvement of various aspects of Palestinians' lives in Israel could be viewed as a history of state power-driven governance strategies and resistance by Palestinians. This power–resistance dynamics renders any conclusions one might draw regarding successes or failures of state policies provisional. For example, has state policy in creating a Druze identity been successful? On the face of it, the answer could be positive. Druze men serve in the army, and security-related occupations have constituted the largest employment sector for them. Moreover, the majority of the Druze population has been reluctant to join Palestinian organizations. However, a research by Halabi (2006) on Druze identity shows that the reality is more nuanced than what Israeli leaders might have hoped for. One prevalent view among Druze men was summed up as follows: 'a proud Israeli on the way to the military camp but a dirty Arab on the way back home' (79–87). Moreover, he reported on differences along gender and geographical lines regarding Arab identification (*ibid.*:57–60). Additionally, the opposition among the Druze community to the creation of a Druze insular identity, which emerged in response to the drafting of Druze men, has not waned.

Such mixed results bring to the fore the limits that state schemes have. However, an analysis of the debates of those in charge of the surveillance and control agencies shows that they had rarely been mindful of the many factors that might disrupt their plans. Only two among the participants kept reminding the rest of the hurdles that their policies might face: the first, Professor Ben-Zion (Dinaburg) Dinur, probably due to his education and his work in Israel as a history professor, highlighted the historical nature of human beings, and in various interventions referred to the Arabs as a historic nation, that being the reason why their conception of pre-1948 Palestine would not fade away quickly, if at all. The second, Issar Harel, the powerful head of the Mossad and the Shin Bet, held a nihilist view and argued that what was broken could not be fixed, referring to the destruction of Palestinian society in 1948.

Indeed, many factors besides the historical backdrop were adversely related to the official Israeli discourse and policy guidelines. Some of these variables were general, such as the subjective images of the world that human beings hold and their resistance to imposed categorizations. Others relate to the conditions of the Palestinian minority. These include the fact that the Palestinians in Israel were part of the Palestinian nation socially, historically and morally. They had relatives, friends, business partners or associates either among the refugees or among the Palestinians in the West Bank and Gaza Strip. The new political order cannot, by setting borders, erase these ties. Besides that, the ghettoization of the Palestinians did not last long, as, through the new means of communications, most significantly radio and television, they were reconnected with the Arab world. Even inside Israel, some of the few remaining national leaders – such as Yani Yani, Elias Kusa and Jabour Jabour – kept challenging state policy and its representations in the *Hasbara*. Their reference to the Palestinian minority as the country's indigenous population comprised a powerful counter-discourse. Following the suppression of the *Al-Ard* nationalist movement in the early 1960s, it seemed for a few years that an organized challenge to the official discourse might have dissipated; yet, this did not last long. In 1971, a nationalist group called *Abna Al-Balad* was established.

Besides that, two main shortcomings of the official policy decreased the likelihood of its success, particularly with regard to the moulding of new identities for the Palestinians. The first, and the main impediment, was the negative nature of the state policy. For example, most policy guidelines, as detailed in the Tolidano plan, indicated a suppressive course of action: to disallow, to prevent, etc. The second was the hollowness and the inappropriateness of the minimal ideology that the regime proposed. This ideology emphasized personal success, 'minding one's own business' and following the directions of the elders and the dignitaries. Such emphases were in opposition to a long-standing socio-moral order, where social solidarity and supporting just causes were venerated. Moreover, this ideology was a dead end, as the Jewish–Arab hierarchy remained overriding. Arabs who accepted this discourse were not treated as equal citizens. Their inferior status stemmed first of all from their national belonging. Even senior dignitaries, such as Arab members of the Knesset (MKs), were secluded and belittled. Beyond that, the fallaciousness of the minimal ideology can neither be hidden nor underplayed. The gap between the official representation of the state – as democratic and built on principles of justice, equality and freedom – and the methods of governance was unbridgeable. In the political realm, this divergence was so glaring that democracy for this minority was no more than a devious spectacle, in which shadows threatening Arabists operated.

Interestingly, this flagrant gap between the official policy and its representation had rarely bothered those in charge of the surveillance and control agencies. The minutes of their meetings and their private messages had rarely touched on questions relating to consciousness, morality, justice and honesty. Rather, their approach had been principally characterized by fanatical realism and instrumental rationality. When questions of moral weight emerged, they were mostly brushed aside. For example, in his response to an army report regarding a military exercise during which Arab citizens were killed, Ben-Gurion criticized the report for including too many printing mistakes (Kafkafi, 1998:358). No reaction was made regarding the carrying out of military training close to the Arab villages. Similarly, in a debate in the Knesset on 5 August 1953 regarding the maltreatment of residents in the village Tira during a search by the army, prompted by false information regarding fire that was allegedly opened at an Israeli jet from the village, Pinhas Lavon, the then Deputy Minister of Defence, stated that 'presumably you don't mean that mahogany furniture or pianos were broken during the search?' (*ibid.*:356).

Indeed, dealing with issues of moral resonance could be counterproductive for the efficiency and the economy of political control. Therefore, questions relating to the morality or the emotions of those who devised or operated the control and surveillance system had largely been overlooked, as their exploration could be damning. The only occasion on which such subjects were bluntly raised was during a debate which took place in the meeting of Mapai's secretariat with the party's MKs on 9 July 1950. It was prompted by a case which David HaCohen brought as an epitome of the state's attitude towards the Palestinians:

> Five months ago we built a main street in Haifa, which had to pass through an Arab [Islamic] cemetery. We brought the Arab community to accept the removal of graves and eighty bags of bones are still until today overstuffed in the mosque because our men are not ready to designate a piece of land where these bones can be buried. There are examples of hundreds of cases of discrimination and brutality. (The Secretariat's Meeting with MKs, 9 July 1950:7/2)

He also highlighted various draconian laws which were passed and aimed to take over Palestinians' property: 'Such laws which we pass for the Arab citizens of the state of Israel couldn't be compared even to the anti-Jewish laws in the Middle Ages, when the Jews were devoid of rights. This constitutes a contradiction between our declarations and our deeds' (*ibid.*:8/2). Even General Emmanuel Moor of the Military Administration expressed unease regarding the attitude towards the Palestinians. While he tried to point to the complexity of 'the existence of citizens with equal rights, who actually do not have equal rights' (*ibid.*:2/3), he went on to declare that '[a]ll the Jewish community beyond its divisions is ready to harm this population; terrible and unfortunate incidents are occurring' (*ibid.*:3/3). Meanwhile, MK Zalman (Aharonowitz) Aran expressed desperation: 'I have to stress that this issue is very important to me and I cannot deal with it morally; it is a process of despair' (*ibid.*:3/4). His hopelessness stemmed from his inability to justify the official policies:

> Morally I reject this thing absolutely and there is not a thing which can justify it. I know that there is a security problem and I do not speak about infiltrators. I know existing considerations. ... Morally speaking we are a movement that should not tell lies and we don't want to lie, in this issue however we live in a total lie. ... I don't speak about the attitude of individuals towards the Arabs; I speak about the general line. I reject this approach. ... I don't accept the justifications which were given. ... We have no right to request other (better) attitude toward Jewish minorities in other countries on the basis of what we are doing here to the Arabs. I think retrospectively that we are falsifying all our arguments against Gentiles' attitudes toward the Jews. (*Ibid.*)

Ben-Zion (Dinaburg) Dinur, who served as Minister of Education and Culture in the third to the sixth governments (1952–55), also objected to the official policies and their implementation. He criticized the main goal of expelling the Palestinians in case an appropriate opportunity emerges and expressed unease regarding the army's mishandling of Palestinians:

> What does it mean that we fought for our right to exist? People have been living here for one thousand and five hundred years and we want to expel them; this means that we justify all what has been done to the Jews. ... What does it mean that we appoint Iraqi and Moroccan youth who mess up with other people's lives... We are responsible for everything. We should say that there is a need for strong hand of the state and whoever harms an Arab must be punished; I accuse the legal system and the spirit of regime; since there is legal discrimination and this will destroy the state. (*Ibid.*:5/4)

Yet, MK Shmuel Dayan thought that his colleagues were insincere and their arguments were contradictory with their existence. He stated:

> Some party members who are sitting here have a social-moral theory and continue [to advocate] this line and this judgement; our ears are not listening and our eyes are not seeing what we are doing. We are doing the opposite of what we say around this table. If Zima [Zalman Aran] and Dinaburg and others stand for what they say, they ought to be consistent and say that the Arabs in Gaza, 300–400 thousands, who are there and are trying to infiltrate should be allowed [to return] and get their houses back. Has Dinaburg, as a man of morals been consistent, he should have advocated this. It can be said that we are immoral, we took their houses, and they are in Gaza willing to burst into their houses in which they lived for hundreds of years and you are preventing them from getting

> into their houses, you shoot them. Do you have any other way to prevent them from getting in? Can you do this by a magical stick? I want to hear for once a clear answer, in what way can we prevent hundreds of thousands of uprooted people from returning, what way is available other than by weapons? I was offended by your talk about these youths. ... They are representative of the state and they do what they do in its name. They are soldiers and they follow orders, if they get other orders they will behave differently ... maybe there are some corrupt young men, but what is the relevance of this here?
>
> I don't know where we shall end up if we want to be right and moral. The question is: are there morals in war. In war there are no morals. We fought like all the other Gentiles; we occupied and took to ourselves the houses of Jaffa and Qatamun (a neighbourhood in Jerusalem). I adhere to the same approach like you, I am confused and I don't know what morals are. (*Ibid.*:1–2/5)

Given the disruptive nature of humanizing those who were the object of surveillance and political control, such reflective debate and self-examination had not continued, and instead, categorizations and labelling were employed. The use of detached labels and the lumping of populations into abstract categories and binaries (particularly that of friend–foe) have constituted a convenient shield for those who devised and implemented the policies of surveillance and control.

Having described throughout this book the various aspects of the official policy towards the Palestinians and the ways in which political control was implemented and reflected in the conclusion on the mindset of those who took part in its formation, I hope another contribution of this research would be recognized: its new interpretative paradigm for state–minority relations. Through this perspective, a reinterpretation of existing data could ensue, an endeavour that could help in shedding light on areas of failure and success that the official policy might have met in certain periods. Moreover, a future research could explore trends of continuity or change in the official policy beyond the discussed period and examine whether some of its aspects were implemented in the West Bank and Gaza Strip after their occupation in 1967. Additionally, future research might compare the Israeli policies of population management and control with other states which contain unwelcome minorities or with historical cases such as colonialism.

Bibliography

Websites

Knesset web pages of Arab MKs

- Saif Al-Deen Al-Zu'bi:
www.knesset.gov.il/mk/eng/mk_eng.asp?mk_individual_id_t=251
- Salih Khnayfis:
www.knesset.gov.il/mk/eng/mk_eng.asp?mk_individual_id_t=422
- Labib Abu-Rukun:
www.knesset.gov.il/mk/eng/mk_eng.asp?mk_individual_id_t=233
- Faris Hamdan:
www.knesset.gov.il/mk/eng/mk_eng.asp?mk_individual_id_t=420
- Amin Jurjora:
www.knesset.gov.il/mk/eng/mk_eng.asp?mk_individual_id_t=345
- Elias Nakhleh:
www.knesset.gov.il/mk/eng/mk_eng.asp?mk_individual_id_t=520

The Emergency Regulations' website: www.israellawresourcecenter.org/websitematerials/mapsg/mapsg1der1945.html.

Kirshbaum, David A. *Israeli Emergency Regulations & the Defense (Emergency) Regulations of 1945*. Website: www.israellawresourcecenter.org/emergencyregs/essays/emergencyregsessay.htm.

Mikunis, Shmuel. Knesset website: http://www.knesset.gov.il/mk/eng/mk_eng.asp?mk_individual_id_t=507

The Provisional Council of State. (19 May 1948) *Law and Administration Ordinance*. Website: http://israellawresourcecenter.org/israellaws/fulltext/lawandadministrationord.htm

Archival

- The Labour Party Archive at Beit Berl will be referred to in short as *LPA*.
- *The Lavon Archive* of the Histadrut in Tel-Aviv, will be referred to in short as *The Lavon Archive*.

Abd al-Raziq, Twfiq. (4 March 1962) 'Letter to Yaakov Eini', *LPA*, Files 26/12/15.

Abu-Hijla, Abd Al-Raziq. (4 January 1966) 'To Meir Mishal: List of the Names of Teachers and the Employees in Public and Governmental Sectors in the Villages of Petah Tikva Region, the Villages Kafr Qasim, Bara, Juljulia', *LPA*, Files 26/17/13.

Abu-Mukh, Abd. S. (25 December 1964) 'Letter: To Mapai's Headquarter, the Arab Department', *LPA*, Files 26/7/20.

The Academic Secretariat, the Hebrew University. (1964) 'The List of Students of Minority Background (Arabs and Druze) in 1964', *LPA*, Files 3/1.

Agassi, Eliyahu. (29 August 1956) 'Letter to the Cinema Department: To Hahaver Arie Brzam', *The Lavon Archive*, Document No. IV-208-1-8559.

The Arab Affairs' Committee. (12 September 1957) 'The Protocol of the Meeting', *LPA*, Files 7/32.

The Arab Affairs' Committee. (30 January 1958) 'The Protocol of the Meeting', *LPA*, Files 7/32.

The Arab Affairs' Committee. (14 August 1958) 'The Protocol of the Meeting – The Military Government', *LPA*, Files 7/32.

The Arab Affairs' Committee. (24 February 1959) 'The Protocol of the Meeting', *LPA*, Files 7/32.

The Arab Affairs' Committee. (11 August 1960) 'The Protocol of the Meeting', *LPA*, Files 7/32/60.

The Arab Affairs' Committee. (5 May 1961) 'The Protocol of the Meeting', *LPA*, Files 7/32/60.

The Arab Affairs' Committee. (1 February 1962) 'The Protocol of the Meeting', *LPA*, Files 7/32/60.

The Arab Affairs' Committee. (4 May 1962) 'The Protocol of the Meeting', *LPA*, Files 7/32/60.

The Arab Affairs' Committee. (16 May 1968) 'The Stenographic Protocol of the Meeting-Secret', *LPA*, Files 7/32/68.

The Arab Affairs' Committee. (6 June 1968) 'The Protocol of the Meeting ', *LPA*, Files 7/32/68.

The Arab Affairs' Committee. (20 June 1968) 'Stenographic Report of the Meeting', *LPA*, Files 7/23/68.

The Arab Department. (15 March 1962) 'Daily Report', *LPA*, Files 26/13/8.

The Arab Department. (24 March 1962) 'Daily Report', *LPA*, Files 26/13/8.

The Arab Department. (25 March 1962) 'Daily Report', *LPA*, Files 26/13/8.

The Arab Department. (15 May 1962) 'Daily Report', *LPA*, Files 26/13/8.

The Arab Department. (15 June 1962) 'Daily Report', *LPA*, Files 26/13/8.

The Arab Department. (n.d.) 'The Problem with the Military Government' [a discussion paper], *LPA*, Files 26/11.

The Arab Front. (17 September 1958) 'A Communiqué to the Public Opinion in Israel', *LPA*, Files 26/14/9.

Barkatt, Reuven. (4 September 1956) 'Cultural Secretary, Russian Embassy: Inviting You to the Premiere of Majnun Layla', *The Lavon Archive*, Document No. IV-208-1-8559.

Barkatt, Reuven. (4 September 1956) 'To Dr. Thomas H. McGrail: Cultural Attache, American Embassy: Inviting You to the Premiere of Majnun Layla', *The Lavon Archive*, Document No. IV-208-1-8559.

Barkatt, Reuven. (4 September 1956) 'To Robert E. Gramble, Second Secretary, British Embassy: Inviting You to the Premiere of Majnun Layla', *The Lavon Archive*, Document No. IV-208-1-8559.

Barkatt, Reuven. (5 September 1956) 'To HaHaver Moshe Sharett: Letter of Invitation to the Arabic Play Majnon Lila', *The Lavon Archive*, Document No. IV-208-1-8559.

Barkatt, Reuven. (5 September 1956) 'To the Minister of Labor M. Namir: Letter of Invitation to the Arabic Play Majnon Lila', *The Lavon Archive*, Document No. IV-208-1-8559.

Barkatt, Reuven. (5 September 1956) 'To the Foreign Minister, Golda Meir: Letter of Invitation to the Arabic Play Majnon Lila', *The Lavon Archive*, Document No. IV-208-1-8559.

Barkatt, Reuven. (5 September 1956) 'Mlle E. Fischer, Attache Culturel, Ambassade de France: Inviter a Assister a la Premier de'Majnun Layla', *The Lavon Archive*, Document No. IV-208-1-8559.

Bassal, Mussa. (29 April 1957) 'To the Inhabitants of Kafr Yassif: The Letter of Resignation from His Position as Deputy Mayor that Mussa Bassel Sent to the Mayor', *LPA*, Files 26/14/23.

Cohen, Ra'anan. (23 March 1975) 'Letter to Meir Zarmi, the Labor Party's General Secretary: Elections for Raina's Local Council – A Request for Funding', *LPA*, Files 26/16/7.

Cohen, Yaakov. (15 February 1956) 'Letter to Ata Company Ltd', *The Lavon Archive*, Document No. IV-208-8559.

The Committee of the Victims, Haifa. (30 September 1961) 'Letter: To the Secretariat of the Workers' Party of Eretz Yisrael', *LPA*, Files 26/16/15.

The Central Committee of the Eretz-Yisrael Communist Party. (14 May 1948) 'Memorandum to the Provisional State Council and Haganah Commanders', *The Lavon Archive*, Document No. IV-230-1-945.

The Confined Committee of the Arab Affairs' Committee. (30 March 1958) 'A Master Plan for Action Among the Arab Minority in Israel: Decisions for Implementation', *LPA*, Files 26/14/11.

The Confined Committee of the Arab Affairs' Committee. (18 August 1959) 'The Meeting of the Headquarter', *LPA*, Files 26/14/11.

The Confined Committee of the Arab Affairs' Committee. (29 June 1960) 'Summary of the Meeting', *LPA*, Files 26/14/11.

The Confined Committee of the Arab Affairs' Committee. (25 October 1960) 'Summary of the Meeting of the Confined Committee in Haifa', *LPA*, Files 26/14/11.

The Confined Committee of the Arab Affairs' Committee. (11 November 1960) 'Summary of a Meeting', *LPA*, Files 26/14/11.

The Confined Committee of the Arab Affairs' Committee. (25 November 1960) 'Summary of a Meeting', *LPA*, Files 26/14/11.

The Confined Secretariat of the Arab Affairs' Committee. (7 September 1959), 'Summary of the Meeting of the Meeting Headquarter', *LPA*, Files 26/14/11.

The Confined Secretariat of the Arab Affairs' Committee. (19 March 1964) 'The Protocol of the Meeting', *LPA*, Files 26/14/11.

Dan-Gur, Yusif. (29 June 1971) 'To The Advisor on Arabs Affairs in The Prime-Minister's Office – Jerusalem: Students and Students' Organizations in Tel-Aviv', *LPA*, Files 26/13/15.

Dawood, Ya'qub. (23 August 1958) 'A Report on the Meeting of the Arab Front in Kafr Yassif, on Saturday 23/8/1958', *LPA*, Files 26/14/9.

Eini, Yaakov. (23 February 1959) 'Towards the Elections for the Fourth Knesset: A Review and Suggestions: The Preparations for the Elections and a Detailed Plan for the Knesset and the Local Councils, 1959', *LPA*, Files 26/14/3.

Eini, Yaakov. (31 March 1959) 'Letter to: Havir Micha Lindenstrauss', *LPA*, Files 3/1.

Eini, Yaakov. (16 June 1960) 'Letter to Beyamin Lezoush: Appeal to the High Court of Justice Against the Mayor of Kafr Yassif [internal number 23]', *LPA*, Files 26/14/23.

Eini, Yaakov. (24 July 1962) 'The Situation of Kafr Yassif's Local Council in the Aftermath of Yan Yani's Death', *LPA*, Files 26/14/23.

Eini, Yaakov. (2 January 1964) 'Loan for Tayibe's Local Council for the Building of 23 Classes', *LPA*, Files 26/12/15.

Eini, Yaakov. (19 May 1964) 'Letter to Reuven Barekitt', *LPA*, Files 26/14/23.

Eini, Yaakov and Falpan, Simha. (n.d.) 'The Draft of the Agreement' [internal number 32]', *LPA*, Files 26/14/23.

Fa, 'A. R. (28 September 1975) 'Letter to: Ra'anan Cohen: Request for Help with the Minister of Communication', *LPA*, Files 26/15/12.

Falk, Zeev. (28 April 1964) 'Response: Your Letter to The Deputy of the Interior Minister', *LPA*, Files 26/14/23.

Ghara, Sharif. (12 January 1966) 'Letter to Mr Amnon Linn', *LPA*, Files 26/7/10.

Hamdan, Faris. (14 May 1965) 'Letter: To His Honor the Prime Minister Mr. Levi Eshkol', *LPA*, Files 26/13/14.

The Histadrut's Arab Department. (1965) 'A Review of the Histadrut's Activity Among Arab Members During 1965', *The Lavon Archive*, Document No. IV-208-1-13300.

The Histadrut's Arab Department. (n.d.) '[Report]: The Activities of the Economic Section of the Arab Department Acting Beside the Histadrut's Executive, Submitted to the Subcommittee of the Knesset's Arab Affairs Committee', *The Lavon Archive*, Document No. IV-208-1-5814.

Hushi, Abba. (27 May 1960) 'Plan for Action of the Workers' Party of Eritz Yisrael Among the Arab Population – Internal Document, Not for Publication', *LPA*, Files 7/32/60.

The Islamic List, Kafr Yassif. (n.d.) '[Elections] Leaflet', *LPA*, Files 26/14/23.

Kafr Yassif's Local Council, the Coalition. (n.d.) 'The Program of the Coalition for the Management of Kafr Yassif's Council', *LPA*, Files 26/14/23.

Kafr Yassif's Local Council, the Coalition. (n.d.b.) 'The Political Program of Kafr Yassi's Local Council Coalition', *LPA*, Files 26/14/23.

Kardosh, Aneas. (September 1960) 'Leaflet: The Committee of Arab Students at the Hebrew University in Jerusalem', *LPA*, Files 26/13/15. [A Summary translated to Hebrew].

Katz, Zvi. (17 November 1971) 'Letter: To Mr. Meir Mishal: B. J. Al-Haj. – "Arara"', *LPA*, Files 26/12/8.

Katz, Zvi. (1 December 1971) 'To Havir Meir Mishal: Answers and Clarifications', *LPA*, Files 26/12/8.

Khaw. A. M. (9 March 1966) 'Letter to Mr. Meir Mishal', *LPA*, Files 26/7/20.

Khaw. A. M. (21 June 1966) 'Letter to Mr. Meir Mishal', *LPA*, Files 26/7/20.

Khuri, Fawzi. (1 May 1960) 'Letter to Yaakov Eini', [internal number 22], *LPA*, Files 26/14/23.

Khuri, Fawzi. (n.d.) 'Letter to Hananiah' [internal number 29]. *LPA*, Files 26/14/23.

Kusa, Elias. (4 April 1958) 'Letter to: The Honorable Persons, the Mayor and the Council Members of Kafr Yassif; Copies to All the Arab Local Authorities, 4.4.1958', *LPA*, Files 26/14/23.

'Letter to Yaakov' (n.d.) *LPA*, Files 26/14/23.

Lindenstrauss, Micha. (27 March 1959) 'Letter to: Havir Yaakov Einni', *LPA*, Files 3/1.

Lindenstrauss, Micha. (19 April 1959) 'Personal – A Letter to Yaakov Eini: The Jewish Arab Society Attached to Mapai Students' Cell', *LPA*, Files 3/1.

Lindenstrauss, Micha. (8 July 1959) 'Letter to Mr. Yaakov Eini: A Proposed Manifesto for the Jewish Arab Students Society', *LPA*, Files 3/1.

Lindenstrauss, Micha. (7 December 1959) 'Elections for the Arab Students' Committee: A Letter to Yaakov Eini', *LPA*, Files 3/1.

Linn, Amnon. (7 November 1963) 'Letter to Abba Hushi: My Resignation from the Management of the Election Campaign in Kafr Yassif', *LPA*, Files 26/14/23.

Linn, Amnon. (1968) 'Our Activities Among the Arabs and the Druze in the State of Israel', *LPA*, Files 7/32/68.

'The Local Council, Kafr Yassif' (n.d.) *LPA*, Files 26/14/23.

'The Local Authority in Kafr Yassif' (26 May 1957), *LPA*, Files 26/14/23.

Mapai and Mafdal Representatives. (n.d.) 'Agreement for the Formation of a Coalition in Kafr Yassif's Local Council Between Mapai and Mafdal', *LPA*, Files 26/14/23.

Mishal, Meir. (14 March 1962) 'Daily Report', *LPA*, Files 26/13/8.

Mishal, Meir. (3 July 1962) '[Report]: The Village of Rena', *LPA*, Files 26/16/7.

Mishal, Meir. (15 October 1962) 'Um al-Fahim: A Report to Yaakov Eini', *LPA*, Files 26/13/18.

Mishal, Meir. (1 November 1962) 'Report: The Village of Jaljulia', *LPA*, Files 26/17/13.

Mishal, Meir. (27 September 1966) 'Letter to Amnon Linn: The Local Council, Jat, The Triangle, Coup-de-tat', *LPA*, Files 26/7/10.

Mishal, Meir. (1967) 'Letter to MK Amnon Linn: Hostile [Persons] Who Were Accepted to the Arab Seminar in Haifa', *LPA*, Files 3/1.

Mishal, Meir. (20 March 1972) 'Letter to David Zakharia: The Election of the Arab Students' Committee at Tel-Aviv University', *LPA*, Files 26/13//15.

Mishal, Meir. (n.d.) 'Letter to Amnon Linn: Hostile Persons and Convicted Persons in Affiliation the Fatah, Espionage and Fleeing the Country', *LPA*, Files 26/13/18.

Mishal, Meir. (n.d.b.) 'Letter to the Haver "Eini"', *LPA*, Files 3/1.

Mol, M. 'A N. and Palmon, Y. 'An Outline of a Meetings that Was Carried Out Between and on 21 and 25 of August, 1949'. *The Lavon Archive*, Document No. IV-208-1:5815.

Muadi, Jaber Dahish. (14 December 1960) 'Letter to Uri Lubrani', *LPA*, Files 26/10/23.

The Political Committee – Bureau – [of Mapai]. (10 November 1948) 'Protocol of the Meeting', *LPA*, Files 2-025-1948-11.

The Political Committee – Bureau – [of Mapai]. (19 January 1950) 'Protocol of the Meeting, *LPA*, Files 2-025-1950-13.

The Political Committee [of Mapai]. (24 January 1952) 'Protocol of the Meeting', *LPA*, Files 2-026-1952-10.

The Political Committee [of Mapai]. (3 August 1952) 'Protocol of the Meeting', *LPA*, Files 2-026-1952-11.

The Political Committee [of Mapai]. (10 June 1953) 'Protocol of the Meeting', *LPA*, Files 2-026-1953-13.

The Popular Front, The Executive Committee. (29 October 1958) 'A Communique: [Leaflet that Was Distributed in Arabic and Hebrew, 2 pages]', *LPA*, Files 26/14/9.

The Popular Front. (n.d.) 'Towards a Solution to the Problems Facing the Arab People in Israel', *LPA*, Files 26/14/9.

The Popular Front, Kafr Yassif Branch. (n.d.) 'Communiqué to the Masses of Our Village', *LPA*, Files 26/14/23.

Progress and Work (n.d.) 'A Leaflet: Beware of Those Who Have No Self-Respect ... My Arab Bother ... This Is Your Enemy ... Beware ... Oh My Brother Beware', *LPA*, Files 26/13/12. Translation, But Most Likely 1959 or 1961; *LPA*, Files 26-13-12 – the Party of Salih Khnayfis.

Q. Abd Al-A. (11 October 1960) 'Letter to Yaakov Eini', *LPA*, Files 26/13/15.

Q. Abd Al-A. (22 December 1961) 'Teachers' Opinions on the Elections for the Teachers' Union', *LPA*, Files 3/1.

'Report of the Meeting Regarding the Elections of Kafr Yassif's Local Council', (3 November 1963) *LPA*, Files 26/14/23.

'Report of the Meeting Which Took Place on 10 February 1964 for Reviewing the Situation in Kafr Yassif', (10 February 1964) *LPA*, Files 26/14/23.

'A Review of the Histadrut's Arab Department' (n.d.) *LPA* (in the political committee's files).

Safyiah Hussein, Khuri Najeeb Labeeb, Bassal Mussa and Shehadeh Saleem. (12 October 1958), 'Letter to Mr. Yani Yani', *LPA*, Files 26/14/23.

The Secretariat of the Arab Affairs' Committee. (24 June 1964), 'Protocol and a Summary of a Coordination Meeting', *LPA*, Files 26/14/11.

The Secretariat of the Arab Affairs' Committee. (n.d.), 'Protocol and a Summary of the Meeting', *LPA*, Files 3/1.

The Secretariat's Meeting with[Mapai's] MKs. (18 June 1950) 'Protocol of the Meeting', *LPA*, Files: Gemil-3; C/3.

The Secretariat's Meeting with [Mapai's] MKs. (9 July 1950) 'Protocol of the Meeting', *LPA*, Files: Gemil-3; C/3.

Shehadeh, Rafeq. (29 May 1964) 'Letter to: Haaver Baraktt, Mapai's Secretary', *LPA*, Files 26/14/23.

Shehadeh, Rafeq. (13 June 1964) 'Letter to: The Prime Minister and to The Speaker of the Knesset', *LPA*, Files 26/14/23.

Shulman, E. (21 September 1949) 'Letter to Mr. Benor: Candidates for Teaching Positions', *The Lavon Archive*, Document No. IV-208-1/5815.

Stevisky, Leo. (30 January 1967) 'Letter to Amonon Linn: The Nomination of New Mukhtars Among Bedouin Tribes in the Negev', *LPA*, Files 26/13/9.

Tibi, A. S. (13 June 1963) 'Letter to Yaakov Eini: My CV', *LPA*, Files 26/12/15.

Tuma, Josef. (15 November 1963) 'Secret Letter to: Yaakov Eini', *LPA*, Files 26/14/23.

The United Block, Kafr Yassif. (n.d.) 'Election Leaflet [written in verses]', *LPA*, Files 26/14/23.

The United Block, Kafr Yassif. (n.d.b.) '[Election] Leaflet: Invitation for a Public Meeting on Saturday 1 February 1964', *LPA*, Files 26/14/23.

Yani, Yani. (15 October 1960) 'Letter to: His Highness, The Prime Minister', *LPA*, Files 26/14/23.

Yani, Yani. (29 September 1961) 'Letter to: Their Highness; The Minister of Defense, The Minister of Police and The Minister of Interior', *LPA*, Files 26/14/23.

Yani, Yani. (8 March 1962) 'Letter to: His Highness the Prime Minister – Jerusalem', *LPA*, Files 26/14/23.

Yani, Yani, (n.d.) 'Letter to the Head of the Department of Illumination and Enlightening', *LPA*, Files 26/14/23.

The Youth's Committee. (28 November 1962) 'Protocol of the Meeting', *LPA*, Files 26/8/3.

Zakharia, David. (29 November 1970) 'Letter to Werba: Changes and Additions of Polling Stations', *LPA*, Files 26/13/9.

Zakharia, David. (24 June 1971) 'Letter: to Dani Korin', *LPA*, Files 26/13/15.

Zakharia, David. (11 March 1973) 'Letter: To Mr. Amnon Golan', *LPA*, Files 26/7/12.

Reports by unidentified authors

Arabba. (n.d.) [notes on the elections], *LPA*, Files 26/16/1.

'The Election for the Knesset Among the Negev Bedouins', (n.d.), *LPA*, Files 26/13/9.

'The Eichmann Affair in Jat School', (29 May 1960), *LPA*, Files 26/7/10.

'An Evaluation of the Situation: Khirbet Al-Byar', (n.d.), *LPA*, Files 26/7/6.

'An Evaluation of the Situation: Maker', (n.d.), *LPA*, Files 26/11.

'An Evaluation of the Situation: Tamra', (n.d.), *LPA*, Files 26/15/11.

'Kafr Qasim, Elections for the Local Council', (n.d.), *LPA*, Files 26/17/9.

'Kafr Yassif', (1 July 1963), *LPA*, Files 26/14/23.

'A List of Teachers in Kafr Qasim School', (September 1960), *LPA*, Files 3/1.

'A List of the Teachers in 'Arabba', (n.d.), *LPA*, Files 26/16/1.

'The Nomination of a Local Council in Kafr Qasim – Candidates', (11 November 1958), *LPA*, Files 26/17/9.

'Summary of the Meeting Regarding Tayibe's Local Council', (15 September 1963), *LPA*, Files 26/12/15.

'Teachers: The Democratic and Islah Lists', (25 May 1962), *LPA*, Files 3/1.

Newspapers

Amnon, K. (6 July 1958) 'Maki and Arab Nationalists Are Expected to Announce the Establishment of the "Front" Today', *Al-Hamishmar*.

Amnon, K. (7 July 1958) 'An Arab Nationalist Front was Established by Maki', *Al Hamishmar*.

Asadi, Mayson. (7 May 1999) 'The Crime Which Shook the Inner Most Feelings of the Arab Citizens', *Al-Ittihad*, pp. 6–9.

Clark, Peter. (11 August 2008) 'Obituary: Mahmoud Darwish', *The Guardian*. Electronic version: www.guardian.co.uk/books/2008/aug/11/poetry.israelandthepalestinians.

Darwish, Yoel. (30 December 1960) 'Additional Young Druze Men Fled the Country', *Davar.*

Darwish, Yoel. (12 January 1961) 'Another Two Druzes Disappeared from Isifya', *Davar.*

Davar. (11 August 1958) 'Complains on Discrimination in Various Fields Were Aired by the Spokesmen of the "Arab Front"'.

Davar. (24 February 1960) 'The Operational Plan and Regulations Were Confiscated from al-Ard'.

Davar. (30 June 1960) 'Parallel Classes for Arab Pupils Will Be Opened in Ironi Alef in Haifa'.

Davar. (24 October 1960) 'An Extreme Nationalist Teacher in the Secondary School in Kafr Yassif'.

Davar. (20 November 1960) 'There Is No Organizing Body that Helps Minority Youth Fleeing'.

Davar. (12 December 1960) 'Druze Young Man Who Fled to Gaza Revealed IDF Secret'.

Davar. (28 December 1960) 'An Arab Teacher Accused of Tearing Herzl Picture in the School'.

Eini, Yaakov. (3 July 1962) 'Among Arab teachers', *Hapoel Hatzair.*

Eini, Yaakov. (17 March 1964) 'Our Achievement in Kafr Yassif and the Defeat of Maki [ICP]', *Hapoel Hatzair.*

Ha'aretz. (7 July 1958) 'Orders of Supervision Were Issued Against Dignitaries Who Initiated the Establishment of the "Arab Front"'.

Haro'veni, Meir. (9 August 1960) 'Arab Students from the North Boycotted a Histadrut Meeting', *Lamerhav.*

Jerusalem Post. (19 January 1959) 'Non-Communists Quit the Popular Front'.

Maariv. (10 January 1960) 'Arab Teacher Who Tore Herzl's Picture Was Fined'.

Melman, Yossi and Raviv, Daniel. (21 February 1988) 'A Final Solution to the Palestinian Problem?' *The Guardian Weekly*, p. 19.

Al-Mussawar. (9 October 1960) 'The Freedom of Opinion Danger to the Security of the State' [A Hebrew translation available in *LPA*, Files 26/13/15].

Nakdimon, Shlomo. (11 August 1958) 'Nationalist Elements Operating the "Arab Front"', *Hirut.*

Sharoni, G. (25 March 1962) 'Othman Raised His Finger', *Maariv.*

Shehadeh, Raja. (2002) 'Mahmoud Darwish', *BOMB Magazine*, 81/Fall. On the web: http://bombsite.com/issues/81/articles/2520.

Yoaz, Yuval and Kourie, Jack. (20 May 2007) 'Shin Bet: Citizens Subverting Israel Key Values to Be Probed', *Haaretz.*

Al-Yom. (12 December 1960) 'A Druze Young Man Fled to Gaza Strip'.

Al-Yom. (15 January 1961) 'The Sentencing of Five Youth Who Tried to Cross to Gaza'.

Jabotinsky, (Vladimir) Ze'ev. (1923/1937) 'The Iron Wall: We and the Arabs', *Jewish Herald (South Africa)*, 26 November. On the internet: www.marxists.de/middleast/ironwall/ironwall.htm.

Zvi, N. (21 January 1959) 'The Arab Front Falling Apart', *Al-Hamishmar.*

Books and articles

Abu El-Haj, Nadia. (2002) *Facts on the Ground: Archaeological Practice and Territorial Self-Fashioning in Israeli Society*, Chicago: University of Chicago Press.

Abu-Ghosh, Subhi. (1972) 'The Election Campaign in the Arab Sector', in Alan Arian (ed.), *The Elections in Israel – 1969*, Jerusalem: Academic Press, pp. 239–52.

Abu-Saad, Ismael. (2006) 'Palestinian Education in Israel: The Legacy of the Military Government', *Holy Land Studies: A Multidisciplinary Journal*, 5(1):21–56.

Agamben, Giorgio. (2005) *State of Exception*, Chicago: University of Chicago Press.

Alatas, Syed Farid. (2006) *Alternative Discourses in Asian Social Science*, London: Sage.

Alatas, Syed Hussein. (1974) 'The Captive Mind and Creative Development', *International Social Science Journal*, 36(4): 691–99.

Al-Haj, Majid and Rosenfeld, Henry. (1988) *Arab Local Authorities in Israel*, Tel-Aviv: The International Centre for Peace in the Middle East.

Althusser, Louis. (1984) *Essay on Ideology*, London: Verso.

Apple, Michael. (1990) *Ideology and Curriculum*, London: Routlege.

Asad, Talal. (1975) 'Anthropological Texts and Ideological Problems: An Analysis of Cohen on Arab Villages', *Economy and Society*, 4(3):251–82.

Avivi, Shimon. (2007) *Copper Plate: Israeli Policy Towards the Druze 1948–1967*, Jerusalem: Yad Ben-Zvi [in Hebrew].

Azaryahu, Maoz and Golan, Arnon. (2001) '(Re)naming the Landscape: The Formation of the Hebrew Map of Israel 1949–1960', *Journal of Historical Geography*, 27(2):178–95.

Azoulay, Ariella and Ophir, Adi. (2008) *This Regime Which Is Not One: Occupation and Democracy Between the Sea and the River (1967–)*. Tel-Aviv: Resling [in Hebrew].

Bauml, Yair. (2007) *A Blue and White Shadow: The Israeli Establishment's Policy and Actions Among Its Arab Citizens: The Formative Years 1958–1968*, Haifa: Pardes Publishing House [in Hebrew].

Beinen, Joel. (1977) 'The Palestine Communist Party 1919–1948', *Middle East Research and Information Project (MERIP)*, 55:3–17.

Bentham, Jeremy. (1995) *The Panopticon Writings*, London: Verso.

Benvenisti, Meron. (2000) *Sacred Landscape: The Buried History of the Holy Land Since 1948*, Berkeley: University of California Press.

Benziman, Uzi and Mansour, Atallah. (1992) *Subtenants*, Jerusalem: Keter Publishing House.

Cohen, Abner. (1965) *Arab Border-Villages in Israel*, Manchester: University of Manchester Press.

Cohen, Hillel. (2004) *An Army of Shadows: Palestinian Collaborators in the Service of Zionism*, Jerusalem: Ivrit Publishing House [in Hebrew].

Cohen, Hillel. (2006) *Good Arabs: The Israeli Security Services and the Israeli Arabs*, Jerusalem: Ivrit Publishing House [in Hebrew].

Cohen, Hillel. (2008) *Army of Shadows: Palestinian Collaboration with Zionism, 1917–1948*, Berkeley and Los Angeles: University of California Press.

Cohen, Hillel. (2010) *Good Arabs: The Israeli Security Agencies and the Israeli Arabs, 1948–1967*, Berkeley and Los Angeles: University of California Press.

Curtis, Bruce. (2002) 'Foucault on Governmentality and Population: The Impossible Discovery', *Canadian Journal of Sociology*, 27(4):505–33.

Dahl, Robert. (1971) *Polyarchy: Participation, and Observation*, New Haven: Yale University Press.

Danin, Ezra. (1987) *Unconditional Zionist*, Jerusalem: Kidum. Vol. 2 [in Hebrew].

Davis, Uri and Lehn, Walter. (1983) 'Landownership, Citizenship and Racial Policy in Israel', in Talal Asad and Roger Owen (eds), *Sociology of the Developing Societies: The Middle-East*, London: Macmillan, pp. 145–58.

Deleuze, Gilles. (1992) 'Postscript on the Societies of Control', *October*, 59:3–7.

Dowty, Alan. (1999), 'Is Israel Democratic? Substance and Semantic in the "Ethnic Democracy" Debate', *Israel Studies*, 4(2):1–15.

Dudai, Ron and Cohen, Hillel. (2007) 'Triangle of Betrayal: Collaborators and Transitional Justice in the Israeli–Palestinian Conflict', *Journal of Human Right*, 6:37–58.

Eilam, Yigal. (2002) 'The Myth of the "Few Against the Many" in 1948', *Palestine-Israel Journal*, 9(4). On the Web: www.pij.org/details.php?id=107.

Eyal, Gil. (2006) *The Disenchantment of the Orient: Expertise in Arab Affairs and the Israeli State*, Stanford: Stanford University Press.

Falah, Ghazi. (1985) 'How Israel Controls the Bedouins in Israel', *Journal of Palestine Studies*, 14(2):35–51.

Falah, Ghazi. (1996) 'The 1948 War Israeli-Palestinian War and Its Aftermath: The Transformation and De-signification of Palestine's Cultural Landscape', *Annals of the Association of American Geographers*, 86:256–85.

Fanon, Franz. (1961) *The Wretched of the Earth*, New York: Penguin.

Firer, Ruth. (1985) *The Agents of Zionist Education*, Haifa: Afik [in Hebrew].

Firro, Kais. (1999) *The Druzes in the Jewish State: A Brief History*, Leiden: Brill.

Firro, Kais. (2001) 'Reshaping Druze Particularism', *Journal of Palestine Studies*, 30(3):40–53.

Fischbach, Michael. (2011) 'British and Zionist Data Gathering on Palestinian Arab Landownership and Population During the Mandate', in Elia Zureik, David Lyon and Yasmeen Abu-Laban (eds), *Surveillance and Control in Israel/Palestine*. London: Routledge, pp. 297–312.

Foucault, Michel. (1981) 'The Order of Discourse', in Robert Young (ed.), *Untying the Text: A Post-Structural Reader*, Boston: Routledge & Kegan Paul, pp. 48–78.

Foucault, Michel. (1991) *Discipline and Punish: The Birth of the Prison*, London: Penguin Books.

Foucault, Michel. (2000) 'Governmentality', in James D. Faubion (ed.), *Power*, New York: The New Press, pp. 326–48.

Foucault, Michel. (2004) *Society Must Be Defended*, London: Penguin.

Foucault, Michel. (2009) *Security, Territory, Population*, New York: Palgrave Macmillan.

Freely, Maureen. (2 May 2007) 'Why They Killed Hrant Dink', *Index on Censorship*, 36:15–29.

Gavison, Ruth. (1999) 'Jewish and Democratic? A Rejoinder to the "Ethnic Democracy" Debate', *Israel Studies*, 4(1):44–72.

Ghanim, Hunaida. (2009) *Reinventing the Nation: Palestinian Intellectuals in Israel*, Jerusalem: The Hebrew University Magnes Press [in Hebrew].

Giroux, Henry and Purpel, David. (1984) *The Hidden Curriculum and Moral Education: Deception or Discovery?*, Richmond: McCutchan.

Gordon, Neve. (2008) *Israel's Occupation*, Berkeley: University of California Press.

Gramsci, Antonio. (1986) *Selection from Prison Notebooks*. Q. Hoare and G. N. Smith (eds), London: Lawrence & Wishart.

Guha, Sumit. (2003) 'The Politics of Identity and Enumeration in India c. 1600–1990', *Comparative Studies in Society and History*, 45(1):148–67.

Halabi, Rabah. (2006) *Citizens of Equal Duties: Druze Identity and the Jewish State*, Tel-Aviv: Hakibbutz Hameuchad [in Hebrew].

Jiryis, Sabri. (1971) 'Recent Knesset Legislation and the Arabs in Israel', *Journal of Palestine Studies*, 1(1):53–67.

Jiryis, Sabri. (1976) *The Arabs in Israel*, London: Monthly Review Press.

Jiryis, Sabri. (1981) 'Domination by Law', *Journal of Palestine Studies*, 11(1):67–92.

Kafkafi, Eyal. (1998) 'Segregation or Integration of the Israeli Arabs: Two Concepts in Mapai', *Journal of Middle East Studies*, 30:347–67.

Kimmerling, Baruch. (2001) *The Invention and Decline of Israeliness: State, Society and the Military*, Berkeley and Los Angeles: University of California Press.

Korn, Alina. (1995) 'Crime and Law Enforcement in the Israeli Arab Population Under the Military Government, 1948–1966', in S. Ilan Troen and Noah Lucas (eds), *Israel: The First Decade of Independence*, New York: State University of New York Press, pp. 659–79.

Kretzmer, David. (1987) *The Legal Status of the Arabs in Israel*, Tel-Aviv: The International Centre for Peace in the Middle-East.

Kretzmer, David. (1990) *The Legal Status of the Arabs in Israel*, Boulder: Westview.

Landau, Jacob. (1993) *The Arab Minority in Israel, 1967–1991: Political Aspects*, Oxford: Clarendon Press.

Leibler, Anat and Breslau, Daniel. (2005) 'The Uncounted: Citizenship and Exclusion in the Israeli Census of 1948', *Ethnic and Racial Studies*, 28(5):880–902.

Lijphart, Arend. (1984) *Democracies: Patterns of Majoritarian and Consensus Government in 21 Countries*, New Haven: Yale University Press.

Lijphart, Arend. (1994) 'Democracies: Forms, Performance, and Constitutional Engineering', *European Journal of Political Research*, 25(1):1–17.

Linn, Amnon. (1999) *Stormy Skies: Jews and Arabs in Israel*, Tel-Aviv: Karni [in Hebrew].

Lockman, Zachary. (1996) *Comrades and Enemies: Arab and Jewish Workers in Palestine, 1906–1948*, Berkeley: California University Press.

Lustick, Ian. (1980) *Arabs in the Jewish State: Israel's Control of a National Minority*, Austin: University of Texas Press.

Lyon, David. (2007) *Surveillance Studies: An Overview*, Cambridge: Polity.

Lyon, David. (2009) *Identifying Citizens: ID Cards as Surveillance*, Cambridge: Polity.

Marshall, Thomas Humphrey. (1950) *Citizenship and Social Classes*, Cambridge: Cambridge University Press.

Masalha, Nur. (1991) 'A Critique of Benny Morris', *Journal of Palestine Studies*, 21(1):90–7.

Masalha, Nur. (1992) *Expulsion of the Palestinians: The Concept of 'Transfer' in Zionist Political Thought, 1882–1948*, Washington, DC: Institute of Palestine Studies.

Masalha, Nur. (1996) *An Israeli Plan to Transfer Galilee's Christians to South America: Yosef Weitz and 'Operation Yohanan' 1949–53*, University of Durham, Centre for Middle Eastern and Islamic Studies: Occasional Paper No. 55.

Masalha, Nur. (2009) '60 Years After the Nakba: Historical Truth, Collective Memory and Ethical Obligations', *Kyoto Bulletin of Islamic Area Studies*, 3(1):37–88. A Special issue on "Nakba after Sixty Years: Memories and Histories in Palestine and East Asia", in Akira Usuki and Aiko Nishikida (eds).

Meir, Avinoam. (1988) 'Nomads and The State: The Spatial Dynamics of Centrifugal and Centripetal Forces Among the Israeli Negev Bedouin', *Political Geography Quarterly*, 7:251–70.

Morris, Benny. (2004) *The Birth of the Palestinian Refugee Problem Revisited*, Cambridge: Cambridge University Press.

Ophir, Adi, Givoni, Michal and Hanaifi, Sari. (eds) (2009) *The Power of Inclusive Exclusion: Anatomy of Israeli Rule in the Occupied Palestinian Territories*, New York: Zone Books.

Ozacky-Lazar, Sarah. (2002) 'The Military Government as an Apparatus of Control of Arab Citizens in Israel: The First Decade 1948–1958', *Hamizrah Hehadash*, 43:103–32.

Pappe, Ilan. (1995) 'An Uneasy Coexistence: Arabs and Jews in the First Decade of Statehood', in S. Ilan Troen and Noah Lucas (eds), *Israel: The First Decade of Independence*, New York: State University of New York Press, pp. 617–58.

Pappe, Ilan. (2006) *The Ethnic Cleansing of Palestine*, Oxford: Oneworld.

Pappe, Ilan. (2011) *The Forgotten Palestinians: A History of the Palestinians in Israel*, London: Yale University Press.

Parizot, Cedric. (2001) *Gaza, Beersheba, Dhahriyya: Another Approach to the Negev Bedouins in the Israeli-Palestinian Space. Bulletin du Centre de Recherche Français de Jérusalem*. No. 9. [English Translation].

Parsons, Laila. (2000) *The Druze Between Palestine and Israel 1947–1949*, London: Macmillan.

Peretz, Don. (1958) *Israel and the Palestine Arabs*, Washington, DC: The Middle East Institute.

Peretz, Don. (1991) 'Early State Policy Towards the Arab Population, 1948–1955', in Laurence J. Silberstein (ed.), *New Perspectives on Israeli History*, New York: New York University Press, pp. 82–102.

Pinkus, Benjamin. (2007) *Special Relations: The Soviet Union and Its Allies and Their Relations with the Jewish People, Zionism and the State of Israel 1939–1959*, Beersheba: Ben-Gurion University Press [in Hebrew].

Powell, G. Bingham. (1982) *Contemporary Democracies: Participation, Stability, and Violence*, Cambridge: Harvard University Press.

Reiter, Y. (2009) *National Minority, Regional Majority: Palestinian Arabs Versus Jews in Israel*, Syracuse: Syracuse University Press.

Rekhess, Elie. (1991) 'Initial Israeli Policy Guidelines Towards the Arab Minority, 1948–1949', in Laurence J. Silberstein (ed.), *New Perspectives on Israeli History*, New York: New York University Press, pp. 103–23.

Robinson, Andrew. (2005a) 'Towards an Intellectual Reformation: The Critique of Common Sense and the Forgotten Revolutionary Project of Gramscian Theory', *Critical Review of International Social and Political Philosophy*, 8(4):469–81.

Robinson, Ronald. (1972) 'Non-European Foundations of European Imperialism: Sketch for a Theory of Collaboration', in Roger Owen and Bob Sutcliffe (eds), *Studies in the Theory of Imperialism*, New York: Longman, pp. 117–42.

Robinson, Shira. (2005b) *Occupied Citizens in a Liberal State: Palestinians Under Military Rule and the Colonial Formation of Israeli Society, 1948–1966*, Stanford University, unpublished doctoral dissertation.

Ro'i, Yaacov. (1968) 'The Zionist Attitude to the Arabs 1908–1914', *Middle Eastern Studies*, 4(3):198–242.

Rosenthal, Ruvik. (2000) 'Who Killed Fatma Sursor: The Background, the Motivations and the Unfolding of the Kafr Qassem Massacre', in Ruvik Rosenthal (ed.), *Kafr Kassem: Myth and History*, Tel-Aviv: Hakibbutz Hameuchad [in Hebrew].

Sa'di, Ahmad. (1992) 'Between State Ideology and Minority National Identity', *Review of Middle East Studies*, 5:110–130.

Sa'di, Ahmad. (1995) 'Incorporation Without Integration: Palestinian-Citizens in Israel's Labour Market', *Sociology*, 29(3):429–51. Reprinted in Moshe Semyonov and Noah Lewin-Epstein (eds), *Stratification in Israel* (2004), New Brunswick and London: Transaction, pp. 231–52.

Sa'di, Ahmad. (1997) 'Modernisation as an Explanatory Discourse of Zionist-Palestinian Relations', *The British Journal of Middle Eastern Studies*, 24(1):25–48.

Sa'di, Ahmad. (2001) 'Control and Resistance at Local Level Institutions: A Study of Kafr Yassif's Local Council Under the Military Government', *Arab Studies Quarterly*, 23(3): 31–47.

Sa'di, Ahmad. (2003a) 'The Incorporation of the Palestinian Minority by the Israeli State, 1948–1970: On the Nature, Transformation and Constraints of Collaboration', *Social Text*, 21(2):75–94.

Sa'di, Ahmad. (2003b) 'The Koenig Report and Israeli Policy Towards the Palestinian Minority, 1965–1976: Old Wine in New Bottles', *Arab Studies Quarterly*, 25(3): 51–61.

Sa'di, Ahmad. (2004a) 'Construction and Reconstruction of Racialised Boundaries: Discourse, Institutions and Methods', *Social Identities*, 10(2):135–49.

Sa'di, Ahmad. (2004b) 'Trends in Israeli Social Science Research on the National Identity of the Palestinian Citizens of Israel', *Asian Journal of Social Sciences*, 32(1):140–60.

Sa'di, Ahmad. (2005) 'The Politics of 'Collaboration': Israel's Control of a National Minority and Indigenous Resistance', *Holy Land Studies: A Multidisciplinary Journal*, 4(2):7–26.

Sa'di, Ahmad. (2010) 'Communism and Zionism in Palestine-Israel: A Troubled Legacy', *Holy Land Studies: A Multidisciplinary Journal*, 9(2):169–83.

Sa'di, Ahmad and Abu-Lughod, Lila (eds), (2007) *Nakba: Palestine, 1948 and the Claims of Memory*, New York: Columbia University Press.

Said, Edward. (1978) *Orientalism*, London: Peregrine Books.

Said, Edward. (1983) *The World, the Text and the Critic*, Cambridge: Harvard University Press.

Schmitt, Carl. (2005) *Political Theology*, Chicago: University of Chicago Press.

Scott, James. (1985) *Weapons of the Weak: Everyday Forms of Peasant Resistance*, New Haven: Yale University Press.

Scott, James. (1992) *Domination and the Arts of Resistance: Hidden Transcripts.* New Haven: Yale University Press.

Segev, Tom. (1984) *1949: The First Israelis*, Jerusalem: Domino.

Segev, Tom. (1998) *1949: The First Israelis*, New York: An Owl Book.

Smooha, Sammy. (1982) 'Existing and Alternative Policy Towards the Arabs in Israel', *Ethnic and Racial Studies*, 26(1):71–98.

Smooha, Sammy. (1990) 'Minority Status in an Ethnic Democracy: The Status of the Arab Minority in Israel', *Ethnic and Racial Studies*, 13(3):389–413.

Smooha, Sammy. (1997) 'Ethnic Democracy: Israel as an Archetype', *Israel Studies*, 2(2):198–241.

Smooha, Sammy. (2002) 'The Model of Ethnic Democracy: Israel as a Jewish and Democratic State', *Nations and Nationalism*, 8(4):475–503.

Stendel, Ori. (1973) *The Minorities in Israel: Trends in the Development of the Arab and Druze Communities 1948–1973*, Jerusalem: The Israeli Economist.

Swirski, Shlomo and Hasson, Yael. (2006) *Invisible Citizens: Israel Government Policy Towards the Negev Bedouin*, Tel-Aviv Adva Center.

Thomas, Martin. (2008) *Empires of Intelligence: Security Services and Colonial Disorder After 1914*, Berkeley: University of California Press.

Wiemer, Reinhard. (1983) 'Zionism and the Arabs After the Establishment of the State of Israel', in Alexander Scholch (ed.), *Palestinians over the Green the Line*, London: Ithaca Press, pp. 26–63.

Yiftachel, Oren. (2006) *Ethnocracy: Land and Identity Politics in Israel/Palestine*, Philadelphia: University of Pennsylvania Press.

Yonah, Yossi, Abu-Saad, Ismael and Kaplan, Avi. (2004) 'De-Arabization of the Bedouin: A Study of an Inevitable Failure', *Interchange*, 35(4):387–406.

Yu, Wang and Cohen Hillel. (2009) 'Marketing Israel to the Arabs: The Rise and Fall of the al-Anbaa Newspaper', *Israel Affairs*, 15(2):190–210.

Zureik, Elia. (1979) *Palestinians in Israel: A Study in Internal Colonialism*, London: Routledge & Kegan Paul.

Index

Page numbers in **bold** refer to figures, page numbers in *italic* refer to tables.